# Guide to Executive Compensation

## Legal and Regulatory Compliance Issues

Sharon Reece
Kelsey N.H. Mayo
Jesse A.A. St. Cyr

AMERICAN BAR ASSOCIATION
Business Law Section

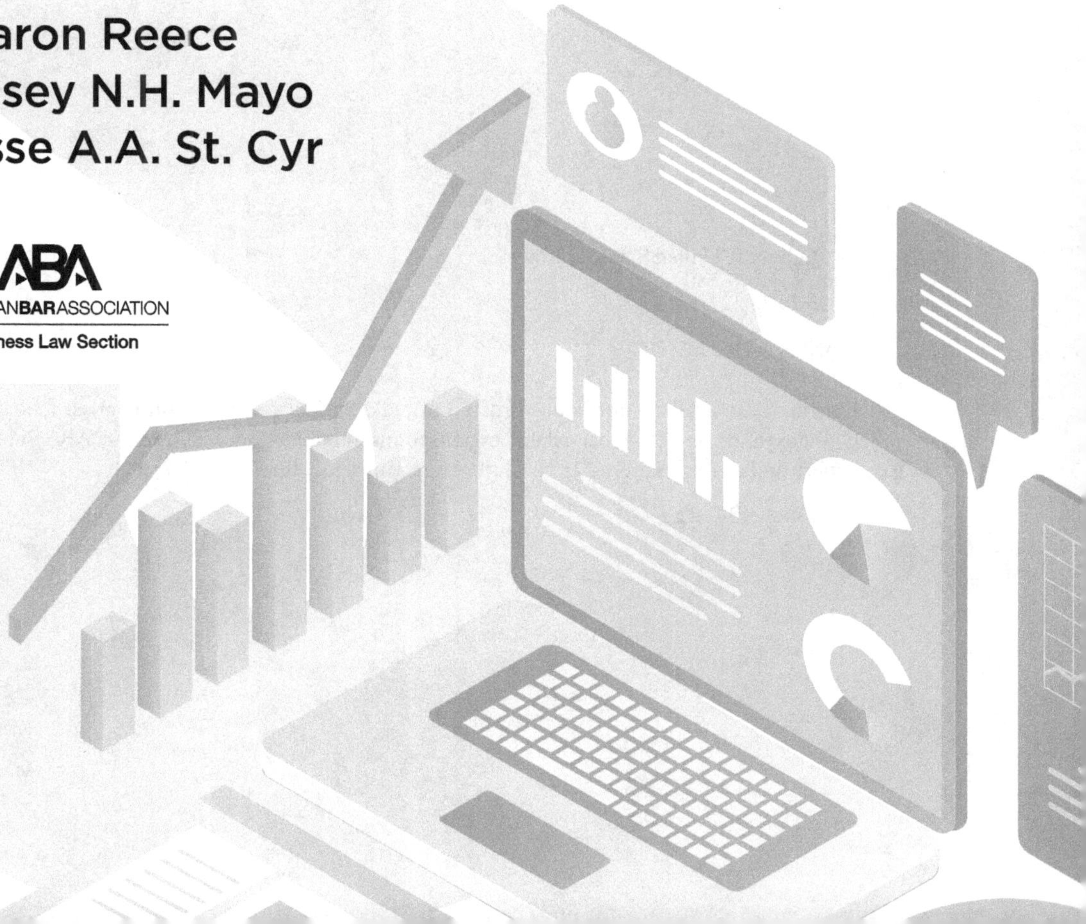

Cover design by Catherine Zaccarine.



Printed in the United States of America.

26 25 24 23 22 5 4 3 2 1

ISBN: 978-1-63905-107-6

Sharon Reece: To my husband, Dr. E. Albert Reece, for his unwavering support.

Kelsey N.H. Mayo: To Hugh Davis, my law partner and mentor who, with patience and perseverance, made me a better lawyer and person.

Jesse A.A. St. Cyr: To my wife, Julie.

# Contents

# Foreword

I am delighted to have been invited to write a foreword to this excellent and very helpful book. I will claim, proudly, to be its godfather, as I introduced the authors to each other, and I could not be more pleased with the result. Sharon Reece and Kelsey Mayo each has a wealth of knowledge and experience in this unusually complex area of law, involving as it does fundamental issues of statutory and decisional law under the Internal Revenue Code, ERISA and the federal securities laws, supplemented by copious administrative guidance.

The book is both comprehensive and clearly written, and accordingly I recommend it to all who venture into the area of executive compensation, whether they be experts or novices, plan participants or plan sponsors, or advisors to any of these. I have been an ERISA lawyer for more than 40 years, and have advised many clients on different aspects of executive compensation, but reading this book gave me new insights and reminded me of many things I had forgotten or never knew. I will keep it readily available as a reference.

I hope you enjoy it, and profit from reading it, as much as I have done.

David Pratt
Jay and Ruth Caplin Distinguished Professor of Law, Albany Law School
Fellow, American College of Employee Benefits Counsel

Albany, New York

# Acknowledgments

Thank you to attorneys Adam Meeham from the Employee Benefits law firm of Smith and Downey, P.A., Hannah Munn from Poyner Spruill, and Kevin Ceglowski from Poyner Spruill for their important contributions to this book. Additional thanks to Jennifer Smith, Esq. Research Fellow at the University of Maryland Francis King Carey School of Law, for her extraordinary research and her dedication to this project. We also wish to acknowledge Myra Carter, Elyshia Menkin, Lili Nizankiewicz, and Antoinette Tardy for their invaluable administrative assistance in the preparation of this book.

Finally, as authors, we wish to thank the publisher and editorial staff, in particular, Richard Paszkiet and Caitlin McCauley, for their patience and their support for the entire project.

# Contacts

We hope you find this book helpful. We welcome your comments, which you may send to Sharon Reece at sreece@law.umaryland.edu, Kelsey Mayo at kmayo@poynerspruill.com, or Jesse St.Cyr at jstcyr@poynerspruill.com.

CHAPTER 1

# Introduction to Executive Compensation

## Section 1.1 Purpose of this Book

The purpose of this book about executive compensation is to provide those who do not frequently interface with, or practice executive compensation, with the tools to navigate this complex area of law in a user-friendly manner. As you will see, executive compensation is more complex than many practitioners anticipate initially. Therefore, this book will provide an overview of many key areas of the law, and will highlight opportunities and pitfalls that are common in executive compensation. The book will not, however, serve as a single comprehensive source of the law—as that would take many more volumes of text. Rather, it highlights the most essential rules and laws that you should be familiar with when navigating an executive compensation matter.

This book is intended to aid lawyers, accountants, business owners, and tax and human resource professionals, who are assisting companies implement executive compensation, or shape policies in the form of incentive pay, equity compensation, and/or deferred compensation plans. The book also may be relevant to students in business, law, accounting, human resources, tax and other disciplines and assist them in learning about the compliance risks associated with executive compensation programs. Of course, nobody should ever stop learning, so this book also is intended for members of the public who are interested in the area.

## Section 1.2 What is Executive Compensation?

One fundamental question is: what is the executive compensation that we will be discussing in this book. Executive compensation could be most simply defined as anything of value that a company would like to provide to a key employee. This could be everything from base salary to incentive compensation to perquisites. As we discuss in chapter 2, these are all items subject to negotiation in the context of an executive's employment agreement or offer.

The executive's pay package may consist of both current compensation and deferred compensation. Current compensation is anything paid immediately, such as salary, vacation pay, etc. Deferred compensation, on the other hand, is not paid immediately, for example, certain incentives and retirement plans. Generally deferred compensation is governed by a plan or written arrangement, which may be either a qualified or a nonqualified plan. Qualified plans, in this context, refer to the company's 401(k) plan, 403(b) plan, and/or pension plan (including a cash balance plan). The nonqualified plans are all other forms of deferred compensation.

This book will focus on the legal and regulatory compliance of only those non-qualified incentive and deferred compensation components of an employee's compensation package—that portion of the package provided in the form of incentive pay, equity compensation, and/or deferred compensation plans.

## Section 1.3 Stakeholders in Executive Compensation

Executive compensation is a critical topic for companies of all sizes. If it is a public company, there could be literally hundreds or thousands of shareholders demanding that the board of directors find the best and brightest executives to lead the company. If it is a start-up company, the owners may be facing cash flow challenges inherent when the owner wants to reinvest in the business to grow, while also attracting and retaining the talented individuals who will allow the business to grow. If the company is a non-profit, sometimes the altruistic pitch is not enough to get the talented executive to leave the lucrative compensation common in the for-profit market behind. In all cases, the parties may be balancing the desire for current compensation, tax deferral, security, and flexibility.

However, it is not only the two parties to the agreement that have an interest in executive compensation. Executive compensation is also important to the crafters of public policy. Legislators and regulators must decide what rules must be satisfied for the executives and companies to reap the tax benefits related to executive compensation. Generally, the rules reflect the collective judgment in balancing the need to generate current tax revenue in Congressional budgeting, a desire to protect the non-executive workforce from inappropriate executive behavior, and the ability of the parties to legitimately negotiate deferred compensation. As discussed throughout this book, executive compensation is carefully regulated and it behooves companies to shape their policies and practices in accordance with these regulations.

## Section 1.4 Which Employees Should Receive Executive Compensation?

The term **executive** in executive compensation is not a term of art. Executive compensation may be provided to nearly any key employee of the organization and should be provided to any individual the company desires to attract and retain. Certain arrangements—such as certain short-term incentive plans, change in control plans, and equity plans may be offered to any such employee in the organization. However, as explained in chapter 5, certain types of executive compensation plans must be limited to only the top group of management and key employees—those that might be considered C-suite employees or, in larger organizations, include the next level of the reporting hierarchy, sometimes called vice presidents or executive vice presidents, or a similar title. Thus, it is critical when providing compensation to a key employee for the company, to determine whether that particular arrangement may be offered to the employee, and then ensure that the program is designed and administered in compliance with the applicable rules and regulations.

Regulators and legislators who make rules regarding executive compensation generally ignore titles and instead focus mostly on how the compensation is structured. Thus, when considering whether a compensation arrangement might be regulated—focus first on the type of compensation and then on the title of the individual.

However, this doesn't mean that it isn't important to identify the executives or key employees in a particular workforce—since the company may want to invest more time and money in attracting and retaining those employees. In addition, there are different considerations for establishing an effective compensation program for executives, than for establishing compensation for rank-and-file workers. As an example, if an employer wants to match its employees' 401(k) retirement plan deferrals up to 5 percent of total compensation, it often can do so and fully deduct that 5 percent match for all rank-and-file employees. The company might not be able to do the same for its executives or highly compensated employees.[1] Due to the limitations of the qualified plan, the company may want to put in a nonqualified plan to provide additional benefits for its highly paid employees who were limited in the 401(k) plan.

Finally, the company should consider what groups of employees may be privy to important trade secrets and other proprietary information. The company may use enhanced compensation and benefit programs in exchange for certain protective covenants (e.g., non-competes, non-solicitations, and the like)—some of which may be subject to the regulations discussed throughout this book.

## Section 1.5 The Employers

Different employers use various considerations to determine how and why they are compensating their executives in a certain manner. Some of these considerations are most important for purposes of designing the executive compensation programs (e.g., short term versus long term).

1. Qualified plans have certain limits—such as compensation limits, deferral limits, and annual contribution limits—that may prevent the company from giving the executive the full 5% contribution.

The determination of whether a company is a for-profit versus a not-for-profit entity is a major distinction for purposes of determining which rules might apply to the compensation arrangement. Some companies are created specifically to achieve a profit for its shareholders, and all of that profit will be taxable. The company may or may not be taxed at the corporate level, but if so, there is often a comparison of the corporate tax rate versus the individual tax rate. On the other hand, not-for-profit companies must meet certain requirements and generally do not have to pay any tax on its revenues. Many people do not typically think of executive compensation in the public sector, but the public sector does compete with the private sector for talent and similarly consider executive compensation to attract and retain top employees. This distinction between for-profit and non-profit is critical because non-profit employers (both public and private sector) have to comply with additional rules because the legislators believe they don't have the same incentives to pay current compensation as for-profit employers.

In addition, the executive compensation practices of publicly held companies are subject to additional scrutiny and federal security rules. Public companies are those that are required to be registered under the Securities Exchange Act of 1934 because they have made a public offering of their stock. The book will explain, in a later chapter, the securities rules that impact public companies' pay practices. Any compensation professional will need to work closely with the company's securities advisors in order to ensure that any compensation granted to executives is being appropriately designed, disclosed, and approved.

The ensuing chapters will focus on the legal and regulatory compliance of the non-qualified incentive and deferred compensation components of an employee's compensation package.

*CHAPTER* **2**

# Negotiating the Executive's Employment Agreement

## Section 2.1 Perspectives

When negotiating an employment agreement, it is important to help your client keep the long-term perspective in mind. Ultimately, the two parties to an employment agreement want the same outcome. The employer wants the executive to work for the company on terms that (1) are lucrative enough to retain the executive, (2) will incentivize achievement of the company's objectives, and (3) can be properly administered. The parties naturally come at this shared objective with different interests that need to be balanced.

Employers that clearly define their mission and their short-term and long-term goals and objectives, are usually in the best position to build a workforce that is carefully designed to meet the focused needs of the company. Hiring decisions are usually the result of board/management meetings that identify specific needs that must be filled to facilitate the growth of the organization. Notes and minutes that clearly reflect those discussions can be helpful in the event that an employer is ever involved in litigation that requires the organization to justify a decision not to hire an applicant or to fire an executive.

### A. Executive: Balance Negotiation with Long-Term Relationship

The executive wants to maximize compensation potential, minimize uncertainty in compensation, and achieve maximum protection and flexibility. However, in pursuing that objective, the executive runs the risk of creating an unshakable impression or image of one who is unreasonably and completely self-interested at the expense of the company. Most companies do not expect executives to work for free and understand and expect negotiation. However, demands that are out of industry norms, or perceived as one-sided, may create a lasting negative impression. Even if the parties do agree on terms eventually, that negative impression may have long-lasting negative effects for the executive—such as difficult relations with a senior executive and/or the board.

## B. Employer: Balance Recruitment with Philosophy and Administration

The company, on the other hand, has an interest in minimizing compensation, retaining discretion for pay, and maximizing the conditional nature of compensation (e.g., paying for performance). However, the company must balance those protective desires with the need to recruit and retain necessary talent. A company that pays less than market, or provides less certainty regarding compensation, may find it difficult to attract and/or retain desired talent.

Some companies find themselves at the other end of the spectrum and are so committed to a particular executive that they are tempted to accede to nearly any demand from the executive. This inclination must be balanced. If the company brings in an executive at a significantly higher rate or with meaningfully richer benefits that are not aligned with the company's compensation philosophy as applied to other executives, it may create discontent, departures, and/or the need to increase compensation and benefits across the board.

Finally, the company should carefully evaluate its ability to manage the desired arrangement. A company that agrees to offer new benefits or new incentive structures to an executive, is less likely to have procedures in place to ensure the compliance and consistent application of those arrangements. To avoid disputes with the executive and the pitfalls of compliance issues discussed in later chapters, the company needs to be prepared to properly administer any arrangement to which it agrees.

# Section 2.2 Provisions

An entire book might easily be dedicated to all the provisions the executive and a company may wish to negotiate in an agreement, and the pros and cons of different approaches. This section will discuss some of the most common provisions and positions the parties might consider, outside of the compensation itself.

## A. Position/Duties

The first step is establishing what the employer is looking for in a candidate and identifying carefully the particular job duties and the ideal candidate to fill those job duties. A disconnect between what the employer is seeking and what the executive believes the employer is seeking can lead to early problems no matter what the compensation may be. That is why it is important to have a clear job description. Job descriptions should be written before the hiring process begins. While drafting these descriptions can be a tedious process, they serve numerous key functions:

1. A job description will help determine and identify the skills and qualifications needed to fulfill the carefully identified duties of the position at issue.

2. A job description will identify the essential functions of the position at issue, which will be crucial in the event that the applicant or the executive has a disability and is in need of an accommodation under the Americans with Disabilities (ADA) and Americans with Disabilities Amendments Act (ADAA).
3. A job description will help a newly hired executive understand the expectations of his or her new employer.
4. A job description will help set realistic expectations for compensation and/or the philosophy of compensating executives.
5. A job description can help remind a faltering executive of his or her expectations, thus increasing the likelihood of reforming such an executive or, in the alternative, providing a clear justification for the need to terminate the executive if he or she is deemed to no longer be a desirable presence in the workplace.

By taking care of some of these issues up front with the job description, it will be much easier to then transition this over to the employment agreement or offer letter, at the appropriate time.

The job position or duties section of the agreement typically includes the executive's title, reporting structure, principal place of employment, and a statement that the executive must devote all of his or her working time and effort to the company. It should obligate the executive to follow all the company's policies, procedures, and standards, as they may be established and modified by the company from time to time. The executive should commit to follow the instructions and directives promulgated by the company's board. Finally, the job description should include a statement that to the extent any provision of the agreement conflicts with any company handbook, or other company policy, the terms of the agreement shall supersede the conflicting policy.

## B. Reporting Relationship

The reporting structure in the organization should be made clear from the outset of any relationship. A failure to effectively communicate who the executive shall report to and/or who will report to the executive may lead to problems. The executive's employment agreement should reflect the reporting structure. If there is no employment agreement, the employee's offer letter and/or job description should reflect the reporting structure.

The reporting relationship, of course, will depend on the position for which the executive is being hired. Typically, a Chief Executive Officer will report to the company's board of directors. Other C-Suite level executives like the Chief Financial Officer (CFO), Chief Operating Officer (COO), Chief Marketing Officer (CMO), etc., typically report to the Chief Executive Officer with an additional acknowledgement that they must follow reasonable instructions from the board. Lower-level executives report to more senior executives.

## C. Term of Agreement

A key aspect of executive employment agreements, in contrast to the employment arrangements of most other employees, is the agreements often are for a term rather than at will. A typical term provision provides for (1) a defined initial term of employment; (2) renewal terms that typically happen automatically absent a notice of termination from either the executive or employee and typically continue the same agreement terms as those in place during the initial term; and (3) a cross-reference to the termination sections of the agreement explaining how either the company or executive may end the employment relationship before the expiration of either the initial term or a renewal term.

## D. Severance and Related Mitigation and Offset Issues

Generally, executives will expect and negotiate for severance arrangements to provide additional compensation at or after the end of their employment with a company. The specifics of these arrangements vary widely, but several principles are typical. First, an executive's severance will typically be owed, if the executive is terminated without cause or if the executive terminates the agreement for good reason. Cause and good reason must be carefully defined in the employment agreement, because any ambiguity is typically going to be construed against the company (recall the company is typically taking the lead in drafting the agreement). If the company terminates the executive for cause, it is common for the agreement to call for a complete forfeiture, or in some cases a mere reduction, in the severance owed to the executive.

When drafting the agreement, the company and executive should consider, negotiate, and draft language explaining what happens to the severance obligation if the executive's employment ends because of death or disability. The specific components of a severance package may include cash compensation (paid in a lump sum or over time), continuation of health care and other insurance benefits, rights associated with stock-based compensation, and additional fringe benefits such as vehicle, technology, and relocation payments.

Given the large financial obligations severance can represent in a departing executive situation, companies are reluctant to allow executives to keep large severance payments if they are immediately reemployed and again highly compensated. For that reason, many agreements contain offset language tied to the cash compensation, health care continuation benefits, or both. Those clauses typically require the departed executive to report to the company if he or she obtains new employment and, in some cases, to report the specifics of new earnings. If the executive fails to mitigate the need for the company to continue making the severance payments, or otherwise triggers the offset language, the clause will allow the company to stop the stream of severance payments and, in some cases, recoup amounts paid already. The offset clauses are often tied to the provisions of restrictive covenants in the employment agreement, such as non-compete, non-solicitation, and non-disparagement covenants.

Finally, executive employment agreements invariably will require the executive to execute a general release in favor of the company in order to receive any severance benefits. This is frequently addressed in the employment agreement in one of two ways. Either the company reserves the right to require the executive to execute a general release agreement in a form prepared by and satisfactory to the company, or the company prepares a sample general release agreement in advance and attaches it as an exhibit to the employment agreement. The release should include a reminder of, and reference to, the executive's ongoing obligations under any restrictive covenants that survive the end of the employment relationship.

## E. Restrictive Covenants

Most executive employment agreements have restrictive covenants to protect the company both during the term of the executive's employment and after the agreement ends. A key aspect for companies to consider is that non-compete and non-solicitation laws will be governed by state law. This has two key effects—first, the potential scope of an enforceable restrictive covenant may be dramatically different depending on the applicable state law, and second, the choice of law provision in the agreement will be vitally important to the scope and enforceability of the restrictive covenants.

Understanding it is impossible to forecast the effect of the terms of any non-compete or non-solicitation covenant because of the varied state laws, some general principles do apply. The more senior an employee, the more likely a court may be to enforce restrictive covenants and to enforce them at the upper limits of time and territory restrictions otherwise allowable under state law. In addition, most executive employment agreements tie severance payments to compliance with these non-compete and non-solicitation covenants. Some states will allow forfeiture of severance provisions. This means a company can claw back severance or not pay it at all. This is separate from any attempt by the employer to obtain an injunction enforcing the covenants under contractual provisions not restricted by the reasonableness requirements state law imposes on non-compete covenants. In other words, a company can condition severance payments on non-competition restrictions that exceed the activities, time, and territory scope otherwise allowed by state law, so long as the company only seeks to recover or avoid paying the severance benefits and does not ask a court to prevent the former executive from working in violation of those restrictions. Regardless of the particular state law applicable to the contract, the company should make sure it understands the maximum allowable scope of restrictive covenants under those laws. The company often will want to draft covenants as close as reasonable to the maximum scope to protect itself from the future activities of departed executives.

An executive's non-disparagement obligations during employment typically will be covered by two layers of protection in favor of the company: (1) a for-cause termination right if the executive disparages the company and

(2) the executive's fiduciary duty to act in the company's best interest. An executive who disparages his or her current employer risks termination for cause and an associated loss of severance benefits. Post termination of employment, the non-disparagement obligation should be covered by a specific covenant in the employment agreement that survives the end of employment and as a standalone provision in the general release agreement the executive must sign to receive any severance benefits.

In addition, an executive may try to negotiate a mutual non-disparagement provision—ensuring that the company does not make negative statements against the executive. Mutual non-disparagement provisions generally are not included unless specifically requested by the employee and often are resisted by companies at the outset of an agreement but more readily accepted as part of a separation agreement. It may also be advisable to limit application of the non-disparagement provision to certain individuals within the company because it may be impracticable or impossible to limit the conduct of all employees, particularly in large organizations.

# Section 2.3 Compensation Package

There are numerous ways to design the executive's total compensation package. These will need to balance the parties' tax objectives, cash flow considerations, and the desire to tie compensation to performance and retention.

## A. Compensation Elements

The typical executive cash compensation component consists of base salary, short-term bonuses, and long-term bonuses. Cash compensation often is set by reference to some relevant indicators in sophisticated comparability data. This comparability data typically is drawn from surveys of the compensation packages of executives performing similar or nearly identical duties in similar or nearly identical businesses.

Typically, an executive's most important welfare benefit is health coverage. This coverage may take the form of: (1) comprehensive health coverage for the executive and the executive's family (typically the same as the rank-and-file plan), (2) an executive medical plan that covers services not covered by the general plan; (3) reimbursement of the executive's copays, deductibles, and out-of-pocket costs incurred under the general plan; and/or (4) annual comprehensive "executive level" physicals. Practitioners should note, some of these plans will be taxable to the executive because they are discriminatory. In addition, the Patient Protection and Affordability Act of 2010 (ACA) also imposed nondiscrimination rules for insured health arrangements, but delayed those rules' effective date until the Department of Treasury issued final regulations. As of 2021, no regulations were proposed, but employers should keep in mind that they may apply in the future.

Additionally, executives often participate in the same short-term disability plans as rank-and-file employees. Employers and executives should review these plans, however, to consider the extent to which the plans' terms continue the disabled executive's actual cash compensation (base salary plus incentive compensation), rather than only the base salary. This is especially critical in those situations in which performance-based compensation represents a significant portion of the executive's total cash compensation component. If the rank-and-file plan does not provide adequate protection, the company may provide a carve-out disability plan for its executives. These carve-out plans may be individual, portable policies owned by the executives. Premiums on those policies often are paid by the employer and taxed to the executives or paid by the executives with after-tax dollars to ensure that any benefits paid under the policies will be tax free. Those policies may also have more favorable provisions, such as shorter waiting periods and a preferred occupation disability definition.

Although most executives participate in their employers' rank-and-file group-term life insurance plans, these plans may be inadequate to provide the level of death benefit coverage needed to sustain the needs of the survivors of a typical executive. Therefore, many companies will offer either a self-insured or fully insured supplemental death benefit for executives.

A more recent addition to the menu of executive compensation program components is long-term care insurance. The employer may deduct the premium costs as they are incurred, the executive is not taxed on either the value of the coverage or the benefits actually received, and no nondiscrimination rules apply, so the benefit may be offered only to key executives. Note, however, long-term care insurance cannot be offered as a pre-tax elective benefit. If the executive pays for it with salary deferrals, those deferrals will still be taxable to the executive.

## B. Deferred Compensation versus Current Compensation

At first blush, many assume that executives would want only current compensation and the company might be motivated to prefer deferred compensation. However, executives may prefer some element of deferred compensation—particularly if they are highly paid and/or nearing retirement—and the company may prefer current compensation for deductions and simplicity. Current compensation should be preferable to the executive to the extent: (1) it is needed for the executive's current expenditures; (2) the executive believes his or her current marginal tax rates are lower than future marginal tax rates; and/or (3) the benefit cannot be provided through a qualified retirement plan and the company's future solvency is a risk. Similarly, the executive may prefer deferred compensation when: (1) current compensation provides sufficient short-term cash flow; (2) the executive believes his or her future marginal tax rate will be lower than his or her current marginal tax rate; and (3) the benefit is provided either through a well-funded qualified plan, or the company's solvency is of little to no concern.

A company may prefer deferred compensation in circumstances where anticipated cash flow is higher in future years than it is currently—such as start-ups, companies in a design and development phase, and those anticipating a near-term sale. Those companies may wish to retain current cash and pay executives upon the liquidity event (e.g., upon the launch of a product or sale of the company). Also, just as the executive may be concerned with tax consequences, the timing of the company's deduction may be a factor in its compensation preference. Current compensation and qualified retirement plan contributions result in current deductions, while nonqualified deferred compensation results in a deduction in a later year. As a result, a company may prefer the current deduction if it believes current tax rates are higher than they will be in the future. The first tier of the executive's deferred compensation benefits generally is provided through the employer's qualified plans. Although these plans enjoy several very important tax and other advantages—immediate deduction of contributions by the employer, tax-deferred growth on plan assets, availability of rollovers for distributions, bankruptcy protection for plan assets—the statutory limits on the amounts of deferred compensation that may be provided by qualified plans, make them inadequate to meet all of the typical executive's deferred compensation needs.

Therefore, many companies also offer executives a nonqualified deferred compensation plan (NQDCP), which is intended to enhance the executive's deferred compensation picture. These nonqualified plans may contain both employer contribution and voluntary executive contribution features. The employer contribution feature typically serves the dual purpose of providing important supplemental deferred compensation to the executive and providing a golden handcuff that discourages the executive from leaving the employ of the employer. Employers and executives look to the combination of the nonqualified plan benefits, the qualified plan benefits, and Social Security benefits to provide an adequate, aggregate level of retirement income to the executives.

## C. Nonqualified versus Qualified Deferred Compensation Arrangements and Plans

It is also important to understand that deferred compensation may be provided in at least two different ways: qualified plans and nonqualified plans. Qualified plans are arrangements with the most favorable tax consequences (for both the employer and employee). Plans such as 401(k) plans, qualified pension plans, and 403(b) plans generally fall into this category. All these arrangements allow the employee to defer income tax until receipt of the benefit, while the company is permitted to take an immediate deduction for its contributions. In exchange for this favorable tax treatment, the tax code applies a host of requirements the plan must meet, including nondiscrimination requirements for most employers. Eligible 457(b) arrangements (applicable only to tax-exempt employers) are hybrid arrangements that receive similar favorable tax treatment, and must comply with numerous requirements, but do not have the nondiscrimination requirements of qualified plans.

Essentially every other arrangement for deferring compensation may be grouped into the category of nonqualified arrangements. These arrangements are not subject to the nondiscrimination requirements that qualified plans are, but, nonetheless, are subject to a myriad of tax rules that restrict the design of these plans. Failure to properly design, document, and/or administer these plans can result in significant tax penalties.

## D. Incentive Compensation

Incentive compensation can form a significant portion of an executive's compensation. As a result, a significant amount of negotiating may center around these provisions. Incentive compensation can run from annual, performance-based bonuses, to multi-year, long-term incentive arrangements. They may be purely cash payments, or they may include equity in the company, and may include some element of retention by including a vesting or payment schedule. The general philosophy of incentive compensation is often driven by the company. However, executives desiring to sweeten the compensation package often find success in negotiating for an increase in the potential incentive compensation or negotiating an equity award.

In negotiating the incentive compensation, a point of tension often arises regarding how the incentive compensation will be determined from year to year. The company naturally wants to retain discretion to set and adapt to current business goals and needs. On the other hand, the executive wants some certainty or promise that objectives will be understandable, attainable, and fairly determined. There are many variations in how the parties resolve this tension—however, the most common include: (1) setting a minimum potential amount of incentive compensation in the contract; (2) stating in the contract the general criteria and their weights in determining performance; (3) requiring objectives to be set and communicated before the performance period: and/or (4) allowing the executive some level of input on the performance requirements set each year.

## E. Fringes (Taxable and Non-Taxable) and Perquisites

Fringe benefits and other perquisites are common requests from executives. The executive's counsel primarily should be mindful of the taxability of the benefit and ensure the executive understands the tax consequences or appropriately negotiates a gross-up payment for the taxability. Similarly, the company also needs to ensure it understands the taxability of benefits and appropriately reports them to the executive. In addition, the company should carefully assess other potential impacts of agreeing to the request—such as any nondiscrimination requirements, impacts on qualified plans (such as whether the taxable benefit must be treated as compensation for those benefits), and ensuring payroll providers are ready and able to properly manage the reporting.

## F. Equity-Based Compensation

Finally, executives of for-profit organizations may negotiate for equity-based compensation. Tax-exempt organizations do not have equity and therefore executives of those organizations do not receive equity compensation. Equity awards often come in the form of incentive stock options, non-statutory or nonqualified stock options, discounted stock options, restricted stock, restricted stock units, stock appreciation rights, or phantom stock, as explained in later chapters.

# Section 2.4 Documentation

Documentation of the employment arrangement can come in a wide range of forms—from single-page offer letters to lengthy employment agreements. The important point for both sides is to understand that despite their differences all documentation should be reviewed and negotiated carefully.

## A. Offer Letters

Many companies and executives enter the employment relationship with only an offer letter. These letters are often only a few pages and outline the basic terms, without the detail that causes employment agreements to go on for pages. While this simplicity is attractive, counsel for both the executive and the company should be careful to ensure there is sufficient specificity, particularly with respect to payments potentially subject to IRC § 409A. The potency of Section 409A will be discussed in later chapters. Often, a payment that could be exempt from IRC § 409A lacks sufficient terms in the offer letter to meet the exemption, thereby creating a potential tax issue for the executive, and lack of flexibility for both parties. Offer letters work best when the parties agree the executive is entitled to benefits, severance, and/or incentive compensation under terms that are already outlined in a robust plan/policy document. This permits a simple offer letter, while ensuring the more nuanced terms of the tax code are satisfied.

Occasionally the parties will enter the relationship under an offer letter with the intent to negotiate a more robust agreement. While this is an acceptable practice, the parties must be aware of common pitfalls, such as ensuring there is adequate consideration by the executive for new restraints (such as restrictive covenants) and avoiding unintentional substitutions that could create IRC § 409A violations with the resulting unintended tax consequences for the executive.

## B. Agreements

Of course, almost all executives will have the terms of their employment memorialized in a written agreement. The agreement is the document controlling the terms of the executive's employment, laying out the rights and responsibilities of both the executive and the company, and explaining compensation terms and conditions under which the executive's employment may end. In almost all cases, the agreement will supersede the offer letter, rendering the offer letter ineffective.

Typically, the agreement will be drafted by the company's attorneys after consultation with the company's other executives or board of directors, and then presented to the executive for review by the executive and his or her attorneys. It is important that both sides view the terms of the agreement with a long lens, as executive employment agreements are often the key documents governing disputes over what amounts an executive must be paid when employment is terminated, and, before that, when, why, and how the employment may be terminated.

*CHAPTER* **3**

# Tax Aspects of Executive Compensation

## Section 3.1 General Rules: Timing of Employee Income Inclusion and Employer Deduction

Compensation paid to executives in the form of cash or other rights are generally ordinary business expenses for which the company may take a deduction.[1] There are a number of special rules for certain arrangements, however, the general rule is the employer will be permitted to deduct deferred compensation in the same year the employee includes the amount in income.[2] Absent a special exception in the Internal Revenue Code (IRC), the employee (as a cash basis taxpayer[3]) will take the amount into income in the year he or she receives the compensation—whether that compensation is in the form of cash, property, rights, etc. and whether that receipt is actual or constructive receipt.[4] While a right may be taxable compensation, the creation of an executive compensation plan that includes a mere promise to pay in the future, generally is not a right that will be immediately taxable to the executive, unless one of the principles or exceptions discussed below accelerate the taxation. Thus, an employer's grant of deferred compensation today, generally, will not result in a current deduction for the employer.

However, if an amount is not deferred compensation, the employer is allowed to deduct the expense in the ordinary course (for example in the year it accrues, assuming the company is an accrual basis taxpayer) without regard to the year in which the employee takes the amount into income.[5] Generally, if the amount is paid within two-and-one-half months after the fiscal year in which it

1. I.R.C. § 162 (2018).

2. I.R.C. § 404(a)(5) (2018). If the company's tax year is not the calendar year, the deduction is taken in the year that includes the end of calendar year in which the employee takes the amount into income. Note, also, that funded arrangements have specific requirements regarding the maintenance of individual accounts in order for amounts to be deductible.

3. I.R.C. § 446 (2018).

4. I.R.C. §§ 61, 83, 451 (2018).

5. *See* Rev. Rul. 88-68, 1988-2 C.B. 117.

is granted to the employee, the amount will not be deferred compensation.[6] As discussed later, this two-and-one-half month concept is potentially applicable in both the IRC 409A[7] and 457(f)[8] contexts. However, those rules generally measure the two-and-one-half months from the year in which the substantial risk of forfeiture lapses, whereas the deduction rule may be measured from the year in which the right was granted.[9]

Finally, the IRC may limit the amount of deferred compensation a particular company is able to deduct. For instance, publicly held corporations are permitted to deduct only $1,000,000 in compensation for its covered employees[10] and health insurance issuers may be limited to a $500,000 deduction in certain years.[11] The rules applicable to publicly traded companies will be discussed in more detail in later chapters. Tax deduction for executive compensation is covered in the next chapter.

# Section 3.2 Principles

## A. Constructive Receipt

The doctrine of constructive receipt is a somewhat intuitive anti-abuse principle. Although an individual is a cash basis taxpayer, meaning he or she accounts for income when it is received, the principle of constructive receipt prevents the taxpayer from manipulating the taxability of compensation by electing when to receive the income. In essence, the constructive receipt doctrine provides that if the individual has a substantially unrestricted right to receive the compensation upon request, then the amount is taxable to the individual.[12] For example, if the employee has the right to receive $50,000 at any time, merely by requesting the company pay that to him or her, then the employee has constructive receipt of that $50,000 and it should be taxable in the year the employee acquired that right; he or she cannot choose the year in which taxation occurs by deferring payment to a year in which he or she feels better positioned taxwise.

On the other hand, if the employee's ability to control the receipt of compensation has substantial limitations or restrictions, or the employee has only a future right to receive the income, that income will not be considered constructively received. Historically, an employee who had the right to receive income in a year was permitted to defer receipt of it before the beginning of the year without

---

6. *See* I.R.S. Priv. Ltr. Rul. 2000-09-013 (Nov. 26, 1999).
7. I.R.C. § 409A (2018).
8. I.R.C. § 457(f) (2018).
9. *See* I.R.S. Tech. Adv. Mem. 1999-23-045 (Oct. 9, 1999).
10. I.R.C. § 162(m) (2018).
11. I.R.C. § 162(m)(6) (2018).
12. I.R.C. § 451 (2018).

creating a constructive receipt issue. IRC Section 409A codified this ability to defer taxability,[13] albeit with certain limitations discussed in later chapters.

While this principle might seem only theoretical or unlikely to arise in an executive compensation situation, the issue does arise more frequently than expected. As an example, this principle may create tax considerations where the executive has the ability to sell back unused paid time off, is able to voluntarily terminate employment and receive severance, or can dictate when a payment from the company can be made.[14]

## B. Economic Benefit

There is a second doctrine relating to executive compensation that is somewhat less intuitive. This doctrine is called the economic benefit doctrine. Essentially, it says that if the individual's right to future compensation is shielded from the company's general creditors, then that amount is taxable to the employee even if the employee does not have a current right to receive the compensation. As an example, if company were to put $50,000 into an irrevocable trust that its creditors could not access, and the amount would be payable to the executive in ten years, the executive would be taxable on that $50,000 immediately.

As applied to deferred compensation arrangements, this means that if the arrangement is funded then the benefit will be includable in the executive's income when the right is either (1) transferrable, or (2) not subject to a substantial risk of forfeiture. For this purpose, the right to compensation is transferrable if the executive's right is not subject to a substantial risk of forfeiture and he or she could transfer it to someone other than the company. A right to compensation (or other property) is subject to a substantial risk of forfeiture if the right is (1) conditioned on the future performance of substantial services or on the nonperformance of services, or (2) conditioned on something other than the performance of services and there is a substantial possibility that the property will be forfeited.[15] Thus, in essence, if a deferred compensation plan is funded, taxation will not be deferred past the time the executive obtains a vested right to that amount, even if it is not paid to the executive until a later tax year.

As a result, most deferred compensation plans (other than qualified plans discussed below) are unfunded.[16] However, unfunded does not necessarily mean that funds are not earmarked for the purpose of paying the deferred compensation benefits. Unfunded means only that the amounts are not protected from the company's creditors. Thus, escrow arrangements that are beyond the reach

13. I.R.C. § 409A(a)(4)(B) (2018).

14. I.R.C. § 409A (2018).

15. *See* Treas. Reg. § 1.83-3(f) (2014); Drysdale v. Comm'r, 277 F.2d 413 (6th Cir. 1960); United States v. Drescher, 179 F.2d 863 (2d Cir. 1950).

16. This is particularly true due to the ERISA-related considerations for exemption, such as a top-hat plan. However, companies that are exempt from ERISA may find funded arrangements more attractive, particularly if the plan pays the executive upon lapse of the substantial risk of forfeiture.

of creditors,[17] letters of credit to secure certain benefits, and irrevocable trusts may create funded arrangements. However, as discussed in later chapters, there are ways to fund the arrangement without running afoul of the economic benefit doctrine, such as rabbi trusts and other vehicles the company's creditors may access.

# Section 3.3 Exceptions in the Tax Code

## A. Qualified Plans

As noted earlier, qualified plans enjoy the most favorable tax treatment. Despite the fact that the benefits are set aside in a funded trust, protected from creditors, the amounts are **not** taxable to the executive until paid from the plan. In addition, as an exception to the normal matching principles of taxation,[18] the company enjoys an immediate deduction in the year of the contribution to the plan (despite the deferred taxation to the executive). As a result, maximizing the permitted benefits under these plans may be most favorable to both parties.

## B. Optional Accelerated Taxation and Deduction on Restricted Property

The general rule that an individual must account for all rights when reporting income, applies equally to rights in property such as a stock option,[19] stock appreciation rights (SAR),[20] or restricted stock unit (RSU).[21] However, when the deferred compensation is a grant of a property, (other than cash or cash equivalents[22]) that is not immediately vested and transferrable, Section 83 may delay the date when income is includible. The employee will take into income the excess of the fair market value of the property over the employee's basis in the property, if any, when the employee's rights become either transferrable or no longer subject to substantial risk of forfeiture.[23]

For this purpose, an amount is subject to a substantial risk of forfeiture if the right to that amount is subject to the performance of future substantial services, refraining from performing substantial services (e.g., a non-compete restriction

17. Rev. Rul. 62-74, 1962-1 C.B. 68.

18. *See* I.R.C. §§ 267(a)(2), 274(e)(2) 404(d) (2018).

19. *See* I.R.C. § 421 (2018)

20. *See* Treas. Reg. § 1.409A-1 (2007).

21. *See* I.R.C. §§ 83, 409A (2018). *See also* Edward Bintz et al., Arnold, Porter Kaye Scholer LLP, *United State: Tax Law Changes to Executive Compensation*, MONDAQ (Jan. 3, 2018), http://www.mondaq.com/unitedstates/x/660388/Employee+Benefits+Compensation/Tax+Law+Changes+To+Executive+Compensation.

22. *See* I.R.C. § 83 (2018).

23. I.R.C. § 83(a) (2018); Treas. Reg. § 1.83-1 (2003).

or retirement requirement), or other conditions related to the purpose of the compensation.[24] This is a facts and circumstances determination.

However, the executive may make an election under IRC Section 83(b) to recognize the income attributable to the property at an earlier date. This allows the company to recognize a deduction sooner and the executive to include a potentially lower amount in income (assuming the executive believes the value of the property will increase over time). Should an executive make a Section 83(b) election, the executive must, generally, file an executed election with the Internal Revenue Service. Because this impacts the deduction for the company, the executive should also provide proof of filing to the company. Often, the Section 83(b) election is a condition of the company's equity compensation arrangement, and the plan specifically notes the executive will be responsible for ensuring that the Section 83(b) election is actually and timely filed with the IRS and for all tax consequences resulting from said election.

## C. Deferred Compensation under Section 409A

Compensation that is subject to IRC Section 409A, but does not meet its requirements, will be taxable to the executive in the first year of failure, (plus a 20 percent penalty tax), even if the amount is not actually or constructively received until a later year. These requirements are in addition to (not in lieu of) the earlier rules. Thus, when designing or reviewing a plan subject to Section 409A counsel for the executive and the employee still must consider the longstanding constructive receipt and economic benefit doctrines as well as the newer rules under Section 409A to ensure their expected tax consequences are met. These rules are discussed at length in later chapters.

## D. Special Rules for Executives of Tax-Exempt Entities

Tax-exempt entities are less concerned with the timing of deductions, as they are exempt from federal taxation. In response, to balance their incentive to defer taxation for executives, the IRC includes a special provision limiting the tax deferral for employees of these tax-exempt entities. Where an executive of a for-profit company may vest in a deferred compensation amount today, receive payment three years from now, and take the amount into income in that later year of payment, an executive of a tax-exempt organization generally would be taxed on that amount in the year the amount vests (or, technically speaking, is no longer subject to a substantial risk of forfeiture), rather than the year in which the amount is received by the executive.[25]

This dramatically changes the design of executive compensation for many non-profit entities as the tax deferral in a nonqualified plan is limited to the amount of time which the executive is willing to remain subject to a substantial risk of forfeiture. This is, at least in part, why the tax code allows tax-exempt entities to have special eligible 457(b) plans that permit the employee to be vested

24. I.R.C. § 83(a) (2018); Treas. Reg. §1.83-1 (2003).
25. I.R.C. § 457(f) (2018).

and still defer taxation until it is actually paid, just with substantial limitations on the amount and timing.[26] These rules are discussed more in a later chapter. However, counsel to a non-profit or an executive of a non-profit should be careful to avoid the unique pitfalls lurking in IRC Section 457 when designing and negotiating the executive's compensation package.

---

26. I.R.C. § 457(b) (2018). *See also Tax-Exempt 457(b) Plans: Key Characteristics and Common Mistakes*, IRS (Apr. 16, 2020), https://www.irs.gov/retirement-plans/tax-exempt-457b-plans-key-characteristics-and-common-mistakes.

*CHAPTER* **4**

# Tax Deductions for Executive Compensation

This chapter focuses on a key employer consideration when providing compensation to employees and other service providers—the tax deductibility of that compensation. As a general rule, compensation is tax deductible to an employer, however there are many rules in the Internal Revenue Code (IRC) that dictate the timing of the deduction, and in some cases limit the amount an employer can deduct. Specifically, this chapter will cover:

- Section 162, which sets forth a general deduction for ordinary and necessary business expenses that covers many types of compensation, including salaries, but includes important limits, such as the limit on excess compensation under Section 162(m).
- Section 83, which provides specific rules for deducting compensation provided in the form of stock, stock options, and other property.
- Section 404, which governs deductions for contributions to retirement plans and payments under nonqualified deferred compensation plans.
- Sections 419 and 419A, which provide rules for deducting contributions to medical trusts.
- Section 280G, which limits deductions for golden parachute payments in mergers and acquisitions.

## Section 4.1 Section 162

IRC Section 162 allows a deduction for ordinary and necessary business expenses, including compensation expenses. Specifically, Section 162 states that "[t]here shall be allowed as a deduction all the ordinary and necessary expenses paid or incurred during the taxable year in carrying on any trade or business, including . . . a reasonable allowance for salaries or other compensation for personal services actually rendered."[1] Accordingly, "reasonable" compensation is deductible when paid or accrued.[2] Generally, employers use Section 162 to deduct payments of salary and cash bonuses, as well as expenses related to certain welfare benefits, such as medical insurance premiums. Compensation that does not qualify as reasonable compensation under Section 162 can still be paid, but it will not be deductible for tax purposes.

## A. Reasonableness under Section 162

Under Section 162, two things must be established for compensation to be considered reasonable, and therefore deductible. First, the payment must, in fact, be made for services rendered.[3] Second, the amount of the payment must be reasonable in relationship to the services performed.[4] If either test is failed, compensation is not reasonable, and, therefore, not deductible.

With respect to the second prong, courts have applied various multifactor approaches to determining the reasonableness of amounts paid.[5] For example, a 2016 Tax Court case, *H. W. Johnson v. Commissioner*, used a five-part reasonableness test followed by the U.S. Court of Appeals for the Ninth Circuit (and many other courts).[6] The court described the factors, stating:

> The Court of Appeals for the Ninth Circuit . . . applies five factors to determine the reasonableness of compensation, with no factor being determinative: (1) the employee's role in the company's success; (2) a comparison of compensation paid by similar companies for similar services; (3) the character and condition of the company; (4) potential conflicts of interest; and (5) the internal consistency of compensation arrangements. In analyzing the fourth factor, the Court of Appeals emphasizes evaluating the reasonableness of compensation payments from the perspective of a hypothetical independent investor, focusing

---

1. IRC §162(a) (2019).
2. I.R.C. § 162(a) (2019).
3. Treas. Reg. §1.162-7.
4. Treas. Reg. §1.162-7(b)(3); *see, e.g.*, Foos v. Comm'r, 41 T.C.M. (CCH) 863, 878 (1981) (explaining that courts have examined numerous factors in determining whether compensation is reasonable including, but not limited to, an employee's qualifications, an employee's contribution to the success of the business, and comparability to other salaries in the company and in the market generally).
5. *See, e.g.*, O.S.C. & Assocs. v. Comm'r, 187 F.3d 1116, 1121 (9th Cir. 1999) (four factors); Dexsil Corp. v. Comm'r, 147 F.3d 96, 100 (2d Cir. 1998) (five factors); Exacto Spring Corp. v. Comm'r, 196 F.3d 833, 834 (7th Cir. 1999) (seven factors); Alpha Medical, Inc. v. Comm'r, 172 F.3d 942, 946 (6th Cir. 1999) (nine factors); Donald Palmer Co. v. Comm'r, 69 T.C.M. (CCH) 1869 (1995), *aff'd*, 84 F.3d 431 (5th Cir. 1996) (nine factors).
6. 111 T.C.M. (CCH) 1418 (2016). *See, e.g.*, Eberl's Claim Serv., Inc. v. Comm'r, 249 F.3d 994, 999 (10th Cir. 2001); Dexsil Corp. v. Comm'r, 147 F.3d 96, 100 (2d Cir. 1998); Owensby & Kritikos, Inc. v. Comm'r, 819 F.2d 1315, 1323 (5th Cir. 1987); Elliotts, Inc. v. Comm'r, 716 F.2d 1241, 1245–48 (9th Cir. 1983); Mayson Mfg. Co. v. Comm'r, 178 F.2d 115, 119 (6th Cir. 1949).

on whether the investor would receive a reasonable return on equity after payment of the compensation.[7]

While compliance with the requirements of Section 162 is economically important for the employer, in practice, disputes with the IRS over the reasonableness of compensation are fairly rare.

## B. Section 162(m): The $1 Million Deduction Limit

While the requirements of the reasonable compensation standard are fairly subjective, Section 162 includes some bright-line limits, including Section 162(m)'s annual $1 million deduction limit for compensation paid by publicly traded companies to certain executives. As with compensation that is not "reasonable" under Section 162, compensation that exceeds the Section 162(m) limit can still be paid, it just will not be deductible to the employer.

Section 162(m) denies a deduction to any "publicly held corporation" for "applicable employee remuneration" paid to any "covered employee" to the extent that the "applicable employee remuneration" for the taxable year exceeds $1,000,000.[8] Each of these terms is more fully explained below.

## C. Publicly Held Corporations

The term "publicly held corporation" under Section 162(m) means any corporation whose securities are required to be registered under Section 12 of the Securities Exchange Act of 1934, or that is *required* to file reports under Section 15(d) of the Exchange Act.[9]

### *(i) Covered Employees*

A person is a "covered employee" subject to the limits of Section 162(m) if the employee is: (1) the principal executive officer (PEO) or principal financial officer (PFO) at any time during the taxable year, or was an individual acting in such a capacity; (2) one of the three highest compensated officers for the taxable year (other than the PEO or PFO); or (3) was a covered employee for any preceding taxable year beginning after December 31, 2016.[10]

### *(ii) Applicable Employee Remuneration*

The "applicable employee remuneration" subject to the limits of Section 162(m) generally means the aggregate amount allowable as a deduction to the publicly held corporation for a taxable year (determined without regard to Section 162(m)(1))

---

7. H.W. Johnson v. Comm'r, 111 T.C.M. (CCH) 1418, 1418 (2016) (internal citations omitted).
8. I.R.C. § 162(m)(1) (2019).
9. I.R.C. § 162(m)(2) (2019).
10. I.R.C. § 162(m)(3) (2019).

for remuneration for services performed by a covered employee in any capacity, whether or not the services were performed during the taxable year.[11]

Prior to the Tax Cuts and Jobs Act (TCJA), the limit on deductibility under Section 162(m) did not apply to certain types of compensation, including certain commissions[12] and certain performance-based compensation.[13] The most notable exception for many corporations was the performance-based compensation exception, which provided a strong financial incentive for employers to emphasize pay-for-performance in their compensation packages for executives. As such, public companies commonly designed their incentive programs so that some, or all, such incentive compensation was exempt from the $1 million deduction limit.

As a result of the TJCA changes, the $1 million limit is a hard limit—all incentive compensation and commission-based compensation paid to covered employees now is subject to the $1 million deduction limit, except for certain compensation that is grandfathered.[14] Under the TCJA, compensation offered under a written binding contract as of November 2, 2017, and not materially modified after that date, was grandfathered and could still take advantage of the performance-based exception. IRS Notice 2018-68 provided helpful guidance on the scope of this grandfather rule.

## Section 4.2 Health and Welfare Benefits under Section 162

As mentioned above, employer-provided health and welfare benefits are generally deductible under Section 162 as long as they are considered ordinary business expenses,[15] which will typically be the case. The timing of the deduction related to these payments is governed by the method of accounting that the employer utilizes: for cash-basis taxpayers, health plan payments (including premiums for insured benefits) are deductible in the year they are actually paid; and for accrual-basis taxpayers, payments are deductible in the year in which costs are accrued.

Some confuse the rules found in Section 105—pertaining to income tax inclusion—with deductibility to the employer. Section 105 is an important consideration for executive offerings because it makes such benefits taxable to highly compensated individuals, if a plan cannot pass certain nondiscrimination tests, but Section 105 does not affect the employer's deduction.

---

11. Treas. Reg. § 1.162-33(c)(3).
12. Treas. Reg. § 1.162-27(d) (2015).
13. Treas. Reg. § 1.162-27(e)(2)(i) (2015).
14. I.R.S. Notice 2018-68, 2018-36 I.R.B. 418.
15. Treas. Reg. § 1.162-10(a) (2020).

# Section 4.3 Section 404: Retirement and Deferred Compensation Plans

The deductibility of employer contributions to fund retirement plans and to provide benefits under deferred compensation plans is governed by Section 404, rather than Section 162.[16]

## A. Contributions to Qualified Retirement Plans

Under Section 162, an employer's deduction for compensation paid to employees usually occurs in the same year employees include the compensation in income for their individual taxes.[17] Under Section 404, tax-qualified retirement plans, such as 401(k) plans and traditional pensions, provide employers the great advantage of being able to deduct contributions in the year they are made, even though employees often do not include the contributions in income until many years later when they receive retirement plan distributions.[18] For instance, if an employer made a $7,500 matching contribution to its tax-qualified plan in 2021 on behalf of a 25-year-old employee, it could take a corresponding deduction for its 2021 tax year. If the employee left this contribution in the tax-qualified retirement plan until age 70, the employee would not include the contribution or related earnings in their income until 2066! This is despite the fact that the employer took a deduction related to the contribution in 2021.

## B. Nonqualified Deferred Compensation Plans

Section 404 also governs employer deductions for compensation paid under nonqualified deferred compensation plans, but nonqualified plans do not receive the same favorable treatment as qualified plans. In general, an employer can take a deduction for compensation paid under a nonqualified deferred compensation plan when the compensation is included in the employee's taxable income.[19] The employer's deduction is equal to the amount included in the employee's income, including any earnings on the deferred compensation.[20] Section 404 and the regulations thereunder require that amounts paid under a nonqualified deferred compensation plan must be ordinary and necessary business expenses under Section 162 to be deductible.[21]

The timing of the employer's deduction under Section 404 differs from Section 162, which allows taxpayers who use the accrual method of accounting

16. IRC §404(a) (2019).
17. IRC §162(a) (2019).
18. IRC §404(a)(1); 404(a)(3) (2019).
19. IRC §404(a)(5) (2019). Section 404(d) and its related regulations subject plans deferring compensation of independent contractors to the same employer deduction rules as plans for employees.
20. *Albertson's, Inc. v. Comm'r*, 42 F.3d 537 (9th Cir. 1994).
21. Treas. Reg. 1.404(a)-1(b) (2019).

to deduct compensation when it is earned and the liability arises, whether or not the actual payment is made.[22] Because of this deduction timing, a company (particularly a closely-held company) might consider a deferred compensation arrangement beneficial only if the employee is taxed at a higher marginal rate than the employer. For example, if an employee is taxed at a 24 percent effective rate, but the employer is taxed at a 35 percent effective rate, the employee avoids an immediate tax of 24 cents for each dollar deferred, but deferral of the deduction increases the employer's tax by 35 cents, leaving the government (assuming all other things are equal) with a net gain of 11 cents per dollar. On the other hand, if an employee is taxed at a 35 percent effective rate, while the employer is taxed at a 0 percent effective rate (such as might be the case if the company's income is offset by losses in the current year or rolled over from prior years), each dollar of deferral reduces the immediate tax liabilities of the employer and employee (collectively) by 35 cents. TCJA's reduction of the corporate tax rate to 21 percent has had an impact on this cost-benefit analysis.

Certain special rules apply to contributions to funded nonqualified deferred compensation plans, but such plans are not commonly used due to the unfavorable tax treatment that applies to employees in funded plans. Plans that use rabbi or other grantor trusts are not considered funded for this purpose, and the employer deduction rules for unfunded plans would still apply.

## Section 4.4 Section 83: Stock, Stock Options, and Other Transfers of Property

In addition to salaries and common benefits such as retirement plans and medical insurance, many employers provide their employees restricted stock, stock options, or other stock-based compensation. The employer's deduction for such compensation is governed by Section 83(h), which states that:

> In the case of a transfer of property to which [Section 83] applies . . . there shall be allowed as a deduction under Section 162, to the person for whom were performed the services in connection with which such property was transferred, an amount equal to the amount included . . . in the gross income of the person who performed such services. Such deduction shall be allowed for the taxable year of such person in which or with which ends the taxable year in which such amount is included in the gross income of the person who performed such services.

While the reference to Section 162 might suggest the deduction rules under Section 83(h) are the same as under Section 162, Section 83(h) differs in at least two ways. Section 83(h) provides different timing for the employer's deduction than Section 162. As noted above, the employer's deduction under Section 83(h) is received in the taxable year of the employer in which or with which ends

22. IRC §162(a); 404(a)(5) (2019).

the taxable year in which the amount is included in the gross income of the employee, rather than according to the employer's method of accounting (i.e., cash basis or accrual). In addition, the statement that "there shall be allowed . . . a deduction . . . to the person for whom were performed the services in connection with which such property was transferred" suggests the employer may receive a deduction even if someone other than the employer, such as a shareholder, transfers the stock used as compensation.

Because the timing and amount of the employer's deduction under Section 83(h) will depend on the type of compensation provided, below are brief overviews of the tax rules applicable to some of the most common forms of equity compensation.

## A. Nonqualified Stock Options

Stock options that do not meet the requirements to be incentive stock options (discussed below) are not taxable to employees at the time they are granted, but they are taxable when exercised.[23] Upon exercise, an employee includes in income the excess of the fair market value of the stock acquired under the option over the price the employee paid to exercise the option and receive the stock. The employer is entitled to a deduction in this amount its taxable year in which the option is exercised.

## B. Incentive Stock Options

Incentive stock options (ISOs) are subject to different deduction rules because of how employees are taxed on ISOs. An employee is not taxed at the grant, vesting, or exercise of an ISO.[24] Further, if the employee holds the stock acquired by exercising an ISO more than two years after the ISO was granted, and more than one year after the ISO was exercised, the ISO will not be included in the employee's income at all.[25] Instead, the amount received in the sale of the stock (minus the exercise price the employee paid to acquire it under the ISO) is treated as a capital gain. In this case, the employer receives no deduction.

However, if the employee sells the stock acquired under an ISO before the holding period has expired (called a "disqualifying disposition"), the employee must include in taxable income for the year of the sale the difference between the exercise price paid for the stock and its fair market value at the time of exercise.[26] Any additional gain on the sale would be treated as capital gain. In this case, the employer would be entitled to a deduction in its taxable year in which the disqualifying disposition occurs in the amount the employee must include in income as a result of the disqualifying disposition.

---

23. Treas. Reg. §1.83-7(a).
24. IRC §421(a) (2019).
25. IRC §422(a) (2019).
26. IRC §421(b) (2019); Treas. Reg. §1.421-2(b).

### C. Stock and Other Property

When stock or other property is transferred to an employee as compensation for the employee's services, it is included in the employee's taxable income in the "first taxable year in which the rights [of the employee] are transferrable or are not subject to a substantial risk of forfeiture."[27] Employers often grant restricted stock as compensation, which is stock of the employer that is subject to a vesting restriction—often a time-based or performance-based vesting schedule.

The fair market value of such stock (minus any amount the employee paid to receive it) is includible in the employee's income in the year in which such vesting conditions are satisfied. Alternatively, an employee can make an election under Section 83(b) to have the fair market value of restricted stock (minus any amount the employee paid to receive it), included in income in the year in which it is granted. In either case, Section 83(h) provides that the employer will be entitled to a deduction equal to the amount included in the employee's gross income for the taxable year of the employer in which or with which ends the taxable year in which the amount was included in the employee's taxable income.[28]

## Section 4.5 Section 419/419A: Funded Health and Welfare Benefit Plans

As discussed earlier, an employer can typically receive a deduction under Section 162 for the cost of health and welfare benefits it provides to its employees. Sections 419 and 419A limit an employer's ability to receive a deduction for pre-funding such benefits through a welfare benefit fund when it has not yet incurred the expense of providing them.

For purposes of Section 419, a welfare benefit fund is any fund that is a part of a plan of an employer, and through which the employer provides welfare benefits (including health benefits) to employees or their beneficiaries.[29] If an employer attempts to prefund liabilities by having assets accumulate in a welfare benefit fund, Section 419 instructs that the employer's contributions to the welfare benefit fund are not deductible under Sections 162, but, so long as the requirements of Section 162 are otherwise met, they are deductible in the year in which they are paid under Section 419 to the extent of the welfare benefit fund's qualified costs.[30] Fortunately, if the amount of employer contributions paid during an employer's taxable year exceeds the amount of the allowable deduction, the employer is allowed a carryover of its excess contributions into the succeeding year.[31]

27. IRC §83(a) (2019).
28. IRC §83(h) (2019).
29. I.R.C. § 419(e) (2019).
30. IRC §419(b) (2019).
31. IRC §419(d) (2019).

# Section 4.6 Section 280G: Limitation on Deduction for Golden Parachute Payments

Section 280G limits an employer's ability to receive a deduction related to excess parachute payments, which are payments made to certain individuals in connection with a change in ownership or control of a company (typically as part of a merger or acquisition) in excess of a specified amount. The financial consequences of Section 280G can be significant for the employer, as discussed below. While beyond the scope of this chapter, Section 4999 also imposes a 20 percent excise tax on the employee receiving such payments.[32]

## A. Companies Subject to 280G

The deduction limits of Section 280G generally apply to C-corporations. S-corporations and companies that could elect to be S-corporation are expressly excluded.[33] While limited liability corporations (LLCs) and partnerships generally are not affected by Section 280G, it is important to bear in mind that a C-corporation's sale of its ownership of an LLC or partnership could result in a change in ownership or control for the C-corporation, thus potentially triggering the limits of Section 280G. In addition, privately held companies otherwise subject to Section 280G are often able to avoid its limits by obtaining shareholder approval for payments.[34]

## B. Disqualified Individuals

If a company is covered by the limits of Section 280G, only payments to certain disqualified individuals are affected. For purposes of Section 280G, "disqualified individuals" are generally: (1) shareholders owning more than one percent of the fair market value of the company's stock, (2) officers of the company (subject to certain limits), and (3) highly compensated individuals (generally the lesser of the highest paid one percent of the corporation's employees or the highest paid 250 employees).[35]

## C. Excess Parachute Payments

To determine whether there are excess parachute payments subject to Section 280G's limit on an employer's deductions, the employer must determine the amount (if any) of parachute payments. A "parachute payment" is generally any payment that meets all of the following conditions: (1) the payment is "in the nature of compensation;" (2) the payment is made to, or for the benefit of, a

32. I.R.C. § 280G (2019); I.R.C. § 4999 (2019).
33. Treas. Reg. §1.280G-1, Q/A-6(a)(1).
34. Treas. Reg. §1.280G-1, Q/A-6(a)(2).
35. Treas. Reg. §1.280G-1, Q/A-15 - Q/A-19.

disqualified individual; (3) the "payment is contingent on a change in the ownership" of a corporation, the effective control of a corporation, or the "ownership of a substantial portion of the assets of a corporation; and (4) the payment has (together with other payments described in (1), (2), and (3) with respect to the same disqualified individual) an aggregate present value of at least three times the individual's base amount."[36]

Parachute payments in excess of the disqualified individual's base amount (rather than three times the base amount) are considered excess parachute payments, and the employer may not receive a deduction for such payments.[37]

## *(i) Payments in the Nature of Compensation*

For purposes of Section 280G, all payments in any form are considered "payments in the nature of compensation if they arise out of an employment relationship or are associated with the performance of services."[38]

## *(ii) Contingent on a Change in Ownership or Control*

A payment is generally treated as contingent on a change in control if payment would not, in fact, have been made had no change in ownership or control occurred, even if the payment is also conditioned on the occurrence of another event.[39]

For this purpose, a change in ownership or control generally occurs when: (1) a person, or more than one person acting as a group, acquires more than 50 percent of the total fair market value or total voting power of the stock of a corporation; (2) either a person, or more than one person acting as a group, acquires (or has acquired during the 12-month period ending on the date of the most recent acquisition by such person or persons) ownership of stock of the corporation possessing 20 percent or more of the total voting power of the stock of such corporation, or a majority of members of the corporation's board of directors is replaced during any 12-month period by directors whose appointment or election is not endorsed by a majority of the members of the corporation's board of directors prior to the date of the appointment or election; or (3) a person, or more than one person acting as a group, acquires (or has acquired during the 12-month period ending on the date of the most recent acquisition by such person or persons) assets from the corporation that have a total gross fair market value equal to or more than one-third of the total gross fair market value of all of the assets of the corporation immediately prior to such acquisition or acquisitions.[40]

---

36. I.R.C. § 280G(b)(2) (2019); Treas. Reg. §1.280G-1, Q/A-2.
37. Treas. Reg. §1.280G-1, Q/A-1 - Q/A-3.
38. Treas. Reg. §1.280G-1, Q/A-11(a).
39. Treas. Reg. §1.280G-1, Q/A-22.
40. Treas. Reg. §1.280G-1, Q/A-27 - Q/A-29.

### (iii) Base Amount

A disqualified individual's base amount is generally the disqualified individual's average Box 1 W-2 or Form 1099 compensation from the company for past five years (or period of service, if shorter).[41] Because the base amount includes only compensation that is includible in gross income, the base amount does not include certain items that otherwise would constitute parachute payments if paid in connection with a change of control.[42] For example, payments in the form of excludible fringe benefits are not included in the base amount, but may be treated as parachute payments.

## D. Certain Exempt Payments

Certain types of payments are not considered parachute payments even if they otherwise fit the definition, include: (1) payments to or from a qualified retirement plan; (2) payments made by a tax-exempt organization (only if tax-exempt before and after transaction) if the organization is subject to the prohibitions against inurement to private individuals; and (3) payments that are reasonable compensation for "personal services to be rendered on or after the date of the change [in control]."[43]

41. Treas. Reg. §1.280G-1, Q/A-34 - Q/A-35.
42. Treas. Reg. §1.280G-1, Q/A-34(c).
43. Treas. Reg. §1.280G-1, Q/A-5.

CHAPTER 5

# Types of Plans: ERISA, Nonqualified Deferred Compensation Plans, and Equity Plans

## Section 5.1 ERISA Coverage

Companies offer a wide variety of benefits to their employees and, generally, know their core arrangements, such as retirement plans and group medical insurance programs, are subject to federal laws including the Employee Retirement Income Security Act of 1974 (ERISA).[1] However, there are common misconceptions that these laws do not apply to special benefits or executive arrangements or that they apply exclusively to those benefits that employers have formalized through a written plan, policy, or other formal steps. In fact, ERISA does apply to a number of executive arrangements, including severance arrangements, and that coverage often surprises business owners.

### A. When is a Plan Subject to ERISA?

A benefit program is subject to ERISA if: (1) there is a plan, fund, or program; (2) that is established or maintained by an employer; (3) for the purpose of providing benefits specifically covered by ERISA; (4) to participants or their beneficiaries.[2]

*Plan, fund, or program*. Generally, it is simple to satisfy the plan, fund, or program component of the ERISA-coverage test—a company's benefit is a plan, fund, or program if a reasonable person could determine the intended benefits, a class of beneficiaries, the source of financing, and the procedures for receiving benefits.[3] These elements do not need to be in writing to establish a plan—they may be determined from how the benefit has been, and is being, administered. Benefits that are not provided on an ongoing basis to similarly situated employees

1. Employee Retirement Income Security Act of 1974 (ERISA), Pub. L. No. 93-406, 88 Stat. 829 (codified as amended at 29 U.S.C. §§ 1001-1461 and scattered sections of 5, 18, and 26 U.S.C.).

2. 29 U.S.C. § 1002 (2018).

3. Donovan v. Dillingham, 688 F.2d 1367 (11th Cir., 1982).

might not be plans.[4] Each benefit should be scrutinized closely because the determination is based on all the facts and circumstances surrounding provision of the benefit.

*Established or maintained by an employer.* The second part of the ERISA-coverage test considers the level of the employer's involvement. If a company contributes funds to provide a benefit to employees, generally this test will be met. Therefore, as an example, a plan or program that provides employees with a set dollar amount to purchase private insurance generally will be maintained by the employer. In contrast, certain voluntary, fully insured, employee-pay-all programs are not subject to ERISA under a safe harbor the Department of Labor (DOL) established.

*Providing an ERISA-covered Benefit.* An employer-provided plan, fund, or program is only subject to ERISA if it provides benefits specifically identified by ERISA as covered benefits. Benefits subject to ERISA generally include:

- Medical, surgical, or hospital care benefits—including, but not limited to, major medical, dental, vision, and prescription drug benefits; health-care flexible spending accounts (health FSAs); health reimbursement arrangements (HRAs), premium reimbursement plans; and certain employee assistance programs (EAPs), executive physical programs, wellness programs, disease-management programs, and cancer policies;
- Benefits in the event of sickness, accident, disability, death, or unemployment—including insured disability income plans, insured sick-pay plans, accidental death and dismemberment (AD&D) plans, and life insurance plans;
- Funded vacation benefits;
- Funded apprenticeship or training benefits;
- Day-care centers;
- Funded scholarship benefits;
- Certain prepaid legal service arrangements;
- Severance and holiday benefits;
- Certain housing assistance benefits; and
- Retirement income or deferral of income to termination of covered employment or beyond.[5]

*Provided to Participants or Beneficiaries.* Finally, to be an ERISA plan, the listed benefit must be provided to a participant or beneficiary. A participant is any employee or former employee of an employer who is or may become eligible to receive a benefit from the plan.[6] Thus, a benefit provided only to retired executives may still be covered by ERISA. A beneficiary is a person designated by the participant, or the terms of a benefit plan, who is or may become entitled to benefits under the plan (such as a spouse or child of an employee). Since self-employed individuals and partners are not considered employees, a plan covering only those

4. Fort Halifax Packing Co. v. Coyne, 482 U.S. 1 (1987).
5. 29 U.S.C. § 1002 (2018).
6. Firestone Tire & Rubber Co v. Bruch, 489 U.S. 101 (1989).

individuals would not be covered by ERISA. However, if the plan covers both employees and self-employed individuals, the plan would be subject to ERISA.[7]

*Exclusions.* If an executive benefit meets the above four elements of the ERISA coverage test, then the next consideration is whether a statutory or regulatory exclusion applies. There are a number of exclusions from part or all of ERISA's rules for plans that would otherwise be subject to ERISA. These exclusions include, but are not limited to, governmental plans; church plans; plans maintained solely to comply with worker's compensation, unemployment compensation, or disability insurance laws; plans maintained outside the U.S. for non-resident aliens; and certain payroll practices. If an exclusion doesn't apply, then the benefit is likely an ERISA-covered plan.[8]

If the benefit is not an ERISA plan, then certain considerations—such as reporting and potential ERISA non-discrimination rules—are not relevant. Common examples of executive benefits that are not covered by ERISA include: unfunded paid time off, annual bonuses, stock options and other equity compensation, and change in control bonus plans.

If you have determined that your plan is covered by ERISA, the next question is what type of ERISA plan do you have? There are two types of ERISA plans: (1) "pension plans" and (2) "welfare benefit plans."[9] The distinction is important because pension plans, in particular, are subject to strict rules and limits on eligibility. An arrangement is an ERISA "pension plan" if it defers compensation to retirement or termination of employment. Common examples of executive arrangements that meet this definition are supplemental executive retirement plans (SERPs) and nonqualified deferred compensation plans (NQDCPs). While severance benefits clearly are designed to defer income to termination and beyond, these generally fall within a special designation as ERISA welfare benefits. DOL regulations provide that a severance agreement will be a welfare benefit plan if the payments are not contingent on retirement, the payments do not exceed twice the employee's annual salary, and the payments are paid over 24-month period post termination.[10]

*Rules for ERISA Pension Plans; Top Hat Group.* Generally, ERISA contains a plethora of rules and nondiscrimination standards that are applicable to ERISA pension plans—these include rules requiring the participation of non-highly-compensated employees and ensuring the plan does not benefit executives impermissibly more than non-highly-compensated employees. Those requirements are obviously incompatible with executive compensation arrangements that are specifically intended to benefit the most highly compensated employees in the company. To permit these arrangements, ERISA contains some specific exclusions from most of the act's requirements—most importantly the non-discrimination rules—for unfunded excess benefit plans[11] and unfunded plans

7. Yates v. Hendon, 541 U.S. 1 (2004).
8. 29 U.S.C. § 4b; DOL Reg. 2510.3-1
9. 29 U.S.C. § 1002 (2018).
10. DOL Reg § 2510.3-2(b).
11. 29 U.S.C. § 1003(b)(5).

maintained for "a select group of management or highly compensated employees" (commonly referred to as a "top hat" group).[12] If an executive compensation plan is an ERISA-covered pension plan, ensuring it is exempt as an excess benefit plan or as a plan that covers only a top hat group is critical to compliance.

An excess benefit plan is relatively straightforward. These plans are maintained solely to provide benefits that cannot be provided in a qualified plan due to maximum benefits limits in IRC § 415. Including features making up for other limited benefits (such as benefits limited by the IRC restriction on compensation) may also be permitted in certain instances.[13]

The definition of a top hat group is unfortunately (and perhaps surprisingly) nebulous. Despite the broad use of the top hat exemption and widespread adoption of top hat plans, there is little definitive guidance on what constitutes a top hat group. However, what we do know is this:

- The positions covered are important—with a focus on whether the employee in such a position would have the ability to meaningfully influence or negotiate the design and operation of the plan.[14]
- The compensation level is relevant. Despite the use of the term "highly compensated employee"—a term of art in the qualified plan world—it does not necessarily mean simply someone who makes more than the compensation threshold used for the qualified plan definition. The compensation in comparison to other employees is generally the relevant consideration.[15]
- The percentage of employees is relevant. While there is no bright line, at least one court surmised that 15 percent of the employee population could be a top hat group, but it might be the upper limit.[16] And another court found that a group consisting of 18.7 percent was too large.[17]

In the past, the Department of Labor has taken the position that the plan must benefit **only** management and highly compensated employees, and the participation of one other individual would mean the plan fails to meet the top hat exemption.[18] This theory has never been ruled on by a court, but emphasizes the care that should be taken when designing a plan to meet the top hat exemption.

Given the lack of clear guidance, practitioners' opinions and advice to clients on what constitutes a top hat group can vary significantly. Failing to meet the top

---

12. 29 C.F.R. § 2520.104-23 (2019); 29 C.F.R. § 2520.104-24 (2002).

13. *See* Gamble v. Grp. Hospitalization & Med. Servs., Inc., 38 F.3d 126 (4th Cir. 1994).

14 U.S. Dep't of Labor, Pension & Welfare Benefit Programs, Opinion Letter 90-14A (May 8, 1990). This factor is treated differently by different circuits with some focusing more on influence and others focusing more on the positions. *Compare* Sikora v. UPMC, 876 F.3d 110 (3rd Cir. 2017) and Bakri v. Venture Mfg. Co., 473 F.3d 677 (6th Cir. 2007).

15. *See* Sikora v. UPMC, 876 F.3d 110 (3rd Cir. 2017) (average income of participants more than nine times the average income of all employees reflected highly compensated status); *see also* Demery v. Extebank Deferred Comp. Plan (B), 216 F.3d 283 (2d Cir. 2000) (more than five times the income of an average worker was not in the gray area).

16. *See* Demery v. Extebank Deferred Comp. Plan (B), 216 F.3d 283 (2d Cir. 2000).

17. *See* Darden v. Nationwide Mut. Ins., 717 F. Supp. 388 (E.D.N.C. 1989).

18. *See* Department of Labor's amicus brief in Bond v. Marriott Int'l Inc., 2016 U.S. App. LEXIS 1499, 61 Employee Benefits Cas. (BNA) 1005 (4th Cir. 2016) (decided on other grounds).

hat exemption could result in a host of problems. Assuming the plan falls in that gray area (rather than being an obvious violation), the most likely consequence would present as a disgruntled employee leaving the organization and asserting a variety of claims that the arrangement violates the law, then using the employer's aggressive position on the top hat definition, the employee negotiates for a more favorable separation package in exchange for a release.

It is important to keep in mind that, unlike excess benefit plans, which are entirely exempt from ERISA, a top hat plan is technically still an ERISA plan; just one that is exempt from many rules. A top hat welfare plan automatically is exempt from all reporting and disclosure other than the requirement to provide the plan document to the DOL upon request.[19] A top hat pension plan must make a particular filing within 120 days of the plan's adoption to secure the top hat exemption.[20] The statement is now filed online[21]—and takes only a matter of minutes to complete—after which the plan is exempt from the ERISA reporting and disclosure scheme. However, a top hat plan must still comply with certain requirements, such as the ERISA rules regarding procedures for participants to make claims.

# Section 5.2 Income Replacement/Retirement Plans

One common goal of executive compensation plans is to replace an executive's income following termination of employment. This section will look at several common arrangements that are used for this purpose, including: severance plans; excess benefit plans; supplemental executive retirement plans; and nonqualified deferral arrangements.

## A. Severance Plans

Severance plans are, perhaps, the most common type of executive arrangement and, as long as they meet the ERISA welfare exception, may be extended to a group larger than the top hat group. The simplest of these arrangements offers to pay an individual a specified amount if he or she is involuntarily terminated by the company without cause. However, in executive compensation additional provisions are often negotiated, including:

- limited definitions of "cause" that would permit the company to refuse severance;
- ability of the executive to terminate for good cause and receive severance; and
- increased severance if termination is in connection with a change in control.

19. 29 C.F.R. §2520.104-24(b) (2002).

20. 29 C.F.R. §2520.104-23(b) (2019).

21. *See, e.g.*, *Top Hat Plan Statement*, Dep't of Labor, https://www.dol.gov/agencies/ebsa/employers-and-advisers/plan-administration-and-compliance/reporting-and-filing/e-file/tophat-plan-filing-instructions (last visited Apr. 12, 2021).

Regardless, when crafting a severance arrangement, it is important to ensure the plan design takes into account applicable laws, such as ERISA's welfare plan provisions, the IRC § 409A involuntary separation exception, and the IRC § 457 separation pay plan exception. (These will be discussed in later chapters).

## B. Excess/Restoration Benefit Plans

An excess benefit plan, also known as a restoration plan, seeks to make up for benefits that cannot be provided in the company's qualified plans due to IRS limits—including the limit on total benefits, the compensation limit, and the deferral limits. To illustrate this type of executive compensation plan, consider the following example:

Company A has a 401(k) plan. In 2020, the tax code provides that the executive can only make $19,500 in elective deferrals ($26,000 if age 50 or older), and in calculating the employer contribution only $285,000 in compensation may be taken into account under the tax code that year, and total contributions to the participant's account cannot be more than $57,000 (plus an additional $6,500 in deferrals if the participant is age 50 or older) that year.

Company A's plan provides for a dollar-for-dollar (100 percent) match on the first 7 percent of each employee's compensation that they defer to the plan. The company also makes a profit-sharing contribution to the plan equal to 4 percent of compensation.

Take an executive who earns $500,000 in 2020. Assuming that he or she wants to maximize the employer contribution, the executive would make the following deferrals and receive the following employer contributions:

| | |
|---|---|
| Deferrals | $35,000 (7 percent of $500,000) |
| Match | $35,000 (100 percent of first 7 percent deferred) |
| Profit sharing | $20,000 (4 percent of $500,000) |
| Total | $90,000 |

Because of the IRS limits, the executive is only able to receive the following:

| | |
|---|---|
| Deferrals | $19,500 ($26,000 if age 50 or older) |
| Match | $19,500 ($19,950 if age 50 or older, because only first 7 percent of $285,000 may be matched) |
| Profit sharing | $11,400 (4 percent of $285,000) |
| Total | $50,400 ($57,350 if age 50 or older) |

Thus, the tax code's limits essentially thwart the executive's and company's intention—resulting in the employee missing out on approximately $25,000 of company contributions ($25,400 if under age 50 and $24,950 if over age 50). An excess benefit or restoration plan would make up for the difference in these outcomes by promising to pay that missed employer contribution outside of the 401(k) plan. As noted above, the executive would have had to make additional deferrals to receive the employer match. Some excess plans require the executive make those deferrals to the excess plan, while others—often for simplicity of administration—simply assume the executive would have made sufficient deferrals and calculate the maximum missed employer contribution. When the 401(k) plan and the excess plan are viewed together, then, the total benefit matches the original intention.

## C. Supplemental Executive Retirement Plans

Supplemental executive retirement plans (SERPs) are similar to excess benefit plans in that they provide a retirement income that is in addition to the company's qualified plan benefits. However, unlike excess benefit plans, SERPs may provide benefits that could have been provided in the qualified plan, but the company elects not to provide them through that method, often due to the nondiscrimination requirements that might make such a benefit expensive to provide to other employees.

For example, assume the company has a cash balance pension plan that provides a 5 percent contribution each year. The company wants to provide the CEO with a total retirement contribution equal to 15 percent of compensation each year. A 15 percent contribution is likely not exceeding the IRS limits on total benefits; thus, the benefit could be provided in the pension plan. However, due to the pension plan's nondiscrimination requirements, benefits to the other employees would need to likewise be increased to permit the CEO to receive that benefit, which would be cost prohibitive. Because top hat executive compensation plans are not subject to nondiscrimination requirements, the company can create a SERP that covers only the CEO to provide the benefit that is not paid under the terms of the qualified plan.

Traditionally, the time and form of payment from the SERP was often tied to the participant's election under the qualified plan—effectively giving the participant control of when and how the SERP was to be paid. This design is no longer permitted under IRC § 409A and care should be taken to ensure the plans are not impermissibly intertwined.

## D. Nonqualified Deferral Arrangements, Including 457(b) Plans

Often, an executive cannot defer enough in the company's qualified retirement plan to adequately save for retirement. This may be due to the tax code limit on participant contributions, total contributions, and/or nondiscrimination testing. In this situation, an executive may wish to save additional compensation for retirement. The executive certainly can do this without involvement of the company, but he or she is saving after paying income tax and will also have to pay tax on the investment earnings. By contrast, if the company provides a method to save outside of the qualified plan, the executive will be able to save before paying income tax and defer payment of taxes to a later date.

This plan may be attractive to an executive who is entitled to receive more cash compensation than he or she currently needs, but it comes with certain risks, including the potential risk of the company declaring bankruptcy or being unable to pay the benefit when due and the executive losing that income to which he or she could have originally taken in cash. To mitigate this risk, these deferral arrangements are often paired with rabbi trusts to provide the executive with some security, although the risk of bankruptcy will always remain.

# Section 5.3 Incentive Plans

## A. Short-Term Incentive Plans

Short-term incentive plans may be the most common executive compensation arrangement around. Very few companies have no bonus or performance-based compensation. A short-term incentive plan is distinguished from other incentive arrangements by the period of time over which performance is measured and the incentive paid. Most commonly, a short-term incentive looks at performance over a twelve-month period, usually the calendar year or the company's fiscal year.

Perhaps because short-term incentive plans are extremely common, many employers believe they do not need assistance documenting or administering these plans. Unfortunately, they are very common sources of IRC § 409A errors. The most basic problems come from a lack of formal documentation with sufficient detail or a lack of appreciation for provisions such as pro-rated bonus when employees are terminated, die, or retire. These plans almost always are designed to meet the short-term deferral exception to IRC 409A and legal counsel should carefully review these plans to ensure those requirements are met, particularly that the time and form of payment are specified clearly.

## B. Long-Term Incentive Plans

Long-term incentive plans (LTIPs) are also common. They are much like short-term plans except they often measure performance over three or more years and set payment thresholds tied to longer-term metrics. These plans may also serve the dual purpose of a retention incentive because an employee who has achieved (or believes he or she will achieve) the performance threshold may be inclined to stay through the date the payment vests (which often is the actual payment date).

The LTIP may set virtually any type of payment and vesting thresholds to align payment with strategic objectives. Often there are multiple payment thresholds, sometimes denoted "threshold," "target," and "maximum" performance. As an example, if a board desires to increase earnings before interest, taxes, depreciation, and amortization (EBITDA) by at least 10 percent over the next five years. It wants to incentivize the executive director to accomplish this goal or, better yet, exceed it. The company adopts an LTIP that provides if EBITDA reaches 110 percent of current EBITDA for three consecutive years, the CEO is credited with 25 percent of current base salary. This would be the target threshold. If EBITADA reaches 112.5 percent of current EBITDA for three consecutive years, the CEO is credited with 35 percent of current base salary. This would be the maximum threshold. And finally, if EBITDA reaches 105 percent, the CEO receives 10 percent of base salary—the threshold performance. The company might also require the CEO remain employed for a number of years after the performance metric is met—both as a retention incentive and also to ensure the performance is appropriately audited.

## C. Change in Control Plan

An incentive plan may be designed to account for one or more specific events the company sees on the horizon. One of the most common arrangements in this category is the change in control plan. A company that is in an industry undergoing consolidation or whose owners are actively seeking (or know they will actively seek) a transaction in the relatively near future may want to incentivize their executives to (a) stay with the company despite the likelihood that they will lose their position upon closing a transaction, and (b) enhance the value of the company to deliver maximum value to owners.

A change in control plan may achieve these objectives by paying the executive a certain amount upon the closing of a transaction—with the amount varying depending on the price obtained. Other conditions on payment may be added, as appropriate, to achieve the company's objectives. For instance, if the payment is merely to provide the executive security in the event of a job loss or demotion in connection with the sale, then the payment might not be made unless the executive terminates within a certain period of time after the transaction.

A common provision unique to change in control plans is to restrict the company's ability to change the terms of the arrangement. While not universally used, these plans often provide the benefits cannot be reduced within a certain period before and/or after a change in control. This provision provides the executive(s) with security that the company will not reduce or terminate the arrangement on the eve of a transaction.

## D. Phantom Stock/Equity Plans

Owners of businesses routinely express a desire for their key employees to act like owners. There are two ways to provide incentives that directly work to achieve this goal: (1) make them owners, or (2) design incentives to mimic ownership. The first option is deceptively simple—but can be a hardship, particularly on small business owners. Actually, granting stock to an employee can create several undesired consequences, including diluting ownership of current employees, creating minority shareholder rights, expense in creating shareholder agreements, and state and federal law requirements. Further, certain entities, such as non-profits and governmental entities, do not have stock to grant to key employees.

Thus, the alternative is to consider an incentive that mimics ownership of the entity. Phantom stock plans mimic the financial upside of being an owner without requiring an actual grant of shares. To illustrate, let us consider a situation where a family-owned business is hiring its first outside CEO. They want to incentivize the new CEO to act like an owner, but do not want to dilute the family's ownership, so they adopt a phantom stock plan under which the CEO is credited with units equivalent to 10 percent ownership. The plan will pay out if the CEO terminates employment at least five years from the grant or if the company is acquired by another entity. In either case, the payout will equal the fair market value of a hypothetical 10 percent interest of the company at the event date, less the fair market value at the grant date.

At the time of grant, the company is worth $1 million (making the CEO's units worth $100,000). A few years elapse, and the CEO grows the business. The family owners are offered $5 million for the company by a competitor. If the owners accept the offer, the phantom stock plan will pay out as follows:

- CEO's units are worth $500,000 at the change of control
- CEO receives $400,000 ($500,000 - $100,000 value at time of grant).

This is approximately the same amount the CEO would have received if he or she purchased stock and then sold the stock during the change of control. However, unlike a stock purchase, the payment from the phantom stock plan will all be taxed as ordinary income. Thus, an executive may negotiate a slightly higher phantom stock grant to compensate for the higher potential tax rate that will apply.

## E. Equity Plans (Stock Grants, Stock Options (ISOs and NSOs), RSU, Restricted Stock, SARs, and Dividend Equivalents)

Finally, there are a host of equity-based incentives. These range from actually granting equity or the right to acquire equities to payments based on some equity-based metric. These plans are most common among publicly traded companies as their equity is readily priced and traded on the market—making the calculation of equity-based payments straightforward and the liquidation of actual equity grants readily available. These hurdles prevent some privately held companies from implementing equity plans—favoring an incentive structure that is less onerous to administer. However, even a privately held company can effectively implement an equity-based incentive plan through well-drafted shareholder agreements and other documentation that sets forth critical terms such as repurchase and put rights and how share value is calculated.

*Stock Grants.* A direct grant of stock in the corporation. The benefit of stock grants is that, absent bankruptcy, the stock generally retains some value. Unlike grants of stock options, stock grants will retain some compensatory value even if the value of the stock falls. This may be accompanied by restrictions on the sale or transfer of the stock.

*Stock Options.* Provides the employee with the ability to purchase stock at an established price for a particular period of time. These may be exercisable immediately or may only be exercisable upon satisfaction of particular conditions (such as a period or service). If a company anticipates significant growth, then the value of the option should become more valuable as the price of its stock increases. On the other hand, if the stock value falls between the grant date and the date the option expires, the reward decreases in value or may become altogether worthless to the executive. Determining the taxes on stock options can be very complicated and especially difficult to relay to employees. A full discussion of the taxation of options is beyond the scope of this text, but practitioners should note that there are two main types of options: incentive stock options (ISOs) and nonqualified stock options (NSOs).

ISOs provide more favorable tax treatment for executives and are subject to additional requirements. They are issued only to employees. No tax is due upon the exercise of the option; taxation occurred only when the employee opts to sell the shares. To realize the favorable treatment, a number of conditions must be satisfied, including: minimum hold time, limiting the period in which the option may be exercised, documentation requirements, and limited modifications.

NSOs do not provide the same favorable tax treatment, but are more flexible. These options can be issued to employees, as well as other service providers, such as independent contractors and directors. The holder is taxed upon exercise of the option.

*RSU.* RSUs are contractual promises to issue stock in the future when performance- or time-based vesting requirements are satisfied. Unlike stock options, RSUs are considered full value awards.

Unlike grants of stock options or restricted stock, RSUs have no general exemption from the regulations on deferred compensation under Section 409A of the tax code. This generally means RSUs either need to comply with 409A or qualify for the short-term deferral exception to 409A.

*Stock Appreciation Rights (SARs).* Like stock options, SARs are an appreciation award because the employee receives the increase in value of the stock from its grant date. However, SARs generally do not involve the purchase or sale of actual shares.

*Dividend Equivalents.* These arrangements pay the executive an amount based on the amounts paid to shareholders as dividend payments.

# Section 5.4 Counsel Considerations

In addition to assisting clients in navigating the myriad of plan options, counsel should ensure that certain questions are answered:

- Is the plan subject to ERISA, and if so, does it meet the requirements of a top hat group?
- Does the plan either clearly meet an exception to IRC 409A or meet the requirements of IRC 409A? (This is discussed in later chapters.)
- Is the plan sufficiently documented to reflect tax code compliance and define the executive's right to payment (and clearly state when payments are forfeited)?

- Does the company and the executive understand the taxation of the arrangement, particularly with respect to FICA/FUTA taxation, 457 taxation for non-profits, and excess compensation rules for publicly-traded companies and non-profits? (This is discussed in later chapters.)
- Does the company have sufficient personnel, sophistication, or vendor assistance to administer this plan properly and avoid errors that result in taxation to the executive?

Ultimately, executive compensation arrangements are fairly flexible in design and will provide value to both the executive and the company if properly selected, designed, and administered.

CHAPTER 6

# Funding Arrangements for Nonqualified Deferred Compensation Plans

As we saw in earlier chapters executive compensation plans also referred to as nonqualified deferred compensation plans (NQDCPs) or top hat plans (THPs), must be an unfunded and unsecured promise from the employer to pay the deferred compensation in the future, to achieve a deferral of taxation for the executive and avoid imposition of ERISA's requirements on non-THPs.

The risks involved in the unfunded and unsecured promise to pay deferred amounts decades in the future, include the possibility that the employer may experience cash flow issues and renege on the promise or may become insolvent or declare bankruptcy. Other areas of concern for the executive are that there may be a change in ownership or management of the employer, and a new owner or manager may not respect the responsibilities of its predecessor. Those risks associated with NQDCPs, create uncertainty among executives and weaken the employers' ability to promote these plans to recruit and retain valuable executives. So, while the executive seeks deferral of taxation until distribution of the benefits, he or she also is interested in having some assurance that the deferred amount will be available at the anticipated distribution date. Formally setting aside assets outside the reach of creditors, to fund the NQDCP, would thwart tax deferral, and subject the plan to the full panoply of restrictions under ERISA.

To mitigate the risks inherent in unfunded promises, employers have sought ways to prefund the obligations to provide some security, without affecting the unfunded status of the plan.

The more popular methods include: setting aside assets in a rabbi trust, purchasing corporate owned life insurance (COLI), using a split-dollar life insurance arrangement, and purchasing an annuity. Other methods include establishing a bookkeeping reserve fund, purchasing stocks and bonds, or using a third-party guarantor for the unfunded promise.

The executive can also contemplate purchasing private insurance to pay the benefits in the event of employer default. Currently, this type of insurance is not as widely available as car or other property insurance and therefore the pricing may be prohibitive.

# Section 6.1 Rabbi Trusts

The most common instrument used in conjunction with the funding of NQDCP that allows achievement of the twin goals of deferral of taxation and a certain level of security, is the rabbi trust. A NQDCP funded by a "rabbi trust" is considered unfunded for purposes of ERISA.[1] A rabbi trust can be revocable or irrevocable.[2] An irrevocable rabbi trust cannot be altered by the employer, or by new ownership after a merger or acquisition.

Use of rabbi trusts has been sanctioned by both the IRS and the Department of Labor (DOL). The IRS specifically sanctioned the use of this specific trust in conjunction with a NQDCP, and made available a template to follow to ensure that the arrangement would preserve the unfunded status of the plan for tax and ERISA purposes. The model rabbi trust issued by the IRS, creates a safe harbor for taxpayers that adopt and maintain such trusts.[3] The model form and procedures provide mandatory language that must be included in the trust document.[4]

The most important aspect of the arrangement was that the assets remain subject to the claims of the employer's creditors in the event of insolvency or bankruptcy.[5] The IRS ruling made it clear that in order not to jeopardize the deferral of taxation, the trust had to limit distribution from the trust to the specific circumstances of paying deferred benefits or paying claims of the employer's creditors in the event of insolvency or bankruptcy.[6] Outside this context of bankruptcy or insolvency the assets in a rabbi trust are preserved for the executives.

The assets of the trust are controlled by a trustee.[7] Some rabbi trusts allow the employee to direct the investment of the trust assets.[8] However the participant must be precluded from assigning, or in any way encumbering, his or her interest in the trust. Some have observed that the main benefit of the rabbi trust is to protect against changes in the plan resulting from a change of control.[9]

Although courts have denied secured creditors access to the funds in the rabbi trust,[10] the rabbi trust document should make it clear that its funds are available for the unsecured creditors of the employer. Merely stating that the assets are subject to the creditors of the employer may generate unnecessary litigation and be interpreted as including the secured creditors.

---

1. *See* Rev. Proc. 92-64, 1992-2 C.B. 422; Rev. Proc. 92-65, 1992-2 C.B. 428; DOL Adv. Op. 92-13A (May 19, 1992).

2. *See* Rev. Proc. 92-64, 1992-2 C.B. 422; Michael S. Sirkin & Lawrence K. Cagney, Executive Compensation 8-04 (2017).

3. Rev. Proc. 92-64, 1992-2 C.B. 422.

4. Rev. Proc. 92-64, 1992-2 C.B. 422; Rev. Proc. 92-65, 1992-2 C.B. 428.

5. I.R.S. Priv. Ltr. Rul. 81-13-107 (Dec. 31, 1980).

6. Bruce J. McNeil, *An Overview of 'Rabbi Trusts'*, Law360 (June 21, 2012), https://www.law360.com/articles/345959.

7. Michael S. Sirkin & Lawrence K. Cagney, Executive Compensation 8-04 (2017). *See also* Rev. Proc. 92-65, 1992-2 C.B. 428.

8. *See* I.R.S. Priv. Ltr. Rul. 88-04-023 (Oct. 30, 1987); I.R.S. Priv. Ltr. Rul. 88-34-015 (May 25, 1988).

9. *See, e.g.*, Bank of Am. v. Moglia, 330 F.3d 942, 944 (7th Cir. 2003).

10. *Id.*

In summary, the advantages to executives of having a rabbi trust as part of a NQDCP include:

- Protection for the executive in a situation where the company uses assets that should be preserved for the NQDCP benefits to meet its other obligations.[11] This protection is enhanced to the extent the rabbi trust is irrevocable.[12]
- Tax deferral is preserved because the rabbi trust is not treated as making the NQDCP a funded or secured arrangement.[13]

A rabbi trust provides a sense of security for beneficiaries of NQDCP without violating the unfunded status of the plan. The employer will get a deduction for the contributed amounts when the employee is taxed, typically at distribution.[14] Note that prior to distribution, the employer will be subject to taxation for any earnings of the trust.[15]

## Section 6.2 Limitations on the Use of Rabbi Trusts

In the past, employers would establish rabbi trusts in offshore jurisdictions that may not readily allow creditors to access assets in the event of insolvency or bankruptcy. Thus, even though the language of the trust would declare that the assets are available to the employer's creditors, there may have been practically no access to those creditors. The American Jobs Creation Act halted this practice by providing restrictions that curtail the manner in which NQDCPs may be funded using offshore rabbi trusts.[16] A rabbi trust established in a foreign jurisdiction, even if ostensibly subject to the claims of creditors, will generate current taxable income, a 20 percent penalty, and interest, all to be paid by the executive.[17] The rule is inapplicable if substantially all of the services to which the nonqualified deferred compensation relates are performed in the foreign jurisdiction.[18]

11. *Rabbi Trust*, Investopedia, https://www.investopedia.com/terms/r/rabbitrust.asp (last visited Apr. 17, 2019).

12. *Rabbi Trust*, Investopedia, https://www.investopedia.com/terms/r/rabbitrust.asp (last visited Apr. 17, 2019).

13. *Rabbi Trust*, Investopedia, https://www.investopedia.com/terms/r/rabbitrust.asp (last visited Apr. 17, 2019).

14 IRC 404(a)(5);Michael S. Sirkin & Lawrence K. Cagney, Executive Compensation 8-04 (2017). *See also* I.R.C. § 404(a)(5) (2012).

15. Michael S. Sirkin & Lawrence K. Cagney, Executive Compensation 8-04 (2017). *See* 26 C.F.R. § 1.404(a)-12(b) (as amended in 1978).

16. *See, e.g.*, I.R.C. § 409A(b)(1) (2012).

17. 409A(b)(1)(2).

18. Thomas Brisendine, Elizabeth Drigotas & Thomas R. Pevarnik, *Deferred Compensation Arrangements*, 385-5th Tax. Mgmt. (BNA) IV.J (U.S. Income 2018) (citing I.R.C. § 409A(b)(1) (2012)).

The law prohibits the springing trust where, assets that may have been placed in a reserve account to informally fund a NQDCP would be segregated and earmarked, should there be a change in the employer's financial health.[19] A rabbi trust that converts to the more secure funded secular trust due to the financial condition of the employer, is also prohibited.[20] The enforcement mechanism for these springing trusts is the triple threat of income taxation, the 20 percent penalty, and interest if these provisions are in the plan.[21]

As an example, assume that an employer adopts a NQDCP for an executive in 2019. The promise is to pay the executive $700,000 upon separation from service. The plan also provides that the employer commits to placing $700,000 in a rabbi trust, to fund the obligation, however, should the financial health of the employer deteriorate, the amounts will be transferred to the more secure secular trust.

Assume that in 2022 the employer contributes the $700,000 to a secular trust because of its precarious financial condition. Subsequently, the executive retires and the trust distributes the $700,000 to the executive. In this scenario, the distributed amounts would be included in the income of the executive in 2019—the year the plan provision was adopted which tied the financial health of the employer to the transfer from the rabbi trust to the secular trust—plus a 20 percent penalty, and interest.[22] Upon actual distribution, there would be no further taxation of the amounts already taxed.

These funding restrictions were implemented largely in response to perceived abuses whereby companies would use offshore rabbi trusts and springing trusts to shield assets set aside to fund nonqualified deferred compensation obligations from the employer's general creditors, while preserving the tax advantages of nonqualified deferred compensation arrangements for their executives.[23]

Congress was also concerned that employers could provide security for executives at the expense of the rank-and-file employees participating in the company's defined benefit plan.[24] Therefore it also included temporal restrictions on the creation of rabbi trusts. The law prohibits the contributions of funds to a rabbi trust during certain periods during which an employer is in chapter 11 bankruptcy proceedings or the employer's defined benefit plan is in at-risk funding status or at risk of being terminated without sufficient assets.[25]

---

19. IRC 409A(b)(2);BNA Benefits Guide: Basics, Executive Compensation Programs, Section 409A Compliance: A Quick How-To Guide 1 (2017).

20. I.R.C. § 409A(b) (2018); Michael S. Sirkin & Lawrence K. Cagney, Executive Compensation § 7.20 (2018).

21. I.R.C. § 409A(b)(1), (5) (2018); Michael S. Sirkin & Lawrence K. Cagney, Executive Compensation § 7.20 (2018).

22. 409A(b)(2); section 409A Handbook 25-11.

23. Samuel Krause & Regina Olshan, *Funding Arrangements, in* Section 409A Handbook (BNA) 25-2 (Regina Olshan & Erica F. Schohn eds., 2016) (citing H.R. Rep. No. 108-755 (2004) (Conf. Rep)).

24. 409A Handbook, 25-18. Defined benefit plans promise a specific benefit at retirement these types of plans are regulated for funding by ERISA and the IRC.

25. IRC 409A(b)(3); Per IRC § 409A(b)(3)(B), and IRC § 430(i) *Nonqualified Deferred Compensation Audit Techniques*, IRS.gov (June 2015), https://www.irs.gov/businesses/corporations/nonqualified-deferred-compensation-audit-techniques-guide. *See also* Pension Protection Act of 2006, Pub. L. No. 109-280, 120 Stat. 780, 856 – 58 (2006).

# Section 6.3 Life Insurance

Several types of insurance products have been developed specifically for use in executive compensation arrangements.

## A. Corporate-Owned Life Insurance (COLI)

The use of corporate owned life insurance (COLI) to support and fund a NQDCP, if structured properly, will maintain the unfunded status of a NQDCP. To maintain top hat status by remaining unfunded, and thus avoid ERISA requirements, the benefits must be provided exclusively through insurance policies that satisfy the relevant state insurance laws, and the premiums must be paid directly by the employer from its general assets.[26]

Under this method of funding the employer purchases individual cash-value life insurance policies on the lives of executives who are covered by a deferred compensation plan. The corporation pays the premiums and is both the owner and the beneficiary of the policies. Upon the death of the insured executive, the death benefits are payable to the employer who can use these amounts to recover the cost of any deferred compensation that it previously paid.[27]

The purchase of a life insurance policy to fund a deferred compensation arrangement is authorized by the IRS.[28] The IRS has given some guidance in structuring the purchase of COLI to provide the funds that would be needed to pay the NQDCP benefits to the employee. The employer should purchase the insurance on the employee's life, pay the premium, and maintain beneficiary status. The policy remains a part of the employer's assets and is subject to the general creditors of the employer, in the event of insolvency or bankruptcy. The employee executive should have no rights at all in the policy, and the deferred compensation arrangement should be provided under a separate arrangement and not be part of the policy. The rights to any benefits under the insurance contract are solely the property of the employer and the proceeds of such contract are payable by the insurance company only to the employer-beneficiary of the policy.[29] The ability to make tax-free withdrawals from the policy is important because the primary payment under a life insurance policy is the death benefit, payable upon the employee's death. However, a NQDCP typically requires payments during the executive's lifetime, therefore with the COLI funding the NQDCP benefits, the employer can utilize the cash accumulation in the life insurance policy to satisfy retirement benefits obligations under the NQDCP.

The employer must also have a true insurable interest in the employee and obtain the employee's consent to be insured.[30] Employers who own

26. 29 C.F.R. § 2520.104-23(d)(2) (2003).

27. Robert E. Madden, Tax Planning for Highly Compensated Individuals ¶ 8.08 (Thomson Reuters Tax & Acct. 2018).

28. Rev. Rul. 72-25, 1972-1 C.B. 127. *See also* Rev. Rul. 68-99, 1968-1 C.B. 193.

29. Rev. Rul. 68-99, 1968-1 C.B. 193.

30. Am. Elec. Power v. United States, 326 F.3d 737 (6th Cir. 2003).

corporate-owned life insurance policies must adequately disclose to employees the details of the coverage and its consequences.[31]

COLI is used to fund less than half of non-qualified deferred compensation plans, likely due in part to insurance and administrative costs.[32]

Concerns with the COLI include the fact that the COLI is only as secure as the financial institution that underwrites the policy. In addition, because the employer owns the policy, the employee has to rely on the employer not cashing out the policy. Despite these concerns, COLI gives executives a measure of psychological security in the plan it is meant to fund.

## B. Split-Dollar Life Insurance

A second type of insurance product used in executive compensation is known as "split-dollar" life insurance. A split-dollar insurance arrangement to purchase life insurance can be used informally to fund the payment of benefits as part of NQDCP compensation package.

As the name suggests, in a split-dollar arrangement the employer and employee split the premium payments, the policy cash value, and the death benefit proceeds. The split-dollar arrangement does not disturb the unfunded status of the NQDCP, provided the documents refer to the employers' general assets for payments of the unfunded promise to pay deferred compensation, and the executive has no rights in the policy. For this "unfunded" status to be achieved in this context, the rights and responsibilities of the employer and employee must be set forth in a separate split-dollar agreement, which is not a part of the NQDCP.[33]

Typically, the face amount of the policy is linked to the executive's compensation and can be twice the compensation. When the deferred compensation amounts become due, the employer will pay the amounts from its general assets, and upon death of the employee, the proceeds of the life insurance policy, will be divided between the employer and survivors of the employee.[34] The death benefits from the split-dollar insurance are tax free.[35]

Executives, sometimes become opportunistic and argue that a NQDCP using life insurance, was in fact funded to achieve certain protections under ERISA. In *Miller v. Heller*,[36] the plaintiffs were former employees that wanted the protections of ERISA and argued that the deferred compensation plan in which they were participants, was funded and, thus, was not exempt from ERISA as an unfunded top hat plan, in which case the protections of ERISA would be

31. I.R.S. Notice 2009-48, 2009-24 I.R.B. 1085 (describing the reporting and disclosure requirements); I.R.C. § 101(j) (2012).

32. David I. Walker, *The Practice and Tax Consequences of Nonqualified Deferred Compensation* 4, 26–27 (B.U. Sch. of L., L. & Econ. Working Paper No. 16-27, Aug. 2, 2016), https://www.bu.edu/law/working-papers/the-practice-and-tax-consequences-of-nonqualified-deferred-compensation/.

33. Robert E. Madden, *Tax Planning for Highly Compensated Individuals* ¶ 8.04 (Thomson Reuters Tax & Acct. 2018).

34. Georgiana J. Slade, *Split-Dollar Life Insurance Arrangements*, 807-2d Personal Life Ins. Tr. (BNA) (Est., Gifts, & Tr. 2018).

35. I.R.C. § 101(a) (2012).

36. 915 F. Supp. 651 (S.D.N.Y. 1996).

retroactively applicable. The plan had both a life insurance aspect and a deferred compensation aspect. They maintained that the life insurance plan assets were intended to fund the deferred compensation plan, thereby making it a funded plan. The defendant employer countered that the deferred compensation plan was unfunded, based on the plan documents that "state[d] that the rights of [plan participants] were those of unsecured creditors and that no assets held by [the company were] held in trust to fund the plan."[37]

The deferred compensation plan in *Miller* promised each participant a lifetime benefit "equal to, at a maximum, 30 percent of [his or her] highest annual salary, plus benefits to a designated beneficiary."[38] The NQDCP was a supplemental plan that included restrictions like a vesting period and a noncompetition clause. The deferred compensation plan did not, however, provide a specific funding mechanism for the benefits. The terms of the plan articulated the lack of specific funding by stating that:

> The rights of the Executive to the Deferred Compensation and of the Beneficiary . . . shall be solely those of unsecured creditors . . . No assets acquired or held by [the company], whether or not in connection with the obligations assumed by it hereunder, shall be deemed to be held under any trust for the benefit of the Executive or the Beneficiary or to be security for the performance of the obligations of [the company], but shall be and remain a general, unpledged, and unrestricted assets [sic] of [the company]. The right of the Executive to the payment of the Deferred Compensation and of the Beneficiary . . . shall not be assigned, transferred, pledged, or encumbered.[39]

The company argued that this language established that the deferred compensation plan was unfunded and, thus, a top hat plan.

The court concluded that the plan was unfunded because the deferred compensation plan language explicitly provided that the participants' rights were "solely those of unsecured creditors," and that none of the company's assets were held in trust or as security for the payment of benefits.[40] The plan satisfied the criteria established by the DOL and by case law for an unfunded plan. Further, the plan made no reference to the life insurance policies, which specifically stated that they were "independent of, and in addition to, any benefits payable under any other agreement."[41] A plan using insurance in conjunction with a deferred compensation plan will be considered funded if the benefits are paid through a specific insurance policy and will be considered unfunded when paid from general assets.[42]

---

37. Miller v. Heller, 915 F. Supp. 651, 654 (S.D.N.Y. 1996).
38. Miller v. Heller, 915 F. Supp. 651, 655 (S.D.N.Y. 1996).
39. Miller v. Heller, 915 F. Supp. 651, 656 (S.D.N.Y. 1996) (quoting the agreement).
40. Miller v. Heller, 915 F. Supp. 651, 656 (S.D.N.Y. 1996).
41. Miller v. Heller, 915 F. Supp. 651, 660 (S.D.N.Y. 1996) (quoting the agreement).
42. Belsky v. First National Life Insurance Co., 818 F.2d 661 (8th Cir. 1987).

## C. Annuity Contracts

An employer-owned deferred annuity contract is another insurance-based funding method that will allow a NQDCP to maintain its unfunded status. The employer would purchase the annuity and use the contracts to fund future benefits. This use of an annuity has been sanctioned by the IRS.[43] This is typically a single premium deferred annuity owned by the employer. Since the employer remains the beneficiary under the annuity policy, it remains an asset of the employer and subject to the claims of its general creditors. The employer who owns the annuity, must also include in taxable income the annual inside build-up in the annuity.[44] In addition, as opposed to life insurance products, annuities are not typically available for preretirement funding.

An employee-owned annuity that is purchased by the employer on behalf of the employee to pay benefits under a NQDCP is not subject to creditors of the employer and therefore will cause the plan to be deemed funded for ERISA and tax purposes.

# Section 6.4 Reserve Fund

The simplest method to informally fund a NQDCP is for the employer to establish an internal reserve account to be used to pay the deferred benefits. However, the funds set aside in this internal method remain at risk and may be lost in a corporate takeover or in bankruptcy. The employee cannot obtain any right of ownership or control over the funds. These amounts are typically invested to generate earnings. A bank or other external entity may be given control over the reserve account to pay benefits, but the funds cannot be removed from the reach of creditors.[45] This reserve arrangement can be made sufficiently irrevocable to the point of removing the funds from the risk of the fluctuations of internal changes within the corporation.[46]

# Section 6.5 Stocks or Bonds

Some employers purchase assets like stocks and bonds which can be sold to assist in paying NQDCP benefits. The downside is that any dividends or interest earned would be taxable currently, and these methods do not protect against the employer using the funds for other projects, or creditors of the employer gaining access to these funds.

---

43. Rev.Rul. 72-25
44. I.R.C. § 72(u)(1)(A) & (B) (2012).
45. *See, e.g.* I.R.S. Gen. Couns. Mem. 39,230 (Jan. 20, 1984).
46. *See, e.g.*, I.R.S. Gen. Couns. Mem. 39, 230 (Jan. 20, 1984).

# Section 6.6 Third-Party Guarantees

A third-party guarantor for the NQDCP benefits can be owners or the parent company of the employer. Such guarantees are mere promises to pay in the event of the refusal or inability of the employer the promised benefits. No funds are formally set aside to satisfy the guarantee.[47] Although this guaranty provides another layer of security for the executive, it is only as good as the financial health of the guarantor.

# Section 6.7 Secular Trusts

A secular trust can be established to hold assets that are earmarked to fund a nonqualified deferred compensation arrangement. Such trust assets cannot be used by the employer for any other purpose,[48] and the executive beneficiary of a secular trust has exclusive rights to the trust assets and its earnings.

More importantly, unlike a rabbi trust, the assets of a secular trust are not available to the employer's creditors in bankruptcy or insolvency. Therefore, a deferred compensation plan using a secular trust creates a funded plan for purposes of the code and ERISA. This means the plan becomes subject to the requirements of ERISA, if it meets the definition of a pension plan or welfare plan. The executive will be currently taxed as contributions are made to the trust or when the executive's interest vests, whichever is later, even though receipt of the compensation itself is deferred until retirement or other termination of services.[49] The tax impacts can be easily managed by providing periodic distributions or tax "gross up" payments to the employee. The ERISA impacts, however, generally are not manageable because an executive compensation plan generally will not satisfy ERISA's non-discrimination requirements. Therefore, this type of trust generally should be contemplated only when the NQDCP is not an ERISA-covered plan (such as a change-in-control only plan). These are most often seen in industries where cashflow is uncertain, such as emerging technology companies.

A secular trust is used when the security of the deferred amounts is a higher priority for the executive than deferral of taxation. The secular trust defers distribution and creates security but does not defer taxation, which means that the secular trust creates a tax liability and is not suitable if the primary objective is deferral of taxation.[50]

---

47. *See, e.g.*, Robinson v. Comm'r, 44 T.C. 20 (1965); Rev. Rul. 70-435, 1970-2 C.B. 100; Berry v. United States, 593 F.Supp. 80 (M.D.N.C. 1984), *aff'd*, 760 F.2d 85 (4th Cir. 1985). *See also* Janet G. Payton, *Corporate Counsel's Primer on Nonqualified Deferred Compensation Plans*, 71 Corp. Counsel's Primers Article I (2d 2006).

48. In keeping with the religious nomenclature of the rabbi trust, the secular trust derives its name from the fact that it is different from a rabbi trust.

49. IRC 402(b)(1); Treas. Reg. 1.402(b)-(1)(a)(1); Michael S. Sirkin & Lawrence K. Cagney, Executive Compensation 8-04 (2017).

50. Michael S. Sirkin & Lawrence K. Cagney, Executive Compensation 8-04 (2017).

The employer benefits from an immediate tax deduction provided the trust maintains separate accounts for each employee.[51] When corporate rates on the employer exceeded individual rates on the employee, the immediate deduction was more beneficial to the employer than the savings to the employee, so in addition to the security, there was a tax strategy in using a secular trust in conjunction with a NQDCP.[52] Currently, the maximum individual rate exceeds the corporate rate, therefore, immediate taxation and deduction has less appeal as a tax strategy.

The secular trust is always irrevocable and therefore, it protects against the change of heart of the employer as well as against the change of control of the employer. When combined with the fact that the trust's assets cannot be subject to the claims of the employer's creditors in the event of insolvency or bankruptcy, these secular arrangements function more like an after-tax savings vehicle for executives who want to defer the receipt of their compensation until retirement and puts the funds outside the temptation for current consumption.

The secular trust is not tax-exempt therefore the trust will generally be taxable on trust income. This will result in double taxation of trust income once to the trust and then again to the employee upon distribution.[53]

By way of contrast, a rabbi trust defers taxation and can be used for all types of NQDCPs (including retirement-type plans), and while its assets remain subject to claims of creditors, it remains the optimum vehicle to fund a deferred compensation plan because these trusts do not taint the unfunded status of the plan and the plan can maintain its flexibility in favor of the executive.

---

51. Michael S. Sirkin & Lawrence K. Cagney, Executive Compensation 8-04 (2017). *See also* 26 C.F.R. §§ 1.404(a) - 12(b)(3) (as amended in 1978); I.R.S. Priv. Ltr. Rul. 92-06-009 (Nov. 11, 1991).

52. *See, e.g.*, A. Thomas Brisendine, Elizabeth Drigotas & Thomas R. Pevarnik, *Secular Trusts*, 385-5th Tax Mgmt. (BNA) (U.S. Income 2018) (stating secular trusts "became even less attractive as marginal individual tax rates rose to a higher level than marginal corporate rates").

53. Michael S. Sirkin & Lawrence K. Cagney, Executive Compensation 8-04 (2017) (internal citations omitted). *See also* Richard Reichler & Jimmy Gatliff, *In General*, 366-2nd State Taxation of Compensation & Benefits (BNA) (U.S. Income 2019).

*CHAPTER* 7

# Origins and Policies of Section 409A and Definitions

Perceived abuses during the decline and ultimate downfall of the Enron Corporation is widely accepted as the catalyst for the enactment of Section 409A of the Internal Revenue Code (IRC). Enron was a natural gas company that enjoyed unprecedented growth in its stock value during the decade of the 1990s and ultimately became bankrupt in 2001. Enron established a sophisticated corporate structure that allowed it to conceal its true financial condition and inflate its stock value.[1]

Enron's conduct with respect to its deferred compensation plans was equally disingenuous. The executives at Enron who participated in the company's nonqualified deferred compensation plans (NQDCPs) were allowed to, and in fact did, accelerate payments of their deferred compensation as the company's financial condition deteriorated. Although this acceleration required the executives to forfeit 10 percent of the principal, often called a "haircut,"[2] executives were still able to preserve a large amount of their benefits and push Enron into an even more precarious financial position, as they drained the company's already dwindling resources. This "raiding" of the company came under even more scrutiny because many of the rank and file employees who were heavily invested in Enron stock (particularly in the company's 401(k) plan), had no similar option to preserve their anticipated benefits.

In contemplating their response to the Enron scandal, Congress recognized that any remedial law should end "existing practices that result in deferral of compensation while providing executives with inappropriate levels of security, control and flexibility."[3] IRC 409A was enacted in 2004 because Congress believed

1. Paul M. Healy & Khrishna G. Palepu, *The Fall of Enron*, 17 J. Econ. Persps. 3, 4 (2003).

2. Robert A. Miller, *Nonqualified Deferred Compensation Plans*, *in* Executive & Director Compensation Reference Guide (BNA) (2018); Kelly S. Kuglitsch, *Spotting Issues Under Section 409A: Perspective and Practice Tips*, 45 Corp. Tax. 3, 4-5 (2018).

3. Alessandra K. Murata, *Reasons for Enactment*, *in* Section 409A Handbook 1-6 (BNA) (Regina Olshan & Erica F. Schohn eds., 2016); *Enron: The Joint Committee on Taxation's Investigative Report*, 108th Cong. 5 (2003) (reporting on the Congressional investigation of the Enron Corporation and related entities regarding federal tax and compensation issues and policy recommendations).

that prior law improperly allowed executives tax deferral in situations where they had too much control over the deferred amounts. This control resulted in the manipulation of deferred compensation plans of troubled companies. IRC 409A's provisions reined in the control executives had over deferred compensation, and levied severe sanctions for violations of its provisions. Section 409A bars acceleration of deferred compensation, subject to regulatory exceptions.[4] It also places restrictions on delays and changes in time and form of distribution.[5]

In addition to addressing perceived abuses from Enron's decline, Congress took the opportunity to curtail other perceived abuses. As we saw in earlier chapters, NQDCPs are unfunded, but the law permits assets to be set aside in a rabbi trust to provide some security that the deferred compensation benefits will be paid, provided the assets remained reachable by the employers' creditors.[6] Prior to Section 409A, some companies would establish these trusts in foreign jurisdictions, which essentially insulated the assets from the reach of creditors.

Section 409A also provides that a trust that is established in a foreign jurisdiction is subject to income tax the year the assets are transferred offshore, despite the fact that the terms of the trust may state that its assets are subject to the claims of U.S. creditors.[7] The rule is inapplicable if substantially all of the services that gave rise to the deferred compensation were performed in the foreign jurisdiction in which the assets were held. In addition, trust income would be taxable in the year the terms of the plan provide that the financial decline of the employer would place the assets in the trust outside the reach of creditors.[8]

## Section 7.1 Important Concepts under Section 409A

IRC Section 409A states that:

> [i]f at any time during a taxable year a [NQDCP]. . . fails to meet the requirements of [Section 409A], or . . . is not operated in accordance with such requirements, all compensation deferred under the plan for the taxable year and all preceding taxable years shall be includible in gross income for the taxable year to the extent not subject to a substantial risk of forfeiture and not previously included in gross income.[9]

This chapter will explore the meaning of nonqualified deferred compensation plan under Section 409A, and the related 409A terms essential to that

4. I.R.C. § 409A(a)(3) (2018).
5. I.R.C. § 409A(a)(4)(C) (2018).
6. Rabbi trusts were discussed in Chapter 6.
7. I.R.C. § 409A(b) (2018).
8. I.R.C. § 409A(b)(2) (2018).
9. I.R.C. § 409A(a)(1)(A)(i) (2018).

definition: plan, deferral of compensation, legally binding right, service provider, and service recipient.

In addition, many Section 409A concepts revolve around certain terms with specific meanings. We will look at the definition of a number of these terms, including: substantial risk of forfeiture, separation from service, change in control, and specified employee. Later chapters may reiterate the definition of certain terms to the extent needed in the particular context.

## A. Nonqualified Deferred Compensation Plan

Section 409A applies to nonqualified deferred compensation plans (NQDCPs). A NQDCP is any plan that "provides for the deferral of compensation."[10] This may be in the form of an agreement between the executive and the company or a unilateral benefit provided for the executive by the company.

It specifically does not include the company's qualified retirement plans, certain IRA-based savings arrangements, 457(b) eligible deferred compensation plans, governmental excess benefit plans, certain other savings vehicles, certain foreign arrangements, and many welfare benefits.[11]

## B. Section 409A Plan

As noted above, a NQDCP must be a plan. The term "plan" for purposes of IRC 409A covers a broad array of arrangements and "includes any agreement, method, program, or other arrangement, including an agreement, method, program, or other arrangement" that is compensatory in nature.[12] The plan does not have to qualify as an employee benefit plan for purposes of ERISA.[13] For Section 409A, the plan includes only one person. While a single arrangement may cover several individuals, Section 409A will apply as though each person were in a separate plan.[14] This distinction becomes critical in many areas of Section 409A. For example, in considering the impact of operational failures, this treatment general results in taxation of only the affected individual and insulates other executives who were not impacted by the failure.

## C. Deferred Compensation

Understanding when a plan does and does not provide for the deferral of compensation is an extremely critical concept under Section 409A. A plan "provides for the deferral of compensation if, under the terms of the plan and the relevant facts and circumstances, the [executive] has a legally binding right during a taxable year to compensation . . . that is or will be payable in a later taxable year."[15]

---

10. Treas. Reg. § 1.409A-1(a)(1) (2020).
11. Treas. Reg. § 1.409A-1(a)(2) - (5) (2020).
12. Treas. Reg. § 1.409A-1(c) (2020).
13. Treas. Reg. § 1.409A-1(c) (2020).
14. Treas. Reg. § 1.409A-1(c) (2020).
15. A. Thomas Brisendine, Elizabeth Drigotas & Thomas R. Pevarnik, *Deferred Compensation Arrangements*, 385-5th Tax Mgmt. IV.D (BNA) (U.S. Income 2018).

This extremely broad definition encompasses an enormous number of compensation arrangements. For example, a commission arrangement under which an employee earns a right to $1,000 dollars on December 31 for sales that quarter, and is paid in the next year is an arrangement that provides for the deferral of compensation under this definition. Similarly, a severance arrangement may provide for the deferral of compensation because the executive provides services today, for the right to payment in a potentially later year after a severance occurs.

The expansiveness of this definition is, however, tempered by a host of exclusions for arrangements that would provide for a deferral of compensation. These exclusions include: deferral of non-taxable items, normal pay practices, deferrals that don't extend more than two-and-one-half months after the end of the year (short-term deferrals), certain stock options and equity incentives, certain transfers of property, certain foreign plans, and certain separation pay plans, among others. Specifics of certain of these exclusions are discussed in chapter 8.

## D. Legally Binding Right

In order to have a deferral of compensation, the employee must have a legally binding right to the deferred compensation. A legally binding right exists if the right is a contract "that is enforceable under the applicable law or laws governing the contract."[16] If facts show that the promised payment can be unilaterally eliminated or reduced by the employer after the compensation is earned there is no legally binding right.[17] However that discretion must generally be unconditional and the facts must reflect there is substantive significance, meaning that the potential reduction isn't an empty threat. If the executive is related to or has effective control over the person retaining the discretion (or that person's compensation), the discretion is treated as lacking substantive significance.

Importantly, a legally binding right is different than being vested. An executive can have a legally binding right to compensation that may be reduced or eliminated by operation of the plan. In such a case, the executive has a legally binding right to compensation, it just isn't nonforfeitable.

## E. Service Provider

Section 409A uses interesting terminology. Rather than applying to employees and employers it applies to "service providers" and "service recipients." Throughout this book, we will refer to "executives" or "employees" instead of "service providers" and to "companies" or "employers" rather than "service recipients," to provide easier context for the reader. However, it is important to recognize the broader

16. Application of Section 409A to Nonqualified Deferred Compensation Plans, 72 Fed. Reg. 19,234, 19,236 (Part III.B. of the Preamble provides a description of a legally binding right). *See also* Regina Olshan, *Coverage, in* SECTION 409A HANDBOOK 2-4 (BNA) (Regina Olshan & Erica F. Schohn eds., 2016); Regina Olshan & Erica F. Schohn, *Other Key Definitions: Service Recipient, Separation from Service, Specified Employee, Change in Control, in* SECTION 409A HANDBOOK 4-5 (BNA) (Regina Olshan & Erica F. Schohn eds., 2016).

17. Treas. Reg. § 1.409A-1(b)(1) (2020).

application. A service provider can be "(1) an individual, (2) a corporation, (3) a subchapter S corporation, (4) a partnership, (5) a personal service corporation, as defined under Code section 269A(b)(1) (or an entity that would be a personal service corporation if it were a corporation), or (6) a qualified personal service corporation, as defined under Code section 448(d)(2) (or an entity that would be a qualified personal service corporation if it were a corporation)."[18] It includes employees, former employees, and certain independent contractors.[19] However, Section 409A applies only to deferred compensation earned by service providers who report their income using the cash receipts and disbursements method of accounting, commonly referred to as the cash-basis method.[20]

## F. Service Recipient

The service recipient is the beneficiary of services provided by an employee, and has the "legally binding right" to pay the compensation.[21] The regulations provide that a service recipient is the entity for which services are performed and all members of its controlled group, as defined in IRC 414(b) and 414(c).[22] The controlled group issue can be critical, particularly in certain transactions. For example, an executive may not have a separation from service when he or she accepts employment at a different subsidiary or moves from a subsidiary to the corporate entity, despite the fact that he or she has had a termination of employment from the original entity.

As noted above, although Section 409A uses the term "service recipient" we will use the term "company" or "employer" to enhance understanding of the various principles.

## G. Substantial Risk of Forfeiture

Although the general principle of Section 409A quoted above, does not mention "substantial risk of forfeiture," a number of Section 409A principles and exceptions turn on this concept. For instance, an amount is taxable under a noncompliant Section 409A arrangement in the first year the amount is no longer subject to a substantial risk of forfeiture, and the short-term deferral period is measured from when an amount is no longer subject to a substantial risk of forfeiture.

According to the regulations, "[c]ompensation is subject to a substantial risk of forfeiture if entitlement to the amount is conditioned on the performance of

---

18. Treas. Reg. § 1.409A-1(f)(1) (2020). *See also* Regina Olshan, *Coverage*, *in* SECTION 409A HANDBOOK 2-10–2-11 (BNA) (Regina Olshan & Erica F. Schohn eds., 2016).

19. Treas. Reg. § 1.409A-1(f) (2020).

20. Regina Olshan, *Coverage*, *in* SECTION 409A HANDBOOK 2-11 (BNA) (Regina Olshan & Erica F. Schohn eds., 2016) *See also* Treas. Reg. § 1.409A-1(f)(1) (2020); A. Thomas Brisendine, Elizabeth Drigotas & Thomas R. Pevarnik, *Deferred Compensation Arrangements*, 385-5th Tax Mgmt. IV.D (BNA) (U.S. Income 2018).

21. Treas. Reg. § 1.409A-1(g) (2020).

22. A. Thomas Brisendine, Elizabeth Drigotas & Thomas R. Pevarnik, *Deferred Compensation Arrangements*, 385-5th Tax Mgmt. IV.D (BNA) (U.S. Income 2018). I.R.C. § 1563(a) (2018) (controlled group of corporations

substantial future services by any person."[23] This is straightforward and exists where an employee has to perform services for a number of years before achieving a non-forfeitable right to the compensation.

A substantial risk of forfeiture also exists if entitlement to the amount is conditioned on the occurrence of a condition related to a purpose of the compensation.[24] The condition must relate to the employee performing services or relate to the employer's business activities or goals, like the attainment of a certain level of earnings, equity value, or completion of an initial public offering (IPO).[25]

However, in either case, the possibility of forfeiture must be substantial. Factors that determine if the risk is substantial and real, include whether the activity that will create the forfeiture is likely to occur. As an example, if an amount is payable on the completion of an IPO it may not be conditioned on a substantial risk of forfeiture if the IPO is certain to occur.[26] If payment is conditioned on the employee's separation from service without cause, the right to the payment is subject to a substantial risk of forfeiture if the possibility of forfeiture is substantial.[27] Evidence that the risk is not substantial might occur, for instance, when a company routinely pays the same severance on voluntary terminations or does not enforce forfeiture conditions.

Importantly, refraining from performing services (such as a covenant not to compete) is not a condition that can create a substantial risk of forfeiture under Section 409A. This is at odds with the fact that this can be a substantial risk of forfeiture under Section 457. Therefore, practitioners should be particularly careful to assess overall tax compliance in situations involving covenants not to compete.

Additionally, salary deferrals generally are not considered to be subject to a substantial risk of forfeiture, unless the amount that may be received is materially greater than the salary deferral.[28]

Adding or extending a substantial risk of forfeiture may be allowed in conjunction with a change in control or other arm's length transactions between unrelated parties.[29] Otherwise, any such addition is disregarded for purposes of applying Section 409A.[30]

As with other technical terminology, to enhance readability, we will refer to the substantial risk of forfeiture lapses, as vesting.

---

23. Treas. Reg. § 1.409A-1(d)(1) (2020).

24. A. Thomas Brisendine, Elizabeth Drigotas & Thomas R. Pevarnik, *Deferred Compensation Arrangements*, 385-5th Tax Mgmt. III.C (BNA) (U.S. Income 2018). *See also* Treas. Reg. § 1.409A-1(d)(1) (2020).

25. Treas. Reg. § 1.409A-1(d)(1) (2020).

26. David E. Kahen & Regina Olshan, *Substantial Risk of Forfeiture*, *in* SECTION 409A HANDBOOK 3-20 (BNA) (Regina Olshan & Erica F. Schohn eds., 2016).

27. David E. Kahen & Regina Olshan, *Substantial Risk of Forfeiture*, *in* SECTION 409A HANDBOOK 3-20 (BNA) (Regina Olshan & Erica F. Schohn eds., 2016).

28. Treas. Reg. § 1.409A-1(d)(1) (2020).

29. Treas. Reg. § 1.409A-1(d)(1) (2020). *See also* David E. Kahen & Regina Olshan, *Substantial Risk of Forfeiture*, *in* SECTION 409A HANDBOOK 3-20 (BNA) (Regina Olshan & Erica F. Schohn eds., 2016); Treas. Reg. § 1.409A-3(i)(5)(iv)(B) (2020).

30. Treas. Reg. § 1.409A-1(d)(1) (2020).

## H. Separation from Service

As described in the next chapter, Section 409A requires the choice of a limited number of payment triggers. One of these triggers is separation from service. This may or may not be the same as when the employee legally terminates employment.

Separation from service for an employee is dependent on the intent of the employer and the employee and the facts.[31] A separation from service is presumed to occur if the employer and employee agree that services will cease altogether or be reduced to 20 percent or less of the previous three years' average.[32] Conversely, a separation is presumed to have not occurred if services continue at a level of 50 percent or more of the previous three years' average.[33] These are presumptions and can be overcome, for example, by evidence that the parties reasonably expected the services to cease, but business necessity resulted in reemployment. Also, the plan is permitted to set a percentage between 20 percent and 50 percent that will be treated as a separation from service, but that must be done upfront (otherwise it will be treated as a subsequent deferral).

Keep in mind, the individual's title or status is not relevant to Section 409A in addition, separation from service applies on the controlled group basis. Thus, a separation from service would not occur if a former employee continues to perform services in another capacity, for example, as a consultant for another related entity.[34] The definition of a related entity is expanded for purposes of separations from service[35]—therefore, special attention is warranted if services are performed for any related entity.

Bona fide leaves of absences, such as military leave and sick leave, are not separations from service, provided the leave does not extend beyond six months, unless there is a special exception.[36] If the leave of absence is due to health-related issues that are expected to last for at least six months, or lead to death, separation from service does not occur unless the absence lasts for at least twenty-nine months.[37]

It is important to note, also, that reemployment will not halt any previous payout that began after a separation from service.[38]

---

31. Regina Olshan & Erica F. Schohn, *Other Key Definitions: Service Recipient, Separation From Service, Specified Employee, Change in Control, in* Section 409A Handbook 4-11 (BNA) (Regina Olshan & Erica F. Schohn eds., 2016).

32. Regina Olshan & Erica F. Schohn, *Other Key Definitions: Service Recipient, Separation From Service, Specified Employee, Change in Control, in* Section 409A Handbook 4-11, 4-14 (BNA) (Regina Olshan & Erica F. Schohn eds., 2016); Treas. Reg. § 1.409A-1(h)(1)(ii) (2020).

33. Regina Olshan & Erica F. Schohn, *Other Key Definitions: Service Recipient, Separation From Service, Specified Employee, Change in Control, in* Section 409A Handbook 4-12, 4-14 (BNA) (Regina Olshan & Erica F. Schohn eds., 2016); Treas. Reg. § 1.409A-1(h)(1)(ii) (2020).

34. Regina Olshan & Erica F. Schohn, *Other Key Definitions: Service Recipient, Separation From Service, Specified Employee, Change in Control, in* Section 409A Handbook 4-17, 4-14 (BNA) (Regina Olshan & Erica F. Schohn eds., 2016); Treas. Reg. § 1.409A-1(h)(1)(ii) (2020).

35. Treas. Reg. § 1.409A-1(h)(3) (2020).

36. Treas. Reg. § 1.409A-1(h)(1)(i) (2020).

37. Treas. Reg. § 1.409A-1(h)(1)(i) (2020).

38. Regina Olshan & Erica F. Schohn, *Other Key Definitions: Service Recipient, Separation From Service, Specified Employee, Change in Control, in* Section 409A Handbook 4-17, 4-18 (BNA) (Regina Olshan & Erica F. Schohn eds., 2016); Treas. Reg. § 1.409A-1(h)(1)(ii) (2020).

Since Section 409A is not limited to employees, the regulations also provide rules regarding when a separation occurs for independent contractors. Similar to the rule for employees, an independent contractor has a separation from service when the parties reasonably expect a good-faith and complete termination of the contractual relationship. This can be tricky for contractors, as it is not always clear if a contract will be renewed. In addition, if the contract is followed by an employment relationship, there is no separation. The regulations do provide a safe harbor, however. The payment will be deemed to be made upon the contractor's separation from service, if the plan provides for payment at least twelve months after the contract expires and the contractor has not performed any services (either as a contractor or an employee) since expiration of the contract.[39]

## I. Change in Control

There are specific rules and options under Section 409A that revolve around whether a change-in-control has occurred. For purposes of Section 409A, a change-in-control event occurs if: (1) a person or group of persons acquires more than 50 percent of the fair market value or voting stock of the service recipient; (2) during a 12-month period a person or group of persons acquire 30 percent or more of the voting stock of the service recipient; (3) during a 12-month period, a majority of the board of directors is replaced with individuals not endorsed by a majority of board members in place before such appointment or election or; (4) a person or group of persons, during a twelve-month period, acquire 40 percent or more of the gross fair market value of the assets of the service recipient.[40] In each of these instances, the plan is permitted to modify the definition by increasing the referenced percentage, but that generally must be done by the time the deferral occurs.

## J. Specified Employee

Specified employees are subject to special payment timing restrictions. The term specified employee is used to describe an employee who, as of the date of separation from service, is a key employee of an employer whose stock is publicly traded on an established securities market.[41] A plan must provide that distributions to a specified employee may not be made before six months after the specified employee separates from service or, if earlier, the date of death.[42] The six-month delay rule, required for payments solely due to the separation from service of a specified employee, must be written in the plan document.[43]

39. Treas. Reg. § 1.409A-1(h)(2) (2020).

40. Treas. Reg. § 1.409A-3(i)(5) (2020).

41. For purposes of this section, a service provider is a key employee if the service provider meets the requirements of I.R.C. §§ 416(i)(1)(A)(i), (ii), (iii) (2018). *See also* Treas. Reg. § 1.409A-1(i)(1) (2020).

42. Regina Olshan & Erica F. Schohn, *Other Key Definitions: Service Recipient, Separation From Service, Specified Employee, Change in Control, in* Section 409A Handbook 4-29 (BNA) (Regina Olshan & Erica F. Schohn eds., 2016); Treas. Reg. 1.409A-1(i)(2)(i) (2020).

43. Treas. Reg. § 1.409A-1(c)(3)(v) (2020).

*CHAPTER* **8**

# Exemptions under 409A

Section 409A of the Internal Revenue Code (Section 409A) and its regulations, form the central nervous system for rules governing executive compensation. The definition of a nonqualified deferred compensation plan (NQDCP) under Section 409A, as any plan providing for the deferral of compensation, is so all encompassing that the exemptions provide welcome relief not only from its complexities, but also from its potential penalties, which are the responsibility of the executive.[1]

## Section 8.1 Exemption for Certain Service Providers

Deferred compensation for certain types of taxpayers is exempt from Section 409A. By definition, Section 409A applies to executives who report their income for federal income tax purposes on the cash receipts and disbursements method of accounting.[2] Therefore, accrual basis taxpayers, who report income when it is earned, and the amount can be determined with reasonable accuracy, are specifically exempt from the restrictions and penalties of Section 409A.[3] Independent contractors who provide significant services to at least two companies which are unrelated to each other, and to the independent contractor are also exempt from 409A.[4] The provision of significant services by the independent contractor will be presumed if up to 70 percent of total revenue is received from such companies.[5]

1. I.R.C § 409A(a)(1)(A)(ii) (2018).
2. Treas. Reg. § 1.409A1(f) (2020).
3. Treas. Reg. § 1.409A-1(f)(1) (2020).
4. Treas. Reg. § 1.409A-1(f)(2) (2020).
5. Treas. Reg. § 1.409A-1(f)(2) (2020).

# Section 8.2 Exemptions for Certain Arrangements

There are two main types of exemptions under 409A: (1) specific exemptions from the definition of NQDCPs; and (2) structural exemptions, where the regulations provide a blueprint for certain plans to avoid IRC 409A. The following plans and arrangements are specifically exempt from the definition of NQDCP under IRC 409A: qualified employer plans; certain employee incentive plans; certain foreign plans; certain 457 plans; and welfare benefit plans.

## A. Qualified Plans

As we saw in earlier chapters, typically qualified employer plans defer taxation on contributions and investment gains, while the employer receives an immediate deduction for its contributions. Included in this category are: pension plans, 401(k) plans, stock bonus plans, profit sharing plans, money-purchase pension plans, cash balance plans, 403(b) plans established by tax exempt nonprofit organizations and certain public educational institutions, 457(b) plans established by tax-exempt and governmental entities, and qualified governmental excess benefit arrangements under IRC 415.[6] A recent new exemption is for qualified equity grants under IRC 83(i).[7] The qualified employer plan exemption also includes simplified employee pensions (SEPs) and savings incentive match plans for employees (SIMPLEs), which are IRA-based arrangements.[8]

## B. Statutory Incentive Stock Options and Employee Stock Purchase Plans[9]

Statutory incentive stock options or the grant of a stock option under an employee stock purchase plan taxed under IRC 422 and 423, respectively, do not constitute a deferral of compensation and are exempt from 409A.[10] These create tax incentives including the fact that the taxable event for participation in these plans, is delayed until disposition of the stock.

---

6. Treas. Reg. § 1.409A-1(a)(2) (2020).

7. This recent exemption is not included in the regulations but was added to the IRC in 2017 as part of the 2017 Tax Cuts and Jobs Act. I.R.C. § 83(i) (2018); A. Thomas Brisendine, Elizabeth Drigotas & Thomas R. Pevarnik, *Deferred Compensation Arrangements*, 385-5th Tax. Mgmt. (BNA) IV.D.1 (U.S. Income 2018).

8. Larger contributions to this type of IRA are permitted than are permitted for individual IRAs. The contribution limit for a SEP in 2021 is the lesser of $58,000 or 25 percent of income. *SEP Contribution Limits (Including Grandfathered SARSEPs)*, I.R.S. (Nov. 12, 2020), https://www.irs.gov/retirement-plans/plan-participant-employee/sep-contribution-limits-including-grandfathered-sarseps. The contribution limit for SIMPLE IRA in 2021 is $13,500; if the employee is 50 years old or older, they can make catch-up contributions up to $3,000. *Retirement Topics—SIMPLE IRA Contribution Limits*, I.R.S. (Nov. 12, 2020), https://www.irs.gov/retirement-plans/plan-participant-employee/retirement-topics-simple-ira-contribution-limits.

9. Treas. Reg. § 1.409A-1(b)(5)(E)(ii) (2020).

10. Treas. Reg. § 1.409A-1(b)(5)(E)(ii) (2020).

## C. Certain Foreign Plans

With respect to foreign plans, the specific exemption relates to treaties, participation in a broad-based foreign retirement plan, and the citizenship or immigration status of the participant.

The regulations provide that the definition of NQDCP does not include any plan or arrangement where contributions and its earnings are excludable from federal income tax based on a bilateral treaty with the United States.[11] Since U.S. taxpayers are subject to tax on worldwide income, this exclusion removes the potential tax penalties for U.S. taxpayers who may participate in a foreign deferred compensation plan that may not be in compliance with IRC 409A.

If nonresidents or persons who are deemed to be U.S. residents due to satisfaction of a physical presence test,[12] rather than due to ownership of a green card, or bona fide residents of U.S. possessions, participate in a broad-based foreign retirement plan, the plan will not be considered a NQDCP for purposes of IRC 409A.[13] If U.S. citizens or resident immigrants possessing a green card, participate in a broad-based foreign retirement plan, the plan will not be considered a NQDCP for purposes of IRC 409A, provided the plan contains nonelective deferrals of modified foreign earned income[14] and the amounts deferred do not exceed the limits for tax qualified defined benefit plans and tax qualified defined contribution under IRC sections 415(b) and (c), respectively.[15] In addition, these participants cannot be eligible to participate in both a broad-based foreign retirement plan and a tax qualified plan.[16]

The term NQDCP does not include totalization agreements made with foreign jurisdictions in order to coordinate benefits under the social security systems of both countries.[17] The goal of these agreements is to minimize any potential double taxation for recipients of these benefits.

---

11. Treas. Reg. § 1.409A-1(a)(3)(i) (2020).

12. "You meet the physical presence test if you are physically present in a foreign country or countries 330 full days during any period of 12 consecutive months including some part of the year at issue. The 330 qualifying days do not have to be consecutive." *Foreign Earned Income Exclusion—Physical Presence Test*, I.R.S. (Dec. 3, 2020), https://www.irs.gov/individuals/international-taxpayers/foreign-earned-income-exclusion-physical-presence-test; I.R.S., Tax Guide for U.S. Citizens and Resident Aliens Abroad, Pub. 54 (Dec. 16, 2020), https://www.irs.gov/pub/irs-pdf/p54.pdf.

13. Treas. Reg. § 1.409A-1(a)(3)(ii) (2020).

14. "The term 'foreign earned income' with respect to any individual means the amount received by such individual from sources within a foreign country or countries which constitute earned income attributable to services performed by such individual during the period described [within]." I.R.C. § 911(b) (2018). *See also About Form 2555, Foreign Earned Income*, I.R.S. (Mar. 24, 2021), https://www.irs.gov/forms-pubs/about-form-2555.

15. Treas. Reg. § 1.409A-1(a)(3((iii) (2020). The limit for defined contribution plans for 2021 under IRC 415(c) is $58,000; pension benefit amounts cannot exceed $230,000 under IRC 415(b). The maximum exclusion for modified foreign earned income in 2021 is $108,700. I.R.S. Notice 2020-79, 2020-46 I.R.B. 1014; *Foreign Earned Income Exclusion*, I.R.S. (Feb. 3, 2021), https://www.irs.gov/individuals/international-taxpayers/foreign-earned-income-exclusion.

16. Treas. Reg. § 1.409A-1(a)(3)(iii) (2020).

17. Treas. Reg. § 1.409A-1(a)(3)(iv) (2020).

To qualify as a broad-based foreign retirement plan, the plan must cover a wide range of employees, including those in the rank and file. The majority of active participants must be nonresidents, resident immigrants due to the substantial presence test, or bona fide residents of a U.S. possession.[18] The plan must provide significant benefits to a substantial number of those covered in this group,[19] and the benefits provided to this group must be nondiscriminatory.[20] In addition, the plan must contain restrictions on accessing the benefits for reasons other than for retirement, hardship,[21] an unforeseen emergency,[22] for analysis educational pursuits,[23] or to purchase a primary residence.[24]

### D. Certain IRC 457 Plans

The term NQDCP does not include length of service award programs that provide pension-type benefits to emergency service volunteers, or their beneficiaries and are offered by state and local governments and other tax-exempt organizations. These payments are typically designed to motivate and improve volunteer services and typically are awarded to firefighters and other emergency intervention personnel.[25]

### E. Welfare Benefit Plans

Many welfare benefit plans are also specifically exempt from the definition of NQDCP and are, therefore, not subject to IRC 409A. These include: plans providing for bona fide vacation leave; sick leave; compensatory time; disability pay plans; death benefit plans; and health savings accounts.[26] It also includes certain medical reimbursement arrangements, which satisfy the provisions of IRC sections 105 and 106 so that both the coverage and benefits are excluded from taxation.[27]

## Section 8.3 Plans and Arrangements Structured to Avoid IRC 409A

Plans and arrangements can be structured to avoid IRC 409A by meeting some or all of the following exemptions:

1. short-term deferrals;
2. stock options and stock appreciation rights (stock rights);

18. Treas. Reg. § 1. 409A-1(a)(3)(v)(A) (2020)
19. Treas. Reg. § 1.409A-1(a)(3)(v)(B) (2020).
20. Treas. Reg. § 1.409A-1(a)(3)(v)(C) (2020).
21. Treas. Reg. § 1.409A-1(a)(3)(v)(D) (2020); I.R.C. § 401(k)(2)(B)(i)(IV) (2018).
22. Treas. Reg. § 1.409A-3(i)(3)(i) (2020).
23. Treas. Reg. § 1.409A-1(a)(3)(v)(D) (2020).
24. Treas. Reg. § 1.409A-1(a)(3)(v)(D) (2020).
25. I.R.C. § 457(e)(11) (2018); Treas. Reg. § 1.409A-1(a)(2) (2020).
26. Treas. Reg. § 1.409A-1(a)(5) (2020).
27. Treas. Reg. § 1.409A-1(a)(5) (2020).

3. restricted property, 402(b) trusts, and 403(c) annuities;
4. certain foreign plans;
5. separation pay plans;
6. certain indemnification agreements;
7. legal settlements; and
8. certain educational benefits.

## A. Short-Term Deferrals

The short-term deferral exemption is one of the most important and frequently used exceptions to IRC 409A.[28] To fall within the short-term deferral exemption, the plan must provide that the deferred compensation will be paid within two-and-a-half months after the end of the executive's first tax year, in which the right to the amount vests, or if later, two-and-a-half months after the end of the company's first tax year in which the right to the amount vests. This payment period is routinely called the "short-term deferral period."

Plans hoping to comply with the short-term deferral exemption can state that amounts will be paid as soon as practicable, but in no event after the short-term deferral period. If the plan is silent with respect to the payment date, the plan will be exempt from 409A if the amount is paid or made available to the employee during the short-term deferral period.[29] Annual bonus programs often are not documented carefully, and therefore, it is important to ensure payments are always made by March 15 after the year to which the bonus relates (particularly if employees are not required to be employed on the payment date to receive the bonus), to ensure the program is exempt from the documentation and other requirements of Section 409A.[30] In order to come within this exemption, the plan cannot provide for a "deferred payment."

If the plan's terms provide for a payment time other than "as soon as practicable" after the vesting date, then the plan's terms must foreclose any possibility that payment could be made at a date beyond the short-term deferral period in order to rely on the short-term deferral exemption. As an example, if a plan provides for payment based on an event that could occur after the short-term deferral period, it has provided for a "deferred payment" and will not come within the short-term deferral exemption even if in actuality the payments are made within the short-term deferral period. In that case, the short-term deferral exemption will not apply because the plan provided for a prohibited "deferred payment." Payments based on a trigger other than lapse of the substantial risk of forfeiture create this possibility that the plan would be considered providing for a "deferred payment."[31]

---

28. P. Garth Gartrell & Steven B. Lapidus, Executive Compensation for Emerging Growth Companies § 2:103 (3d ed. 2017).

29. Treas. Reg. § 1.409A-1(b)(4), ex. 1 (2020).

30. Kevin J. Murphy & Michael C. Jensen, *The Politics of Pay: The Unintended Consequences of Regulating Executive Compensation* 21-22 (Ctr. for Law and Social Science, Research Paper Series No. CLASS18-8, 2018), https://papers.ssrn.com/sol3/papers.cfm?abstract_id=3153147; Michael S. Sirkin & Lawrence K. Cagney, Executive Compensation § 7.16 (2008).

31. Treas. Reg. § 1.409A-1(b)(4)(i)(D) (2020).

Below are examples from the Treasury Regulations illustrating the deferred payment prohibition:

> Example 5: On November 1, 2008, Employer V awards a bonus to Employee E such that Employee E has a legally binding right to the payment as of November 1, 2008. Under the bonus plan, Employee E will forfeit the bonus unless Employee E continues performing services through December 31, 2010. Under the bonus plan, the bonus is scheduled to be paid as a lump sum payment on July 1, 2011. By specifying a payment date after the applicable 2 ½-month-period, the bonus plan provides for a deferred payment. The bonus plan provides for a deferral of compensation, and will not qualify as a short-term deferral regardless of whether the bonus is paid or made available on or before March 15, 2011 (and generally any payment before June 1, 2011 would constitute an impermissible acceleration of a payment).[32]

> Example 6: On November 1, 2008, Employer U awards a bonus to Employee F such that Employee F has a legally binding right to the payment as of November 1, 2008, that is not subject to a substantial risk of forfeiture. The bonus plan provides for a lump sum payment upon Employee F's separation from service. Because the separation from service is an event that may occur after the applicable 2 ½-month-period, the bonus plan provides for a deferred payment and therefore provides for a deferral of compensation. Accordingly, the bonus plan will not qualify as a short-term deferral regardless of whether Employee F separates from service and the bonus is paid or made available on or before March 15, 2009.[33]

Plans otherwise satisfying the short-term deferral exemption will not lose the exemption status if payments are delayed beyond the short-term deferral period, and it is shown the delay was due to an unforeseeable administrative issue or where making the payments on time would jeopardize the employer's financial health and/or its ability to proceed as a business entity. Payments must be made as expeditiously as possible after reasons for the delay have abated.[34] Publicly traded companies may also be allowed to delay payments in certain circumstances where IRC section 162(m) would unforeseeably restrict the employer's deduction.[35] If the short-term deferral exemption does not apply the plan must comply with Section 409A (assuming no other exemption applies).

32. Treas. Reg. § 1.409A-1(b)(4)(iii), ex. 5 (2020).
33. Treas. Reg. § 1.409A-1(b)(4)(iii), ex. 6 (2020).
34. Treas. Reg. § 1.409A-1(b)(4)(ii) (2020); Treas. Reg. § 1.409A-3(d) (2020).
35. *Id.*

## B. Stock Rights

Stock rights can be structured to be exempt from 409A. Granting stock rights like stock options and stock appreciation rights do not require exorbitant upfront costs for the employer, therefore, start-up companies benefit greatly from using stock rights as part of a deferred compensation package. The most common stock right offered as part of a NQDCP is a non-statutory stock option, which grants to the executive the right to purchase company stock over a stated period of time, at a predetermined price.[36] The grant date of the option refers to the date the corporation finalizes the corporate action needed to create a legally binding right to the option.[37] The stock option will not provide for a deferral of compensation and, therefore, will not be subject to Section 409A if all the following conditions are met:

1. The exercise price of the stock option must be at least equal to the fair market value (FMV) of the underlying stock on the date the option is granted.[38] In other words, the stock option cannot be discounted. Section 409A has essentially eliminated the use of discounted stock options as part of a NQDCP.[39]
2. The number of shares subject to the option must be fixed at the time of the grant of the option.[40]
3. The transfer or exercise of the option must be subject to the tax timing rules of IRC § 83. Under IRC § 83, the grant of an option that does not have a readily ascertainable FMV is not a taxable event. However, when the option is exercised there is a transfer of property, the stock, and the FMV must be reported as income at that time.[41]
4. The plan must not provide for a deferral of compensation, other than a deferral of income recognition, until the later of the exercise or disposition of the option, or the time the stock acquired, as a result of the exercise of the option, first becomes substantially vested.[42]
5. The stock subject to the stock option must be common stock of the company for whom the services are provided or that of a parent corporation.[43]

Conditions can be imposed on the exercise of the option without invalidating the grant of the option.[44] Therefore, if an option is granted to purchase stock on a particular date and it requires the holder of the option to be employed on the exercise date and/or requires certain profit benchmarks to be achieved, these

36. Treas. Reg. § 1.409A-1(b)(5)(i)(C) (2020).
37. Treas. Reg. § 1.409A-1(b)(5)(vi)(B) (2020).
38. Treas. Reg. § 1.409A-1(b)(5)(i)(A)(1) (2020); Michael S. Sirkin & Lawrence K. Cagney, Executive Compensation § 2.02 (2018).
39. Michael S. Sirkin & Lawrence K. Cagney, Executive Compensation § 5.02 (2018).
40. Treas. Reg. § 1.409A-1(b)(5)(i)(A)(1) (2020).
41. I.R.C. § 83 (e)(4) (2018).
42. Treas. Reg. § 1.409A-1(b)(5)(i)(A)(3) (2020).
43. Treas. Reg. § 1.409A-1(b)(5)(iii)(B) (2020).
44. Treas. Reg. § 1.409A-1(b)(5)(vi)(B) (2020).

conditions will not affect the validity of the option or its exemption from Section 409A.[45]

Since the value of the stock is an important criterion for the exemption and because valuation can succumb to manipulation, the regulations provide guidance on the valuation of the underlying stock.[46] If the stock is readily tradable on an established securities market, the FMV of the stock can be determined using various methods listed in the regulations, including the last actual sales price before the grant or the first sales price after the grant.[47] Valuation can also be determined using the closing price on the trading day before or on the date of the grant of the option.[48]

If the stock is not readily tradable on an established securities market, the process and methods of valuation must be reasonable based on all the facts and circumstances.[49] A safe harbor method allowed is to use a qualified independent appraiser within a year of the grant date.[50] This would create a presumption that the valuation was reasonable. A private start-up company that has not been in business for at least ten years can use a professional appraiser with considerable experience in valuing businesses.

## C. Stock Appreciation Rights

A stock appreciation right (SAR) grants an employee the opportunity to share in the appreciation and growth in value of a specified number of company shares, between the grant date and the exercise date. The advantage of the SAR from the employee's perspective is that he or she does not have to pay out any funds to realize the gain in the underlying shares,[51] on the other hand, SARs do not grant equity interests in the company. A SAR does not provide for a deferral of compensation and is, therefore, not subject to Section 409A if the:

1. compensation payable under the SAR is limited to the excess of the FMV of the stock on the date of grant and the FMV of the stock on the date of exercise of the stock appreciation right;[52]
2. exercise price of the SAR must be at least equal to the FMV of the underlying stock on the date of grant;[53]
3. underlying stock must be common stock;[54]

---

45. Treas. Reg. § 1.409A-1(b)(5)(vi)(B) (2020).
46. Treas. Reg. § 1.409A-1(b)(5)(iii)(A) (2020).
47. Treas. Reg. § 1.409A-1(b)(5)(iv)(A) (2020).
48. Treas. Reg. § 1.409A-1(b)(5)(iv)(A) (2020).
49. Treas. Reg. § 1.409A-1(b)(5)(iv)(B)(1) (2020).
50. Treas. Reg. § 1.409A-1(b)(5)(iv)(B)(2)(i) (2020).
51. Paul J. Schneider, *Reexamining the Application of Internal Revenue Code Section 409A to Stock Options*, 70 J. FIN. SERV. PROF. 27 (2016).
52. Treas. Reg. § 1.409A-1(b)(5)(B)(1) (2020).
53. Treas. Reg. § 1.409A-1(b)(5)(B)(2) (2020).
54. BNA Benefits Guide: Basics, Executive Compensation Programs, SARs, Phantoms, and Other Stock-Based Plans (2017) (*citing* Treas. Reg. § 1.83-3(i) (2007) & Treas. Reg. § 1.409A-1(b)(5)(i)(B) (2007)).

4. SAR must not have a deferral feature other than the ability to defer income until exercise;[55] and
5. appreciation must be based on a fixed number of shares at date of grant.[56]

Changing the number of shares or shortening vesting periods will not be deemed modifications that will cause the stock rights to lose their exemption status under 409A.

## D. Restricted Property

There is no deferral of compensation under Section 409A where nonvested property (property with restrictions) is transferred to an executive pursuant to a NQDCP, and the transfer would not be taxable under IRC § 83 due to the restrictions.[57] Under IRC § 83, taxation is postponed until the interest vests, that is, it is no longer subject to a substantial risk of forfeiture. Recipients of restricted property can opt to treat the receipt of the property as compensation in the year it is received, even though it is nonvested, nontransferable, and subject to a substantial risk of forfeiture at that time by using the IRC § 83(b) election feature. Strategically, an IRC § 83(b) election often is made on the calculation that later appreciation would be taxed at the more favorable capital gains rates. The election will not affect the exemption under Section 409A.[58]

## E. Certain Foreign Plans

Foreign deferred compensation plans will not be deemed to provide for a deferral of compensation under the following conditions: where the compensation and its earnings,[59] if paid at the later of when the legally binding right arose or the right to the compensation vests,[60] would have been excluded from gross income based on a bilateral treaty with the United States or based on a multilateral treaty to which the United States is signatory.[61] In addition, a foreign plan does not provide for a deferral of compensation if the compensation would not have been includible in income, if paid at the later of, when the legally binding right arose, or the right to the compensation vests, due to any of the following reasons:

1. the executive receiving the payment was a nonresident of the United States and consequently the compensation would have been excluded under IRC § 872;[62]

---

55. Treas. Reg. § 1.409A-1(b)(5)(i)(B) (2020).
56. Treas. Reg. § 1.409A-1(b)(5)(i)(B) (2020).
57. Treas. Reg. § 1.409A-1(b)(6) (2020).
58. Treas. Reg. § 1.409A-1(b)(5)(i) (2020).
59. Treas. Reg. § 1.409A-1(b)(8)(vi) (2020).
60. Treas. Reg. § 1.409A-1(b)(8)(i) (2020).
61. Treas. Reg. § 1.409A-1(b)(8)(i) (2020).
62. Treas. Reg. § 1.409A-1(b)(8)(ii)(A) (2020).

2. the compensation would be considered foreign earned income and would be excluded pursuant to IRC § 911;[63]
3. the compensation would have been excludible under IRC § 893; this would apply to U.S. citizens or permanent residents working in foreign jurisdictions and to foreign workers of a foreign government or international organizations;[64]
4. the compensation was earned by a bona fide resident of Guam, American Samoa, or Northern Mariana Islands and would be excluded from taxation pursuant to IRC § 931;[65] or
5. the compensation was earned by a bona fide resident of Puerto Rico and would be excluded from U.S. taxation pursuant to IRC § 933.[66]

Under a de minimis exemption, nonresident immigrants with U.S. source income can continue to participate in a foreign plan without the impact of Section 409A, provided the deferred amounts do not exceed the limit for 401(k) plans in the U.S. for the relevant tax year.[67] This benefits nonresidents who have a short stint in the United States and allows them to continue to participate and make deferrals in their foreign plans. The plan must cover mainly nonresidents or resident immigrants who do not have a green card and are classified as residents based on the substantial presence test.

Compensation paid under tax equalization agreements, designed to mitigate the impact of double taxation by a foreign government and the United States, do not provide for a deferral of taxation.[68] Payments under these agreements must be made by the end of second year after the U.S. tax return is due.

## F. Separation Pay Plans

A severance benefit arrangement can be negotiated at the time of the executive's departure, negotiated initially in an offer letter, employment agreement, or as part of a change in control plan, or implemented any time under a broader severance program.[69] These arrangements provide for a deferral of compensation and are, therefore, subject to 409A unless they are drafted as separation pay plans, which are exempt from 409A. Payment following an actual separation from service is a prerequisite for the exemption to apply. Of course, a separation

---

63. Treas. Reg. § 1.409A-1(b)(8)(ii)(B) (2020).

64. Treas. Reg. § 1.409A-1(b)(8)(ii)(B) (2020).

65. Treas. Reg. § 1.409A-1(b)(8)(ii)(D) (2020).

66. Treas. Reg. §§ 1.409A-1(b)(8)(ii)(C) & (D) (2020).

67. Treas. Reg. § 1.409A-1(b)(8)(iv) (2020). For 2021, this would be $19,500. I.R.S. Notice 2020-79, 2020-46 I.R.B. 1014; *COLA Increases for Dollar Limitations on Benefits and Contributions*, I.R.S. (Nov. 13, 2020), https://www.irs.gov/retirement-plans/cola-increases-for-dollar-limitations-on-benefits-and-contributions.

68. Treas. Reg. § 1.409A-1(b)(8)(iii) (2020).

69. Joseph M. Yaffe, *Separation Pay Arrangements*, *in* SECTION 409A HANDBOOK 12-3 (BNA) (Regina Olshan & Erica F. Schohn eds., 2016).

from service for purposes of 409A does not occur if the executive continues providing services to another entity that is related to the company.[70]

The following separation pay plans can be structured to be exempt from IRC 409A:

1. collectively bargained separation pay plans;[71]
2. separation pay plans due to involuntary separation from service;[72]
3. foreign separation pay plans;[73] and
4. reimbursement as part of separation pay plans.[74]

## *(i) Collectively Bargained Separation Pay Plans*

To be exempt from IRC 409A, collectively bargained separation pay plans must provide for separation pay based on an involuntary separation from service or pursuant to a window program.[75] They must also relate to employees covered by a bona fide collective bargaining agreement, that meets the following conditions:

1. the separation pay plan is contained within an agreement that the Secretary of Labor determines to be a collective bargaining agreement;
2. the separation pay provided by the collective bargaining agreement was the subject of arm's-length negotiations between employee representatives and one or more employers; and
3. the circumstances surrounding the agreement evidence good faith bargaining between adverse parties over the separation pay to be provided under the agreement.[76]

If a collectively bargained agreement plan covers employees who are performing services for multiple employers, the employees must separate from service from all such employers to receive separation pay. The plan can use any reasonable definition of involuntary separation from service provided the definition was the subject of arm's-length negotiation between the employee representatives and two or more employers.[77] The definition must also be in accordance with the regulations defining separation from service,[78]

---

70. Regina Olshan & Erica F. Schohn, *Other Key Definitions: Company, Separation from Service, Specified Employee, Change in Control, in* Section 409A Handbook 4-6 (BNA) (Regina Olshan & Erica F. Schohn eds., 2016); Joseph M. Yaffe, *Separation Pay Arrangements, in* Section 409A Handbook 12 (BNA) (Regina Olshan & Erica F. Schohn eds., 2016).

71. Treas. Reg. § 1.409A-1(b)(9)(ii) (2020).

72. Treas. Reg. § 1.409A-1(b)(9)(iii) (2020).

73. Treas. Reg. § 1.409A-1(b)(9)(iv) (2020).

74. Treas. Reg. § 1.409A-1(b)(9)(v) (2020).

75. Treas. Reg. § 1.409A-1(h) (2020).

76. Treas. Reg. § 1.409A-1(b)(9)(ii) (2020).

77. Treas. Reg. § 1.409A-1(n)(3) (2020).

78. Treas. Reg. § 1.409A-1(n)(1) (2020).

## (ii) Involuntary Separation Pay Plans

A separation pay plan that provides for separation pay solely upon involuntary separation from service, or based on a voluntary termination for good reason, will not provide for a deferral of compensation and will not be subject to 409A.[79] There are compensation limits to the separation pay plan based on an involuntary separation from service or a window program. The separation pay cannot exceed the lesser of twice the executive's annual compensation for the taxable year preceding the year of separation from service, or twice the compensation limit imposed on tax qualified plans pursuant to IRC 401(a)(17) for the year of separation.[80] The plan must provide that the separation pay be paid within two years after the separation from service.[81]

As an example, assume an executive is terminating employment in 2021. The executive earned $500,000 in 2020; twice that amount is $1,000,000. The IRC §401(a)(17) limitation on compensation for 2021 is $290,000.[82] Twice that amount is $580,000. The maximum amount payable under the Section 409A separation pay exemption is, therefore, limited to the lesser amount, which is $580,000. Any amount paid in excess of that amount will be subject to Section 409A unless another exemption, like the short-term deferral exemption, applies to the excess.

An involuntary separation from service is essentially a firing. It occurs when the company exercises its unilateral and independent authority to terminate an executive's service at a time that the executive was willing and able to continue to provide services.[83] Involuntary separation from service could also take the form of not renewing an expiring employment contract, and the executive was willing and able to execute a new contract.[84] The parties' characterization of the reason for the separation from service represents a rebuttable presumption that the reason for the separation was characterized properly.[85] Many times the parties may frame an executive's departure as a resignation when, in fact, it is a forced exit. This framing should not prevent application of the involuntary separation pay exemption, but the parties should be careful to document the facts surrounding the termination to ensure any applicable presumption could be rebutted upon IRS examination.

A voluntary separation from service for a bona fide good reason can be deemed an involuntary separation from service for purposes of the separation pay exemption. There are two ways to satisfy the requirement of "good reason": (1) Adhere to the general test or (2) utilize the safe harbor provisions describing

79. Treas. Reg. § 1.409A-1(b)(9)(iii), -1(n)(2) (2020).
80. Treas. Reg. § 1.409A-1(b)(9)(iii)(A)(2) (2020).
81. Treas. Reg. § 1.409A-1(b)(9)(iii) (2020).
82. I.R.S. Notice 2020-79, 2020-46 I.R.B. 1014.
83. Treas. Reg. § 1.409A-1(n) (2020)
84. Treas. Reg. § 1.409A-1(n)(1) (2020).
85. Treas. Reg. § 1.409A-1(n)(1) (2020).

"good reason."[86] Using the safe harbor will provide more assurance that a good reason termination falls within the separation pay plan exemption, but deviations from the safe harbor do not necessarily mean the separation pay plan exemption is unavailable.

Under the general test, the plan must specify certain limited conditions that must exist for an executive's voluntary separation from service to be deemed a constructive involuntary separation from service. These limited conditions must be actions taken by the company that result in a material and negative change in the employment relationship and they cannot be conditions intended only to avoid application of Section 409A. This could include a demotion and/or a salary reduction.[87] Other relevant factors include whether the amount and/or the form of payment is the same as that available upon an actual involuntary separation from service, and whether the executive is required to give the company both notice of the existence of the negative condition, and a reasonable opportunity to remedy the condition.[88]

Under the safe harbor good reason requirements, the plan must require the executive to resign within two years after the initial existence of one or more of the following occurrences:[89]

1. a material reduction in the executive's base compensation;[90]
2. a material decrease in the executive's authority, duties, or responsibilities;[91]
3. a material diminution in the authority, duties, or responsibilities of the supervisor to whom the executive is required to report, including a requirement that an executive report to a corporate officer or employee instead of reporting directly to the board of directors of a corporation;[92]
4. a material diminution in the budget over which the executive retains authority;[93]
5. a material change in the geographic location of the executive's workplace;[94] and
6. any other action or omission that constitutes a material breach by the company of the employment agreement with the executive.[95]

86. Treas. Reg. § 1.409A-1(n)(2)(i) (2020); Robert A. Miller, *Nonqualified Deferred Compensation Plans, in* Executive & Director Compensation Reference Guide 52 (BNA) (2018) (*citing* Application of Section 409A to Nonqualified Deferred Compensation Plans, 72 Fed. Reg. 19,234 (Apr.17, 2007)).

87. Treas Reg. § 1.409A-1(n)(2)(i) (2020).

88. Treas. Reg. § 1.409A-1(n)(2)(i) (2020).

89. Treas. Reg. § 1.409A-1(n)(2)(ii) (2020).

90. Treas. Reg. § 1.409A-1(n)(2)(ii)(A)(1) (2020).

91. Treas. Reg. § 1.409A-1(n)(2)(ii)(A)(2) (2020).

92. Treas. Reg. § 1.409A-1(n)(2)(ii)(A)(3) (2020) (including a requirement that an executive report to a corporate officer or employee instead of reporting directly to the board of directors of a corporation).

93. Treas. Reg. § 1.409A-1(n)(2)(ii)(A)(4) (2020).

94. Treas. Reg. § 1.409A-1(n)(2)(ii)(A)(5) (2020).

95. Treas. Reg. § 1.409A-1(n)(2)(ii) (2020).

The executive must be required to provide notice to the company of the existence of the condition within ninety days of the initial existence of the condition, and the company must be provided a period of at least thirty days to remedy the condition.[96] In addition, the amount, time, and form of payment upon the voluntary separation from service must be substantially identical to the amount, time, and form of payment payable due to an actual involuntary separation from service.[97]

Following the safe harbor closely in crafting the good reason provisions will ensure that the arrangement falls within the separation pay exemption. However, many executives are not satisfied with the safe harbor—for instance, it is common for a good reason provision to include a reduction in the executive's total compensation opportunity as opposed to a reduction only in base pay. While it would seem that a small deviation such as this should still fall within the safe harbor rule, practitioners can provide little assurance to clients on this front. Since it is unclear whether a deviation of this type will take the provision out of the separation pay exemption, it is advisable to ensure the program will satisfy Section 409A on its own, rather than relying solely on the safe harbor exemption if deviations are used.

### *(iii) Separation Pay Plan Pursuant to a Window Program*

Separation pay pursuant to a window program can also be exempt from 409A. Window programs are sometimes established by a company in connection with, and in anticipation of an impending separation from service, which could be due to early retirement, a reduction in workforce, or a sale of a business division.[98] The length of the window programs varies significantly depending on the needs of the company, but cannot be longer than twelve months. Employees who voluntarily terminate service during this limited period may receive enhanced separation pay benefits as an inducement to voluntarily terminate. The separation from service will not be considered a window program if a pattern of repeatedly offering similar programs for substantially consecutive periods is discovered. Whether the recurrence of these programs constitutes a pattern is determined based on the facts and circumstances. Although no one factor is determinative, relevant factors include: whether the window program benefits are on account of a specific event like a sale of business; the degree to which the separation pay relates to the event; and whether the event triggering the separation pay is temporary or a permanent aspect of the employer's business.[99]

The same compensation limits applicable to a separation pay plan based on an involuntary separation from service applies to the window program. The separation pay cannot exceed the lesser of twice the executive's annual compensation for the taxable year preceding the year of separation from service or twice the compensation limit imposed on tax qualified plans pursuant to IRC 401(a)

96. Treas. Reg. § 1.409A-1(n)(2)(ii)(C) (2020).
97. Treas. Reg. § 1.409A-1(n)(2)(ii) (2020).
98. Treas. Reg. § 1. 409A-1(b)(9)(iii) (2020).
99. Treas. Reg. § 1.409A-1(b)(9)(vi) (2020).

(17) for the year of separation.[100] The plan must provide that the separation pay be paid within two years after the separation from service.[101]

## (iv) Foreign Separation Pay Plans

A foreign separation pay plan will be exempt from IRC provided the payments comply with the separation pay plans of a foreign jurisdiction.[102]

## (v) Expense Reimbursements

Reimbursement arrangements as part of a voluntary or involuntary separation from service are exempt from Section 409A, as not providing for a deferral of compensation.[103] Reimbursements can be for reasonable outplacement expenses and reasonable moving expenses. Moving expenses include all, or part of, any loss the executive may actually incur due to the sale of a primary residence in connection with separation from service.[104] The plan must provide that the expenses must be incurred within the two-year period after separation from service under the separation pay plan, and paid no later than by the end of the third year after the separation from service.[105] Reimbursements for medical expenses as part of the separation pay, and incurred after separation from service, are also exempt from 409A provided they are deductible medical expenses, and the conditions for continued payment of these expenses is similar to the time limitation periods for continuation of coverage under COBRA.[106]

In-kind benefits provided to the executive after a separation from service, such as the use of tangible personal or real property, are exempt from 409A under the same conditions as expense reimbursements.[107] They must be incurred within two years of separation from service and paid by the end of the third year after separation from service are part of the exemption.[108]

Under a de minimis exemption, a separation pay plan does not provide for a deferral of compensation if the payment does not exceed the elective deferral limits, allowed pursuant to IRC 402(g)(1)(B), applicable in the year of separation from service.[109] These are the same limits which are allowed for certain tax qualified plans like 401K plans.[110]

---

100. Treas. Reg. § 1.409A-1(b)(9)(iii)(A)(2) (2020).

101. Treas. Reg. § 1.409A-1(b)(9)(iii) (2020).

102. Treas. Reg. § 1.409A-1(b)(9)(iv) (2020).

103. Treas. Reg. § 1 409A-1(b)(9)(v)(A) (2020); BNA Benefits Guide: Basics, Executive Compensation Programs, Section 409A: Scope and Exemptions 12-13 (2017)

104. Treas. Reg. § 1.409A-1(b)(9)(v)(A) (2020).

105. Treas. Reg. §§ 1.409A-1(b)(9)(iv), (v)(E) (2020).

106. Treas. Reg. § 1.409A-1(b)(9)(v)(B) (2020). For involuntary termination, the period for COBRA coverage is up to eighteen months. 29 U.S.C. 1162 (2018).

107. Treas. Reg. § 1.409A-1(p) (2020).

108. Treas. Reg. §§ 1.409A-1(b)(9)(v)(C), -1(p) (2020).

109. I.R.C. § 402(g)(1)(B); Treas. Reg. § 1.409A-1(b)(v)(D) (2020).

110. Treas. Reg. § 1.409A-1(b)(9)(v)(D) (2020). For separation from service in 2020, the limit is $19,500. Notice 2020-79, 2020-46 I.R.B. 1014.

## G. Indemnification and Liability Insurance Plans are not Deferral of Compensation

A plan that provides for indemnification or the purchase of an insurance policy to provide payments to an executive, for payments that were made to settle bona fide claims which arose while the executive was acting in his or her capacity as an employee, does not provide for a deferral of compensation, and are exempt from 409A.[111]

## H. Legal Settlements do not Provide for a Deferral of Compensation

An agreement to pay amounts to resolve bona fide employment related legal claims are exempt from IRC 409A.[112] The settlement could be for claims based on wrongful termination, employment discrimination, violations of the Fair Labor Standards Act (FLSA), or worker's compensation statutes, including federal, state, local, or foreign laws.[113] Excludable legal settlements include reimbursements for, or payments of, reasonable attorneys' fees or other reasonable expenses incurred by the executive related to such bona fide employment related claims.[114] See chapter 17 for a further discussion of legal settlements.

## I. Certain Educational Benefits

A plan that provides for taxable educational benefits solely for the employee will not constitute a deferral of compensation and will not be subject to Section 409A. The benefits cannot be provided to any other person including the spouse, child, or other family member of the executive.[115]

111. Treas. Reg. § 1.409A-1(b)(10) (2020).
112. Treas. Reg. § 1.409A-1(b)(11) (2020).
113. Treas. Reg. § 1.409A-1(b)(11) (2020).
114. Treas. Reg. § 1.409A-1(b)(11) (2020); 81 Fed. Reg. 40569, 40580 (June 22, 2016).
115. Treas. Reg. § 1.409A-1(b)(12) (2020).

CHAPTER **9**

# Compliance with 409A

If a nonqualified deferred compensation plan (NQDCP) does not fall within an exemption to Section 409A, and fails to comply with its requirements, the deferred compensation will be included in gross income in the year of vesting, in addition, a penalty of 20 percent of the compensation, plus interest, will apply.[1]

Both the plan document itself and the operation of the plan must be in accordance with Section 409A.[2] Therefore, it is not enough to have a valid NQDCP document, the plan must be operated in accordance with the plan document, and in compliance with Section 409A.

This chapter will focus on the compliance rules of Section 409A that relate to:

1. the timing of the election to defer;
2. the rules governing subsequent changes to an election;
3. the anti-acceleration rules; and
4. permissible distribution events and times.

## Section 9.1 Initial Election to Defer—Amount/Time and Form of Payment

A central element of NQDCPs concerns the timing of the initial election to defer.

Prior to Section 409A, the determination of when an employee could make an election to defer compensation was not straightforward. The IRS offered that to receive a favorable determination with respect to deferral of amounts pursuant to a NQDCP, the election to defer receipt of compensation, had to be made in the calendar year prior to the year the compensation was earned.[3] However,

1. I.R.C. § 409A(a)(1)(A), (B) (2018); Daniel Hogans, *Deferral Election Deadlines Under Section 409A Chart*, Westlaw Practical Law Practice Note (2018).

2. I.R.C. § 409A(a) (2018). *See also Nonqualified Deferred Compensation Audit Techniques Guide*, IRS.gov (June 1, 2021), https://www.irs.gov/pub/irs-pdf/p5528.pdf.

3. Rev. Proc. 71-19, 1971-1 C.B. 698.

case law supported the view that an election to defer could be made at any time prior to the time the employee was entitled to the payment.[4] Section 409A settled the matter by mandating that the plan terms must provide that the initial irrevocable election to defer compensation generally must be made no later than the end of the executive's taxable year, preceding the year in which the compensation is earned.[5] Therefore, to defer compensation paid for services to be performed in the year 2022, the election to defer the receipt of compensation generally must be made by December 2021.[6]

The initial election to defer compensation must include the time and form that the compensation will be payable.[7] However, the medium of payment, whether cash or property, does not have to be selected at the time of the initial deferral election.[8] On the other hand, if the plan permits the company the discretion to disregard the choice of the time and form of payment, such a provision will destroy the irrevocability of the initial election.[9] Despite the rules on irrevocability, changes or a cancellation of the deferral election, deferrals can be made upon the executive's death, disability, or the occurrence of an unforeseeable emergency or hardship.[10]

As stated in previous chapters, NQDCPs can be based on elective salary deferrals or non-elective company deferrals. Elective deferral plans allow executives to elect to reduce receipt of current compensation, and instead defer receiving a portion, or all, of currently earned compensation and/or bonuses, until a future date. In the non-elective type of deferral, the employer establishes a NQDCP that promises additional compensation, the payment of which is deferred to a date in the future, without any concomitant reduction in current compensation.[11]

The initial deferral election rules require the plan to designate the time and form of payment by the later of the time the executive first has a legally binding right to the compensation or, if later, the time the executive would be required to make an election.[12] A legally binding right to compensation refers to

---

4. Veit v. Comm'r, 8 T.C. 809 (1947), *acq.* 1947-2 C.B. 4 (Veit 1); Veit v. Comm'r, 8 T.C.M. (CCH) 919 (1949) (Veit II); Oates v. Comm'r, 18 T.C. 570 (1952), *aff'd* 207 F.2d 711 (7th Cir. 1953), *acq.* 1960-2 C.B. 6; Robinson v. Comm'r; 44 T.C. 20 (1965), *acq.* 1970-2 C.B. xxi, *acq.* 1976-2 C.B. 2; Metcalf v. Comm'r, 43 T.C.M. (CCH) 1393 (1982); Martin v. Comm'r, 96 T.C. 814 (1991); Goldsmith v. United States, 586 F.2d 810 (Ct. Cl. 1978).

5. Treas. Reg. § 1.409A-2(a)(3) (2020). An executive's taxable year is typically the calendar year. Regina Olshan, *Initial Deferral Elections*, *in* SECTION 409A HANDBOOK (BNA) 8-4 (Regina Olshan & Erica F. Schohn eds., 2016).

6. Treas. Reg. § 1.409A-2(b)(9), ex.1 (2020).

7. Treas. Reg. § 1.409A-2(a)(1) (2020); Robert A. Miller, *Nonqualified Deferred Compensation Plans*, *in* EXECUTIVE & DIRECTOR COMPENSATION REFERENCE GUIDE (BNA) 56 (2018).

8. Treas. Reg. § 1.409A-2(a)(1) (2020); H.R. Rep. No. 108-755, at 732–33 (Conf. Rep.).

9. Treas. Reg. § 1.409A-2(a)(2) (2020).

10. Treas. Reg. § 1.409A-3(i)(3) (2020) (defining unforeseeable emergency); Treas. Reg. § 1.409A-3(i)(4) (2020) (defining disability); Treas. Reg. § 1.409A-3(j)(4)(viii) (2020) (describing the cancellation of deferrals following an unforeseeable emergency or hardship distribution).

11. Treas. Reg. § 1.409A-2(a)(2) (2020).

12. Treas. Reg, § 1.409A-2(a)(2) (2020).

the existence of a contractual right to receive the compensation in exchange for specific services to be performed.[13]

A plan may allow an executive to have in place a recurring deferral where an election for one year continues for the ensuing year, unless the election is terminated or modified before the end of the immediately preceding year. These are referred to as evergreen deferrals.[14]

There is some flexibility in the initial deferral rules where the employee is a newly eligible participant. In such cases, the new participant has thirty days from eligibility to elect to defer compensation for services to be performed prospectively.[15] In a non-elective plan, the employer has up to thirty days after the participant becomes eligible to participate, to specify the time and form of payment.[16]

The rules for the initial election to defer are different for performance-based compensation. Performance-based compensation is defined as "compensation . . . the entitlement to which, is contingent on the satisfaction of preestablished performance criteria . . . ."[17] Deferral elections for performance based compensation can be made up to six months before the performance period has ended, provided the employee continuously performs services during that time,[18] and the amount of the compensation is neither readily ascertainable, nor substantially certain to be paid.[19] This means that an employee who participates in an employer's annual performance based bonus plan, from January 1, 2021 to December 31, 2021, may make an initial election to defer by June 30, 2021, provided the employee performed services for the entire period and provided the compensation is not yet readily ascertainable or assured at that time.[20]

## Section 9.2 Subsequent Changes in Time and Form of Payment

Prior to the enactment of Section 409A, the issue of when changes to an initial deferral election could be made was unsettled. Extensions of the initial deferral period and other changes could be made prior to the time the payment was due. The IRS would not issue an advanced ruling with respect to a NQDCP if the plan allowed changes to time and form of payment to be made after the beginning of the year in which the services were performed.[21] The courts, however, were more

---

13. Treas. Reg. § 1.409A-2(b)(9), ex.2 (2020).
14. Treas. Reg. § 1.409A-2(a)(1) (2020). *See, e.g.*, Regina Olshan, *Initial Deferral Elections, in* Section 409A Handbook (BNA) 8-13 (Regina Olshan & Erica F. Schohn eds., 2016) (describing "evergreen deferral elections" as "elections that remain in effect until terminated or modified").
15. Treas. Reg. § 1.409A-2(a)(7) (2020).
16. Treas. Reg. § 1.409A-2(a)(7)(i) (2020).
17. Treas. Reg. § 1.409A-1(e)(1) (2020).
18. Treas. Reg. § 1.409A-2(a)(8) (2020).
19. Treas. Reg. § 1.409A-2(a)(8) (2020).
20. Treas. Reg. § 1.409A-2(a)(8) (2020).
21. Rev. Proc. 92-65, 1992-33 I.R.B. 16.

flexible and allowed changes to extend the initial deferral of compensation to be made at any time before the scheduled payment was due.[22]

Section 409A settled the issue by allowing plans to permit employees to further postpone receipt of payments or alter the time and form of payment under very prescribed conditions.[23] If the employer chooses to allow subsequent further deferrals, and other changes, the executive must give careful thought prior to making changes. The reason for this cautionary note is that the plan document must explicitly provide that such elections must be made no less than twelve months before the original scheduled payment date.[24] Furthermore, the change may not take effect for at least twelve months after it is made, and any further deferral must be extended for at least five years from the original distribution date. This is referred to as the "one-year/five-year rule."[25] An executive must consider whether a subsequent deferral for five years, with the risks involved, because the plans are unfunded, is appropriate in the particular circumstance.

If the distribution of the deferred amounts is scheduled for a fixed date or based on a fixed schedule, any subsequent change in the date must be made at least one year before the originally scheduled payment date and the new payment date must be set for five years later.[26]

Below are examples from the Treasury Regulation:

> Example 15: Subsequent deferral election. Employee N participates in a nonqualified deferred compensation plan. Employee N elects to be paid in a lump sum payment at the earlier of age 65 or separation from service. Employee N anticipates that he will work after age 65, and wishes to defer payment to a later date. Provided that Employee N continues in employment and makes the election by his 64th birthday, Employee N may elect to receive a lump sum payment at the earlier of age 70 or separation from service.[27]
>
> Example 16: Subsequent deferral election rule—change in form of payment from lump sum payment to life annuity. Employee P participates in a nonqualified deferred compensation plan. Employee P elects to be paid in a lump sum payment at age 65. Employee P wishes to change the payment form to a life annuity. Provided that Employee P makes the election on or before his 64th birthday, Employee P may elect to receive a life annuity commencing at age 70.[28]

---

22. *See, e.g.*, Martin v. Comm'r, 96 T.C. 814 (1991) (finding the "circumstances of a shadow stock plan" did not constitute constructive receipt).

23. Treas. Reg. § 1.409A-2(b) (2020); Robert A. Miller, *Nonqualified Deferred Compensation Plans*, *in* Executive & Director Compensation Reference Guide (BNA) (2018).

24. Treas. Reg. § 1.409A-2(b)(1)(iii) (2020).

25. Treas. Reg. § 1.409a-2(b)(1) (2020); BNA Benefits Guide: Basics, Executive Compensation Programs, Section 409A Compliance: A Quick How-To Guide 4–5 (2017).

26. Treas. Reg. § 1.409A-2(b)(1)(iii) (2020).

27. Treas. Reg. § 1.409A-2(b)(9), ex.15 (2020).

28. Treas. Reg. § 1.409A-2(b)(9), ex.16 (2020).

Changing a triggering event for distribution from, for example, separation from service to a change in control must also follow the one-year/five-year rule. The Treasury Regulations provide the following example:

> Example 24: Subsequent deferral election rule—change in time of payment from payment at separation from service to payment at a change in control event. Employee X participates in a nonqualified deferred compensation plan that provides for a lump sum payment at separation from service. Employee X wishes to change the payment provision such that the payment is payable upon a change in control event. A change in the distribution provision to provide for a payment only upon a change in control event will violate the rules governing payment provisions, because the change could result in an acceleration if the change in control event occurs before Employee X separates from service, or a subsequent deferral if the change in control does not occur until after Employee X separates from service. However, provided that Employee X makes such election on or before the date 1 year before a separation from service, Employee X may elect to receive a payment upon the later of a change in control event or 5 years following a separation from service.[29]

These are operational rules and care must be taken to ensure their proper implementation.[30] In the case of a life annuity or installment payments, the deferral must be extended for five years from the date the first amount was scheduled to be paid.[31] Changes after the initial election to provide that payments can be made earlier due to death, disability, or an unforeseeable emergency are exempt from the one-year/five-year rule.[32] This rule seems appropriate since any scenario where these events were not initially included would seem more to be an oversight.

## Section 9.3 Prohibition Against Acceleration of Payments

Prior to the enactment of Section 409A, distributions could be permitted earlier than the time originally selected for a myriad of personal and other reasons and as a quid pro quo, the executive would lose 10 percent of the deferred amount in the process. This loss is referred to as taking a "haircut."[33] Although tax revenue

29. Treas. Reg. § 1.409A-2(b)(9), ex.24 (2020).

30. Robert A. Miller, *Nonqualified Deferred Compensation Plans*, *in* Executive & Director Compensation Reference Guide (BNA) n.148 (2018).

31. Treas. Reg. § 1.409A-2(b)(1)(ii) (2020); BNA Benefits Guide: Basics, Executive Compensation Programs, Section 409A Compliance: A Quick How-To Guide 4–5 (2017).

32. Treas. Reg. § 1.409A-2(b)(1)(ii) (2020); Robert A. Miller, *Nonqualified Deferred Compensation Plans*, *in* Executive & Director Compensation Reference Guide (BNA) 45 (2018).

33. *See, e.g.*, Robert A. Miller, *Nonqualified Deferred Compensation Plans*, *in* Executive & Director Compensation Reference Guide (BNA) (2018) (describing haircut provisions and the impact of 409A).

would be earlier, there was the potential for manipulation where an executive who became aware of the financial problems of an employer could opt, for any reason, to accelerate payment of his or her deferred compensation rather than face the possibility of losing it all. This was seen as presenting an unfair advantage to some, at the expense of other creditors and/or employees in the rank and file.

Under Section 409A, a NQDCP generally cannot allow the acceleration of distributions of deferred compensation unless an exception provided in the regulations applies.[34] A plan can adopt all the exceptions allowed in the regulations or choose certain exceptions without any input from the executive with respect to the exceptions to adopt.[35]

Some of the more commonly encountered exceptions provide flexibility in practical circumstances, for example acceleration of distributions are allowed to comply with domestic relations orders,[36] ethics agreements with the federal government, or to be in compliance with conflicts of interest rules and ethics rules of federal state, local, or foreign governments.[37] Another important exception allows accelerated payments of deferred amounts with respect to IRC 457(f) plans, where tax is due upon vesting.

Accelerated payments can be made to pay certain taxes,[38] or to cash out amounts that do not exceed the dollar limits applicable to elective deferrals of tax qualified plans, like 401(k) plans, pursuant to IRC 402(g)(1)(B).[39] Accelerated distributions in connection with plan terminations are exempt from the antiacceleration rules under special circumstances[40] and are discussed in more detail in chapter 16.

## Section 9.4 Permissible Conditions for Payment

Section 409A allows only six conditions that can trigger a distribution from NQDCPs.[41] These conditions, set forth in both the statute and the regulations, are not self-executing, therefore, the plan must affirmatively state, at the time of

34. I.R.C. § 409A(a)(3) (2018); Treas. Reg. § 1.409A-3(j)(1) (2020); Vorris J. Blankenship, *Employee Benefits & Pensions: Deferred Compensation: The Proposed Sec. 457(f) Regulations and Sec. 409A*, Tax Advisor (June 1, 2017), https://www.thetaxadviser.com/issues/2017/jun/deferred-compensation-proposed-sec-457f-regulations-sec-409A.html.

35. Treas. Reg. § 1.409A-3(j)(4) (2020).

36. Treas. Reg. § 1.409A-3(j)(4)(ii) (2020).

37. Treas. Reg. § 1.409A-3(j)(4)(iii) (2020).

38. BNA Benefits Guide: Basics, Executive Compensation Programs, Section 409A Compliance: A Quick How-To Guide (2017). *See also* Treas. Reg. §§ 1.409A-3(j)(4)(i)–(xiv) (2020).

39. Treas. Reg. § 1.409A-3(j)(4)(v) (2020). For 2021 this amount is $19,500. *Retirement Topics—401(k) and Profit-Sharing Plan Contribution Limits*, IRS.gov (June 26, 2021), https://www.irs.gov/retirement-plans/plan-participant-employee/retirement-topics-401k-and-profit-sharing-plan-contribution-limits.

40. Treas. Reg. § 1.409A-3(j)(4)(ix) (2020).

41. I.R.C. § 409A(2) (2018); BNA Benefits Guide: Basics, Executive Compensation Programs, Section 409A Compliance: A Quick How-To Guide 6 (2017).

the initial election to defer, the circumstances that will trigger a distribution or the date for distribution of the deferred amounts. Note, if payments were made based on a triggering event in the regulations, but that event was not listed in the plan document, the payments would violate the permissible distribution payment rule.

The law allows distributions for any one or more of the following reasons: (1) the employee's "separation from service;" (2) the date the employee becomes "disabled;" (3) the employee's death; (4) a specified date (or pursuant to a fixed payment schedule, such as installments); (5) a "change in control" of the company; or (6) the occurrence of an "unforeseeable emergency."[42]

Events like separation from service, disability, death, change in control, and unforeseen emergencies, are defined in the regulations. The definitions in the plan document can be more restrictive, but not less restrictive than the regulatory definitions.[43]

The selection of separation from service as a distribution event is very common and typical.[44] A separation from service is presumed to occur if there will be a complete cessation of future services to the employer or to the employer's affiliates. If post-separation service continues at the rate of 50 percent or more of the average for the previous three years, there is a presumption that there is no separation from service.[45] Likewise, if there is a reduction in services to 20 percent or less of the average for the previous three years, there is a presumption that there is a separation from service.[46]

If the rate of service post separation is more than 20 percent but less than 50 percent of the average level for the preceding three years, there is a rebuttable presumption that there is no separation from service.[47] The presumption can be rebutted by demonstrating that both the employer and the employee anticipated

---

42. John J. Heber & Steven Novak, *409A Issues in Executive Compensation Contracts and Employment Agreements*, Lewis Brisbois Bisgaard & Smith LLP Newsletter (Sept. 2017), http://lewisbrisbois.cmail19.com/t/ViewEmail/d/15EB63B41C1A6B3C/D62DD85C63D77D102438807772DD75D1?utm_source=Mondaq&utm_medium=syndication&utm_campaign=View-Original.

43. I.R.C. § 409A(a)(2) (2018); Henry C. Blackiston, Michael Dunn & Jonathan D. Karelitz, 2-34 Corporate Compliance Practice Guide § 34.08 (2018). *See also*, Treas. Reg. § 1.409A-3(a)(4) (2020) (a fixed date); Treas. Reg. § 1.409A-3(a)(1) (2020) (separation from service); Treas. Reg. § 1.409A-3(a)(5) (2020) (change in ownership or control of the employer); Treas. Reg. § 1.409A-3(i)(1)(i) (2020) (vesting or lapse of a substantial risk of forfeiture); Treas. Reg. § 1.409A-3(a)(2) (2020) (disability); Treas. Reg. § 1.409A-3(a)(3) (2020) (death); Treas. Reg. § 1.409A-3(a)(6) (2020) (unforeseeable emergency).

44. I.R.C. § 409A(a)(2)(A)(i) (2018); Treas. Reg. §§ 1.409A-3(a)(1), (b), (c), (i)(2) (2020); Dominick Pizzano, *The NDCP Dirty Dozen: Timing is Everything*, Retirement Town Hall Blog (Aug. 31, 2016), https://www.retirementtownhall.com/?p=8466#sthash.GEuXeKev.dpbs.

45. Treas. Reg. § 1.409A-1(h)(1)(ii) (2020); Dominick Pizzano, *The NDCP Dirty Dozen: Timing is Everything*, Retirement Town Hall Blog (Aug. 31, 2016), https://www.retirementtownhall.com/?p=8466#sthash.GEuXeKev.dpbs.

46. Treas. Reg. § 1.409A-1(h)(1)(ii) (2020).

47. Treas. Reg. § 1.409A-1(h)(1)(ii) (2020); Dominick Pizzano, *The NDCP Dirty Dozen: Timing is Everything*, Retirement Town Hall Blog (Aug. 31, 2016), https://www.retirementtownhall.com/?p=8466#sthash.GEuXeKev.dpbs.

a reduction in service to below 20 percent. Post-separation service is scrutinized to ensure that the executive is not engaging in significant consulting services for the employer after the ostensible separation from service.[48] There is no separation from service if the employee is on military leave, sick leave, or other bona fide leave of absence that does not last longer than six months.[49] If the duration is over six months, the executive must "retain[] a right to reemployment with the company under an applicable statute or by contract."[50]

There is a special payment rule for specified employees of a public company, who separate from service. Specified employees are among the top fifty most highly compensated officers of a public company.[51] A public company is defined as a corporation, the stock of which is traded on an established securities market.[52] The plan must provide that payments to a specified employee by reason of separation from service cannot be made until six months after the date of such employee's separation from service (or, if earlier, the date of death of the specified employee).[53] This rule does not apply to distributions to specified employees due to other triggering events under Section 409A or to amounts exempt from Section 409A.[54]

The catalyst for the six-month delay rule was the Enron debacle, where Enron's executives obtained distributions of their deferred compensation benefits in the period leading up to the company's bankruptcy, even though shareholders and other rank-and-file employees lost most of their investment in the company.[55] The six-month delay is an attempt to ensure that executives cannot immediately and expeditiously access deferred compensation upon separation from service.

Disability of the executive can be chosen as a payment event trigger for deferred compensation, provided disability is defined in accordance with the standards set forth in the regulations or are more restrictive.[56] Disability for purposes of the event triggers occurs when an employee is:

> unable to engage in any substantial gainful activity by reason of any medically determinable physical or mental impairment which can be expected to result in death or can be expected to last for a continuous period of not less than twelve months or [the executive] is, by reason of any medically determinable physical or mental impairment which can be expected to result in death or can be expected to last for a continuous

48. Treas. Reg. § 1.409A-1(h)(1)(ii) (2020).
49. Treas. Reg. § 1.409A-1(h)(1)(i) (2020).
50. Treas. Reg. § 1.409A-1(h)(1)(i) (2020).
51. Treas. Reg. § 1.409A-1(i) (2020).
52. Treas. Reg. § 1.409A-1(i) (2020).
53. Alvin D. Lurie et al., Bender's Federal Income Taxation of Retirement Plans § 14.02 (Matthew Bender & Co., Inc. 2018).
54. Michael S. Sirkin & Lawrence K. Cagney, Executive Compensation § 7.09 (2018).
55. *See, e.g.*, *Enron: The Joint Committee on Taxation's Investigative Report*, 108th Cong. 16 (2003) (statement of Lindy L. Paull, Chief of Staff, Joint Committee on Taxation, Washington, DC).
56. Treas. Reg. §§ 1.409A-3(i)(4)(i)–(iii) (2020).

period of not less than twelve months, receiving income replacement benefits for a period of not less than three months under an accident and health plan covering employees of the participant's employer.[57]

A determination by the Social Security Administration that the employee has a disability is not required, but is proof of a disability.[58] A plan may also provide for the payment of deferred compensation upon the event of an executive's death.[59]

A fixed date as a trigger for distribution can be the designation of a single date (e.g., January 2, 2022) or a designated period within single tax year (e.g., 2022, Q1 2022, or December 2022).[60]

A distribution may be paid upon a change in ownership of the employer, a change in effective control, or a change in the ownership of a substantial portion of the assets of the employer. Change in ownership occurs when a person or group of persons acquire more than 50 percent of the total fair market value (FMV) or total voting power of the stock of the company.[61] If a person or group already owns more than 50 percent of the employer, the acquisition of additional stock will not constitute a change in control for purposes of Section 409A. A change in effective control occurs if a person or a group of persons acquire, during a twelve-month period, 30 percent or more of the total voting power of the stock of the employer or the majority of the board is replaced during any twelve-month period by directors whose appointment or election was not endorsed by a majority of the corporation's board before the date of the appointment or election.[62] A change in ownership of a substantial portion of the assets occurs when a person or group acquire, during a twelve-month period, 40 percent or more of the FMV of the assets of the corporation.[63] This definition of a change in control sets the outside limit on what constitutes a change in control. It is common for the plan to specify a more limited definition of change in control—particularly raising the noted percentages to require a more substantial sale of the company's assets or stock to constitute a change in control for payment purposes.

A company may permit the payment of deferred compensation to the executive if the executive experiences an unforeseeable emergency.[64] The plan can provide its own definition of an unforeseeable emergency, however, at a minimum, the emergency must arise from an extraordinary and unforeseeable circumstance beyond the control of the executive, and which causes the executive severe financial hardship, that cannot be alleviated by reimbursement from an insurance company, cessation of future deferrals, or liquidation of the executives

57. I.R.C. § 409A(a)(2)(C)(i) (2018); Treas. Reg. § 1.409A-3(i)(4) (2020).
58. Treas. Reg. § 1.409A-3(i)(4)(iii) (2020).
59. I.R.C. § 409A(a)(2)(A)(iii) (2018); Treas. Reg. § 1.409A-3(a)(3) (2020).
60. Treas. Reg. § 1.409A-3(i)(1)(ii) (2020).
61. Treas. Reg. § 1.409A-3(i)(5)(v) (2020).
62. Treas. Reg. § 1.409A-3(i)(5)(vi) (2020).
63. Treas. Reg. § 1.409A-3(i)(5)(vii) (2020).
64. Treas. Reg. § 1.408A-3(i)(3) (2020).

assets.[65] Examples of unforeseen circumstances include: illness; an accident; funeral expenses of a spouse, a beneficiary, or a dependent or nondependent child;[66] or loss of the executive's property due to casualty, foreclosure, or eviction from the executive's primary residence.[67] The need to pay additional federal state and local taxes, to purchase prescription drugs, or to pay for medical expenses also may qualify as unforeseen emergencies.[68]

The regulations clarify that the desire to purchase a home is not an unforeseen event, however, the need to repair uninsured water damage of a principal residence *is* an unforeseen emergency.[69] The need to defray college-related expenses are not unforeseeable emergencies.[70] The statute gives an executive discretion whether to request the distribution for an emergency, and it gives the company discretion whether to grant such a request.[71]

## Section 9.5 Timing of Payments after Distribution Trigger

Once a distribution trigger is activated, the employer's obligation to make a payment is not discretionary, and the plan document must provide for the actual payment to be made within a designated period or on a designated schedule after the event occurs.[72] This could be on the date of the triggering event but, practically, that would be difficult to administer.[73] Generally, plans provide a schedule of payment(s) based on the triggering event. This schedule must be nondiscretionary and objectively determinable at the time of triggering event. The period specified may be any time during the calendar year in which the triggering event occurs or could be a period of up to 90 days if the period is allowed to cross tax years. For example, see the examples from the regulations below.

> Example 1: Employee A provides services as an employee of Employer Z, but is not a specified employee. Employee A participates in a nonqualified deferred compensation plan providing for a lump sum payment payable on or before December 31 of the calendar year in which Employee A separates from service. The plan provides for a payment upon a separation from service in compliance with this section.[74]

---

65. I.R.C. §§ 409A(a)(2)(A)(vi), (a)(2)(B)(ii) (2018); Treas. Reg. § 1.409A-3(i)(3) (2020).
66. Rev. Rul. 2010-27, 2010-45 I.R.B. 620.
67. Treas. Reg. § 1.409A-3(i)(3)(i) (2020).
68. *Id.*
69. Rev. Rul. 2010-27, 2010-45 I.R.B. 620.
70. Treas. Reg. § 1.409A-3(i)(3)(i) (2020); Rev. Rul.2010-27, 2010-45 I.R.B. 620.
71. Treas. Reg. § 1.409A-3(i)(3)(iii) (2020).
72. Treas. Reg. § 1.409A-3(b) (2020).
73. Dominick Pizzano, *The NDCP Dirty Dozen: Timing is Everything*, Retirement Town Hall Blog (Aug. 31, 2016), https://www.retirementtownhall.com/?p=8466#sthash.GEuXeKev.dpbs.
74. Treas. Reg. § 1.409A-3(i)(vi), ex.1 (2020).

> Example 2: Employee B provides services as an employee of Employer Y, but is not a specified employee. Employee B participates in a nonqualified deferred compensation plan providing for a lump sum payment payable on or before the 90th day immediately following the date upon which Employee B separates from service. Employer Y retains the sole discretion to determine when during the 90-day period the payment will be made. Although the plan does not specify a period during one calendar year in which the payment will be made, the plan provides for a payment upon a separation from service in compliance with this section because the period over which the payment may be made is no longer than 90 days.[75]

If the plan specifies a period of up to ninety days that may cross tax years, then the plan must ensure the executive does not have a right to choose the taxable year of payment.[76] This presents practical NQDCP design issues when the payment is conditioned on execution of a release. A plan that provides payment will be made in the 90-day period following separation from service, but only after execution of the release would effectively permit the executive to ensure selection of the later tax year by withholding return of the release. This may create impermissible discretion that violates Section 409A. Instead, plans that include a release requirement often provide that payment will begin in the later tax year, regardless of when the executive returns the release or that payments will begin on a certain date after separation, subject to recoupment if the executive doesn't execute the release timely. While the former is often preferrable to the company, it often is not practical for the company's payroll to administer (particularly if severance normally continues without interruption) and therefore the latter option may be advisable to avoid operational errors that would create Section 409A violations.

A plan may also establish a schedule of successive payments that is nondiscretionary and objectively determinable. A common example is installment payments—the NQDCP may provide that the amount is paid in three equal installments payable during the first three taxable years following the taxable year in which a separation from service occurs.[77] While the amount and timing of payment under the schedule generally must be determinable at the time of the triggering event, there is limited ability to create payment schedules based on amounts received by the company after separation (such as payments as account receivable are paid) and schedules that include guardrails on the amount of payments that a company will pay to all employees under an arrangement.[78] A company wishing to utilize these special rules should be careful to follow all the

---

75. Treas. Reg. § 1.409A-3(i)(vi), ex.2 (2020).

76. Eric D. Altholz, Verrill Dana LLP, *Section 409A Basics: When is a Payment Date Close Enough?*, Benefits L. Update, (June 12, 2012, 8:36 AM). *See also* Treas. Reg. § 1.409A-3(i) (2020).

77. Treas. Reg. § 1.409A-3(b) (2007).

78. Treas. Reg. § 1.409A-3(i)(1)(ii) and (iii) (2007).

requirements included in Section 409A and would be well advised to consult with experienced 409A counsel as these rules are particularly complex.

Finally, it is important to note that plans may specify different times and forms for each payment trigger, but generally may only specify one time and form of payment for any particular payment trigger. The plan cannot, for example, provide for payment in a lump sum immediately if the triggering event occurs on a Monday, but in a lump sum next calendar year if the event occurs on any other day of the week. While those are both permissible schedules, the plan cannot provide two schedules for that same triggering event.

However, if the plan provides for payment upon death, disability, change of control, or unforeseeable emergency, the plan may provide an alternative payment schedule if the event occurs on or before one (but not more than one) specified date. For example, the plan could provide for payment in lump sum on the first day of the month, following a change in control event that occurs before the executive attains age 55, and in 5 substantially equal annual installments following a change in control event that occurs on or after the executive attains age 55.

In addition, if the plan provides for payment upon separation from service, the plan may specify a different time and form of payment with respect to a separation from service under each of the following conditions:

1. Separations from service during a limited period of time not to exceed two years following a change in control;
2. Separations from service before or after a specified date (for example, attainment of age 55) or combination of a specified date and a specified period of service; and
3. Other separations from service.[79]

While the plan generally must be operated in strict compliance with the written plan document, Section 409A does provide limited forgiveness for small variances in the actual payment timing. Payment will be considered to have been on the date specified in the plan, if it is made on the specified payment date, not more than 30 days prior to the specified date, or on a later date within the executive's same taxable year (or, if later, within 2 ½ months after the specified payment date). To the extent the 30 days prior or 2 ½ after the specified date would cross a tax year, the rule applies only if the executive could not directly or indirectly specify the taxable year in which the payment occurred).[80]

---

79. Any service condition must be determined under a predetermined, nondiscretionary, objective formula, or pursuant to the method for crediting service under a qualified plan sponsored by the service recipient. Treas. Reg. § 1.409A-3(c) (2007).

80. Treas. Reg. § 1.409A-3(d) (2007); Eric D. Altholz, Verrill Dana LLP, *Section 409A Basics: When is a Payment Date Close Enough?*, Benefits L. Update, (June 12, 2012, 8:36 AM).

*CHAPTER* **10**

# Section 409A Corrections

The ability to correct violations of Section 409A of the Internal Revenue Code (IRC) is important because, as we saw earlier, the penalties are severe. An executive that has a right to receive compensation from a nonqualified deferred compensation plan (NQDCP), that does not comply with Section 409A, must report that compensation as income when the right to receive the income is no longer subject to a substantial risk of forfeiture, generally meaning when it vests.[1] In addition to that income tax, the executive must pay an additional 20 percent tax on the compensation. The executive may also owe potentially substantial interest, computed as the federal underpayment rate plus one percentage point—a premium interest penalty.[2] The employer will have to issue a Form W-2 to the participant, and the participant may have to file an amended return, unless the statute of limitations on assessment of the tax has expired. Normally, the IRS has three years after a return is filed to assess a tax unless there is a substantial omission of income.[3] A substantial omission of income exists if the taxpayer omits from gross income an amount in excess of 25 percent of the amount of gross income stated on the return.[4] In this case, the tax can be assessed within six years after the return is filed. Therefore, the statute of limitation has to be considered in determining whether to file an amended return.

Operating the plan and drafting the document in accordance with Section 409A are within the purview of the employer; nevertheless, it is the executive who bears the brunt of the penalties, absent a gross-up agreement with the employer. In a recent case, an executive unsuccessfully brought an action against his employer for failure to operate the plan in compliance with Section 409A. In *Wilson v. Safelite Group, Inc.*, the well-known auto glass repair company, created a deferred compensation plan in 2006 for its top executives.[5] The executives could defer both bonus and salary payments. Wilson deferred over $9 million in bonuses

1. I.R.C. § 409A(d)(4) (2018).
2. I.R.C. § 409A(a)(1)(B) (2018).
3. I.R.C. § 6501(a) (2018).
4. I.R.C. § 6501(e) (2018).
5. 930 F.3d 429 (6th Cir. 2019).

and salary, however, a federal audit found defects in the operation of the deferrals pursuant to Section 409A resulting in additional income tax and penalties.[6]

The executive, Wilson, brought actions in federal and state court and asserted state law claims against Safelite for breach of contract and negligent misrepresentation. Safelite moved for summary judgment, on the grounds that Wilson's state law claims were preempted because the Safelite plan was an employee pension benefit plan within the scope of ERISA.[7] The district court agreed with Safelite and granted the motion after reiterating that the plan was within the scope of ERISA, because it "results in a deferral of income by employees for periods extending to the termination of covered employment or beyond."[8] Upon appeal, the Sixth Circuit affirmed the district court's decision.[9] Since ERISA generally limits the types of claims available, it may create significant barriers to recovery against the employer—this increases the importance of independently reviewing any programs at the outset and potentially negotiating indemnification provisions. State law claims may be available for non-ERISA arrangements, but we are not aware of cases successfully asserting these claims.

Thankfully, a number of common Section 409A violations can be corrected in a manner that lessens or completely avoids the additional income taxation. Section 409A violations generally fall into two categories: (1) an operational error in administering the plan or (2) a documentary error in preparing the terms of the plan document.

Notice 2008-113 addresses the correction of operational failures, and Notice 2010-6 addresses the correction of documentary failures. Utilizing these measures expeditiously to correct violations under IRC 409A is optional, but may mitigate the acceleration of income tax and potential penalties under Section 409A.

# Section 10.1 Correcting Operation Errors under Notice 2008-113

Notice 2008-113 lists overall eligibility requirements to obtain relief.[10] Use of the correction program requires the employer to show that measures have been taken to ensure that the failure will not be repeated,[11] and that the failure was unintentional.[12] Correction measures under this notice also cannot be used if the employee or employer is under audit for a federal income tax matter involving the plan.[13] In addition, the employer cannot seek relief under this notice if

6. Wilson v. Safelite Group, Inc., 930 F.3d 429, 432 (6th Cir. 2019).

7. Wilson v. Safelite Group, Inc., 930 F.3d 429, 433-35(6th Cir. 2019); 29 U.S.C. § 1002(2)(A) (2018).

8. Wilson v. Safelite Group, Inc., 930 F.3d 429, 433 (6th Cir. 2019); 29 U.S.C. § 1002(2)(A)(ii) (2018).

9. Wilson v. Safelite Group, Inc., 930 F.3d 429, 438 (6th Cir. 2019).

10. I.R.S. Notice 2008-113, 2008-51 I.R.B. 1305.

11. I.R.S. Notice 2008-113, 2008-51 I.R.B. 1305 (Section III.B).

12. I.R.S. Notice 2008-113, 2008-51 I.R.B. 1305 (Section III.D).

13. I.R.S. Notice 2008-113, 2008-51 I.R.B. 1305 (Section III.C).

it is in the throes of a financial crisis.[14] Interestingly, if erroneous payments are made to the employee, typically a correction would require repayment to the employer, however, repayment is not required in the situation where the financial condition of the employer casts doubt on whether the compensation will be available when rightfully due.[15] Notice 2008-113 requires the employer to attach to its tax return a statement about correction of the error for the year the failure was discovered.[16]

There are specific failures available for correction under Notice 2008-113, including erroneous payments to the employee or amounts improperly held by the employee, resulting from:

- premature payments before the due date, failure to defer, or insufficient deferral;
- premature payments made more than thirty days before a specified date, due to failure to comply with the thirty-day rule;[17]
- premature payments due to a violation of the six-month delay payment requirement for specified employees who separate from service.

Other specific failures include erroneous retention of amounts by the employer due to:

- failure to make a payment when due after the occurrence of a permissible distribution event, resulting in a continuing erroneous deferral;
- excess deferrals;
- the need to correct stock right issues.

This notice also addresses stock right mistakes. If the intention was to have a stock option or stock appreciation right exempt from section 409A, however, due to an error, the exercise price is set at less than the fair market value (FMV) of the underlying stock at date of grant, this is correctable under Notice 2008-113.[18]

The scope of the relief under this Notice 2008-113 is based on the time the correction is made and whether the employee is an insider.[19] Four categories of failures are correctable under Notice 2008-113.

---

14. I.R.S. Notice 2008-113, 2008-51 I.R.B. 1305 (Section III.E).

15. I.R.S. Notice 2008-113, 2008-51 I.R.B. 1305 (Section III.F).

16. I.R.S. Notice 2008-113, 2008-51 I.R.B. 1305. (Section IX)

17. Recall that this rule allows a mini-acceleration, not earlier than thirty days prior to the specified date.

18. I.R.S. Notice 2008-113, 2008-51 I.R.B. 1305 (Section IV.D).

19. Insider is defined in Notice 2008-113 as:

> A service provider is an insider with respect to a service recipient if the service provider is a director or officer of the service recipient or is directly or indirectly the beneficial owner of more than 10 percent of any class of any equity security of the service recipient, determined in accordance with the rules of the Securities and Exchange Commission under §16 of the Securities Exchange Act of 1934, as amended, 15 USC 78p, without regard to whether the service recipient has any class of equity securities registered under §12 of such Act, 15 USC 78l. See 17 CFR §240.16a-1(a) (beneficial owner) and (f) (officer). In the case of a service recipient that is not a corporation, such rules are applied by analogy.
>
> I.R.S. Notice 2008-113, 2008-51 I.R.B. 1305 (Section III.G).

## A. Failures Corrected in Same Taxable Year the Operational Failure Occurs

The first category concerns failures corrected in the same taxable year the operational failure occurs.[20] Retention of an amount by an employee due to failure to defer or an erroneous payment to the employee, other than an erroneous payment due to violation of the rule relating to specified employees, requires payment to the employer in the time frame in this category. Additional taxes, penalties, and premium interest under Section 409A will not apply.[21] If an insider is involved and the amount exceeds the elective deferral limit for tax qualified plans under IRC Section 402(g)(1)(B), then the insider has to repay the employer with reasonable interest.[22] If hardship is demonstrated, the parties can agree to have the repayment occur over twenty-four months with interest.[23] This reprieve due to hardship, is not available to insiders. The amount is not required to be reported on a Form W-2 as income. The repayment can be done through salary reduction but that salary has to be reported as income prior to the reduction.

If the employer fails to defer, the employer upon receiving the amount can, but is not required to, adjust the account balance for earnings and losses to take into account the time value of money. If the operational failure involves a premature payment to the employee due to payment more than thirty days before the due date, or results from violation of the rules relating to specified employees, repayment is all that is required if done in the time frame of this category, no adjustment can be made for earnings.[24] Notice 2008-113 provides the following example:

> Example 1: Under a nonqualified deferred compensation plan sponsored by Employer, Specified Employee has a legally binding right to a payment of deferred compensation on the first day of the seventh month following Specified Employee's separation from service. Specified Employee separates from service on December 15, 2008, so that the payment is due on July 1, 2009. Employer erroneously pays Specified Employee the amount of deferred compensation on March 1, 2009 (122 days before the original payment due date). Employer discovers the error on May 1, 2009, and Specified Employee repays the amount to Employer on June 1, 2009 (ninety-two days after the erroneous payment). Provided that immediately after such repayment Specified Employee has a legally binding right to receive the amount from Employer on October 1, 2009

20. I.R.S. Notice 2008-113, 2008-51 I.R.B. 1305 (Section IV).

21. I.R.S. Notice 2008-113, 2008-51 I.R.B. 1305 (Section IV.A).

22. I.R.S. Notice 2008-113, 2008-51 I.R.B. 1305; I.R.C. § 402(g)(1)(B) (2018).

23. I.R.S. Notice 2008-113, 2008-51 I.R.B. 1305 (Section IV.A). A hardship is a "distribution [] treated as necessary to satisfy an immediate and heavy financial need of an employee to the extent the amount of the distribution is not in excess of the amount required to satisfy the financial need (including any amounts necessary to pay any federal, state, or local income taxes or penalties reasonably anticipated to result from the distribution)." Treas. Reg. 1.401(k)-1(d)(3)(iii) (2020).

24. I.R.S. Notice 2008-113, 2008-51 I.R.B. 1305 (Section IV.B).

> (ninety-two days after the July 1, 2009, original payment due date) and Employer does not repay the amount to Specified Employee before that date, Specified Employee will not be treated as having failed to comply with § 409A(a)(2)(B)(i) and the terms of the plan and the applicable deferral election solely as a result of the early payment.[25]

To correct an excess deferral in this category, the employer will repay the excess to the employee in the same year in which this operational failure occurred.[26] The employer may pay a reasonable interest to the employee, although that is not required.[27] If an insider is involved, there must be an adjustment to the account balance for earnings, however, adjustment for losses is optional.

Correction of an operational error, with respect to the exercise price of a stock option or stock appreciation right, that was unintentionally set at less than the FMV of the underlying stock at date of grant, requires that the exercise price be reset in the same year of grant and certainly before exercise of the stock right.[28] Correction cannot occur after two years of the grant date. Under case law there may be an opportunity for correction of the discounted stock right pricing if the error is discovered and corrected prior to vesting.[29]

Notice 2008-113 provides the following example:

> Example: On January 1, 2009, Employer grants Employee a stock option to purchase 100 shares of stock, and the stock option otherwise would not provide for a deferral of compensation for purposes of § 409A except that due to an error the exercise price is set at an amount below the fair market value of the stock on January 1, 2009. On July 1, 2009, Employee partially exercises the stock option and purchases 40 shares, but retains a stock option to purchase 60 shares. Provided that before the earlier of January 1, 2009 or the exercise of the remaining stock option to purchase 60 shares, the exercise price of the stock option to purchase 60 shares is reset to a price at or above the fair market value of the underlying stock on January 1, 2009, the stock option to purchase 60 shares may qualify for the relief provided in this section. Because the exercise price was not reset before the exercise on July 1, 2009, the portion of the stock option that was exercised to purchase 40 shares is not eligible for the relief provided in this section.[30]

---

25. I.R.S. Notice 2008-113, 2008-51 I.R.B. 1305 (Section IV.B.5).
26. I.R.S. Notice 2008-113, 2008-51 I.R.B. 1305 (Section IV.C).
27. I.R.S. Notice 2008-113, 2008-51 I.R.B. 1305 (Section IV.C.2.c).
28. I.R.S. Notice 2008-113, 2008-51 I.R.B. 1305 (Section IV.D).
29. *See* Sutardja v. United States, 109 Fed. Cl. 358 (2013); Rosina B. Barker & Kevin P. O'Brien, *Correcting Document Errors, in* SECTION 409A HANDBOOK 30-34 (BNA) (Regina Olshan & Erica F. Schohn eds., 2016).
30. I.R.S. Notice 2008-113, 2008-51 I.R.B. 1305 (Section IV.D.3).

## B. Failures with Respect to Non-Insiders Corrected by Next Taxable Year

The second category concerns failures with respect to non-insiders that are corrected in the taxable year immediately following the year in which the failure occurred.[31] If the error involves amounts erroneously paid to an employee, other than to a specified employee, or the error concerns amounts erroneously held by an employee due to the failure to defer, and the repayment is done in accordance with the timing in this category by an employee who is a non-insider, neither the penalty tax of 20 percent nor the premium interest required by Section 409A will apply. However, the erroneous payment must be paid to the employer with reasonable interest. The employee can have up to twenty-four months to make the payment if hardship, as described in IRC Section 401(k), is shown.[32] The amounts erroneously held by the employee would be reported on a Form W-2 and, on repayment, the employee can take a deduction resulting in somewhat of a wash.[33]

If the failure is due to an excess deferral, after repayment by the employer to the employee, the account balance must be adjusted for earnings.[34] However, the employer need not compensate the employee for any possible forgone interest or loss of other potential investment gain. A Form W-2 would be issued to reflect the additional income to the employee.[35] This failure also requires a statement to be attached to the tax return by the employee. Notice 2008-113 provides the following example:

> Example: Employee makes a timely election pursuant to an account balance plan to defer 10 percent of a bonus otherwise payable in 2010. The bonus is $100,000. Employer erroneously defers 20 percent of the bonus, or $20,000, and pays Employee $80,000 (instead of deferring $10,000 and paying Employee $90,000). Employer pays Employee $10,000 of the account balance under the plan on July 1, 2011. Provided that Employee includes in income the $10,000 payment in 2011, Employee is not required to include any amount in income under § 409A. The remaining account balance must be adjusted for earnings and may be adjusted for losses that were allocable to such $10,000 amount under the plan. However, Employer may not pay Employee interest on the $10,000 erroneous deferral or otherwise compensate Employee for the loss of the use of such funds.[36]

The exercise price of a stock right that was intended to be exempt from Section 409A can be corrected within the time frame of this category before the stock right is exercised.

31. I.R.S. Notice 2008-113, 2008-51 I.R.B. 1305 (Section V).
32. I.R.S. Notice 2008-113, 2008-51 I.R.B. 1305 (Section V).
33. I.R.S. Notice 2008-113, 2008-51 I.R.B. 1305 (Section V.B.3).
34. I.R.S. Notice 2008-113, 2008-51 I.R.B. 1305 (Section V).
35. I.R.S. Notice 2008-113, 2008-51 I.R.B. 1305 (Section V.D.II. a –.d).
36. I.R.S. Notice 2008-113, 2008-51 I.R.B. 1305 (Section V.D).

## C. Operational Failures Involving Limited Amounts Corrected Within Two Years After the Failure Occurs

If the operational failure involves situations of erroneous payments, including premature payments to a specified employee, or failures to defer, and in either case, the amount is not more than the annual limit on elective deferrals to tax qualified plans described in IRC Section 402(g)(1)(B), no repayments are required.[37] However, the erroneous payment of the deferred compensation or the amount not deferred, must be reported as income within two years of the failure. An amended return may have to be filed to include the amount in income. The 20 percent penalty under IRC 409A applies, but only to the limited amount (not the entire amount deferred under the plan), and the premium interest under Section 409A does not apply. If the amount cannot be included in income in the first two years after the failure (because, for example, the tax years are closed and an amended return is unavailable), then this correction is not available.

If there is an excess deferral, and the amount is limited, the employer has two years to make the payment to the employee.[38] A Form W-2 must be issued and there must be earnings and losses adjustments. Notice 2008-113 provides the following example:

> Example 1: Employee makes a timely election to defer 10 percent of a bonus payable in 2008 pursuant to an account balance plan. The bonus is $100,000. Employer erroneously defers only 8 percent of the bonus, or $8,000, and pays Employee $92,000 (instead of deferring $10,000 and paying Employee $90,000). Employer discovers the error on February 1, 2010. As a payment to Employee, Employer must treat the amount as a wage payment for employment tax and reporting purposes, as appropriate, including reporting as income and wages on the 2008 Form W-2. Employer is permitted to report as income under § 409A on the 2008 Form W-2 (or 2008 Form W-2c), Box 12, using Code Z, only $2,000, and Employee is permitted to include in income under § 409A for 2008 only $2,000. Furthermore, Employee is permitted to pay the additional 20 percent tax only with respect to the $2,000 (or $400 in additional income tax), and is not required to pay the premium interest tax. However, to qualify for the relief, Employee must file an original or amended 2008 income tax return reflecting the additional tax on or before December 31, 2010.[39]

---

37. Treas. Reg. § 1.409A-1(c) (2020). For 2021, the annual limit under Section 402(g)(1)(B) is $19,500. I.R.S. Notice 2020-79, 2020-46 I.R.B. 1014.

38. I.R.S. Notice 2008-113, 2008-51 I.R.B. 1305 (Section VI.C).

39. I.R.S. Notice 2008-113, 2008-51 I.R.B. 1305 (Section VI.B).

## D. Other Types of Operational Failures Corrected Within Two Years

Repayments of erroneous payments must be made within the time frame of this category, with interest, if the employee is an insider.[40] The employee has to pay the 20 percent penalty tax under Section 409A without penalty premium interest, unless the employee is an insider. If the violation involves a premature payment to a specified employee repayment must be made within the time frame in this category.[41] A Form W-2 will be issued and no deduction against income is allowed for the repayment year. No adjustment for earnings will be made.

Excess deferrals must be repaid to the employee without compensation for forgone interest, however, the amount must be adjusted for earnings. A Form W-2 must be issued and a statement with an amended return notifying the IRS of the error must be attached to the return for the year the failure is discovered. The employee will owe a 20% percent tax under IRC 409A but no penalty premium interest will apply.[42] Stock right failures cannot use this category for correction.

# Section 10.2 Correction of Documentation Failures under Notice 2010-6

Correction of document failures is guided by Notice 2010-6.[43] Documentary failures expose the participants in a NQDCP to the same sanctions under Section 409A as operational failures. Following the corrective guidelines in this notice can result in a spectrum of implications from full relief, that is, no Section 409A penalties, to full penalties. If the document fails to include a payment trigger altogether, that correction can only be made with penalties. On the other hand, document failures relating to compensation that is non-vested throughout the employer's entire taxable year, can be corrected without Section 409A penalties.[44]

For the employee to obtain relief under Notice 2010-6, certain eligibility requirements must be satisfied. The documentary error must be inadvertent;[45] neither the employer nor the employee must be under audit of a federal income tax for any year the document failure existed;[46] and the employer must correct all "substantially similar" document failures in other plans.[47] In addition, a

40. I.R.S. Notice 2008-113, 2008-51 I.R.B. 1305 (Section VI.D).

41. I.R.S. Notice 2008-113, 2008-51 I.R.B. 1305 (Section VI.D).

42. I.R.S. Notice 2008-113, 2008-51 I.R.B. 1305 (Section VI.D).

43. I.R.S. Notice 2010-6, 2010-I.R.B. 275.

44. Rosina B. Barker & Kevin P. O'Brien, *Correcting Document Errors, in* Section 409A Handbook 31-10 (BNA) (Regina Olshan & Erica F. Schohn eds., 2016).

45. I.R.S. Notice 2010-6, 2010-I.R.B. 275 (Section III.D).

46. I.R.S. Notice 2010-6, 2010-I.R.B. 275 (Section III.C).

47. I.R.S. Notice 2010-6, 2010-I.R.B. 275 (Section III.B)

statement concerning the error must be attached to the employer's tax return in the year of the correction.[48]

Helpfully, Notice 2010-6 clarifies that certain common documentation mistakes do not rise to the level of documentation errors that require correction. Certain document terms that are vague or ambiguous with respect to payment, for example a provision that states that payment will be made "as soon as reasonably practicable" after a permissible event, may not violate Section 409A.[49] Similarly, a provision requiring payment following "termination of employment" may not cause a Section 409A failure (even though not all terminations are valid "separations from service"), particularly when the plan contains a provision indicating the plan will be interpreted consistent with the requirements of Section 409A. Thus, to mitigate the effect of ambiguities, plans typically include a clause stating that the terms of the plan must be interpreted in a manner consistent with Section 409A.

Correction of document failures can be achieved by either removing the nonconforming language or amending the terms of the plan to comply with IRC 409A, before the defective plan provision is activated. The following failures are not correctable under a Notice 2010-6 program:

1. Document failures relating to stock option and stock appreciation rights.[50] However, recall that discounted stock rights can be corrected under Notice 2008-113.
2. Failures in plan terms linking a NQDCP to another NQDCP or to a qualified plan.[51]
3. Plan terms allowing the employee to opt to accelerate payments with a haircut provision.[52]

## A. One-Year Rule

Optimum relief is available under the one-year rule. In short, under the one-year rule a corrected document failure cannot become operative within one year of the correction. If the nonconforming provision in the plan is eligible for relief under Notice 2010-6, and the one-year rule is adhered to, there is a complete avoidance of income inclusion, penalties, and premium interest under Section 409A. As an example, if a plan contains an impermissible definition of a permissible event, and within one year after the correction, the corrected payment event occurs, the one-year rule is not satisfied. In that case, the employee must include 50 percent of the deferred compensation in income under 409A, but is not subject to the 20 percent additional tax, nor the premium interest.

As another example, assume a document provides for payment upon "separation from service," and the definition of "separation from service" does not

48. I.R.S. Notice 2010-6, 2010-I.R.B. 275 (Section XII.A)
49. I.R.S. Notice 2010-6, 2010-I.R.B. 275 (Section IV).
50. I.R.S. Notice 2010-6, 2010-I.R.B. 275 (Section III.G).
51. I.R.S. Notice 2010-6, 2010-I.R.B. 275 (Section III.G).
52. I.R.S. Notice 2010-6, 2010-I.R.B. 275 (Section VII.A.1).

comply with Section 409A, however, the employer brings the definition into compliance on April 1. If the employee has a reduction in services on June 1, that is, within one year of the correction, the one-year rule is violated and the employee will be required to include in income 50 percent of the amount deferred under the plan under 409A as a condition of the correction.

The following are examples of document failures that are subject to the one-year rule:

1. impermissible definition of separation from service;[53]
2. impermissible definition of a change in control event;[54]
3. combination of permissible and impermissible payment events;[55]
4. impermissible alternative payment schedules, for example, a lump sum for involuntary termination and installment payments for voluntary termination;[56]
5. impermissible discretion given to the employee or the employer to change the time, form, or payment, including changes with respect to subsequent deferral elections;[57] and
6. impermissible reimbursements or in-kind provisions;[58]

In addition to these examples, failure to include in the document the requirement for a six-month delay for specified employees is subject to the one-year rule.[59] Correction of this failure requires an amendment providing that an amount payable to a specified employee after separation from service must be made by the later of eighteen months after correction or six months after separation from service.[60] It is best to correct before the separation from service. If an employee separates from service within a year of the amendment, the one-year rule applies.[61] If the one-year rule is flunked then 50 percent of the deferred amount is included in income, plus the 20 percent additional tax, even though payment is deferred for eighteen months.[62]

The following are examples of document failures that can be corrected under Notice 2010-6 but are not subject to the one-year rule, provided the correction is made before the noncompliant provision is triggered.

---

53. I.R.S. Notice 2010-6, 2010-I.R.B. 275 (Section V.A)

54. I.R.S. Notice 2010-6, 2010-I.R.B. 275 (Section V.B). In this failure, 25 percent of the deferred amount will be in income.

55. I.R.S. Notice 2010-6, 2010-I.R.B. 275 (Section VII.A).

56. I.R.S. Notice 2010-6, 2010-I.R.B. 275 (Section VII.C); Rosina B. Barker & Kevin P. O'Brien, *Correcting Document Errors, in* SECTION 409A HANDBOOK 31-23 (BNA) (Regina Olshan & Erica F. Schohn eds., 2016).

57. I.R.S. Notice 2010-6, 2010-I.R.B. 275 (Sections VII.D examples 1 and 2). Correction involves revocation of the discretion.

58. I.R.S. Notice 2010-6, 2010-I.R.B. 275 (Section VII.F).

59. I.R.S. Notice 2010-6, 2010-I.R.B. 275 (Section VIII).

60. I.R.S. Notice 2010-6, 2010-I.R.B. 275 (Section VIII).

61. I.R.S. Notice 2010-6, 2010-I.R.B. 275 (Section VIII).

62. I.R.S. Notice 2010-6, 2010-I.R.B. 275 (Section VIII example 3).

1. Impermissible definition of disability. Correction can be made by either removing this payment event or amending the definition to comply with Section 409A.[63]
2. Ninety-day rule failure.[64] This is where the plan designates a payment period beyond ninety days after the permissible payment event; for example, a plan term providing payment to be made "within 100 days after separation from service." Correction options include either eliminating the time or shortening the period to ninety days before a payment event occurs.
3. Impermissible payment events.[65] Correction must be made before any of the events occur and, if the plan included only impermissible payment events, replaced with the provision that payment will be paid on the later of the employee's separation from service or six years after correction. The affected employee must include 50 percent of the deferred amount in income.
4. Plan provides for payment periods upon a permissible payment event but conditions the payment upon employee action like signing a release.[66] Example 3 in Section VI of Notice 2010-6 exemplifies this:

> Example 3 (impermissible payment provision making timing of payment after a permissible payment event dependent upon employee action). Employee M is an employee of Employer whose employment agreement entitles Employee M to $100x upon a separation from service (defined to comply with §1.409A-1(h)). Employee M's employment agreement provides that the amount is payable within 90 days of Employee M's separation from service, but not until Employee M executes and submits a release of claims and any period during which Employee M may revoke the release pursuant to applicable law has expired before the end of the 90-day period. If Employee M fails to execute the release the amount is forfeited. On April 1, 2011, Employer and Employee M amend Employee M's employment agreement to provide for payment of the amount on the 90th day following Employee M's separation from service provided that Employee M has executed and submitted a release of claims and the statutory period during which Employee M is entitled to revoke the release of claims has expired on or before that 90th day. Employee M has a separation from service with Employer on June 1, 2011, and Employee M executes and submits a release of claims on June 30, 2011. Employer pays Employee $100x on August 30, 2011.
>
> Conclusion: Because Employer and Employee M corrected the amendment before Employee M's separation from service, and because Employer paid the amount in compliance with the amended plan

63. I.R.S. Notice 2010-6, 2010-I.R.B. 275 (Section V.C).
64. I.R.S. Notice 2010-6, 2010-I.R.B. 275 (Section VI.A).
65. I.R.S. Notice 2010-6, 2010-I.R.B. 275 (Section VII.B).
66. I.R.S. Notice 2010-6, 2010-I.R.B. 275 (Section VI.B).

provision, Employee M is not required to include any amount in income under §409A solely due to the pre-correction plan provision.[67]

5. Impermissible discretion to company to accelerate payment.[68] This can be corrected by removing the discretion before the earlier of the employer's action on the discretion, or before an actual payment is made, pursuant to exercise of the discretion. Of course, if the plan gives the employee the discretion to accelerate payment, no redemption in the form of correction is available, and the full panoply of Section 409A penalties will apply.[69]

Where the document failure involves the initial deferral election, the employer can revoke the faulty deferral period prior to the appropriate initial election deferral period.[70] There will be no penalties if the employee has not made an election under the defective provision. If the employee has made an election, the plan terms can still be corrected up to two years after the irrevocable election. If document failure relates to subsequent deferrals there will be no penalties to the employee who has not activated the defective subsequent deferral election rule under the plan.[71]

67. I.R.S. Notice 2010-6, 2010-I.R.B. 275 (Section VI example 3).

68. I.R.S. Notice 2010-6, 2010-I.R.B. 275 (Section VII.E).

69. Rosina B. Barker & Kevin P. O'Brien, *Correcting Document Errors, in* Section 409A Handbook 31-28 (BNA) (Regina Olshan & Erica F. Schohn eds., 2016).

70. I.R.S. Notice 2010-6, 2010-I.R.B. 275 (Section IX).

71. I.R.S. Notice 2010-6, 2010-I.R.B. 275 (Section VII.D).

*CHAPTER* **11**

# Withholding and Reporting Tax

When entering into any sort of executive compensation arrangement, the parties must be mindful of taxation. This chapter will look into how the company will need to withhold on reported compensation, when the compensation is reported for payroll taxation (spoiler alert: it's not always at the same time as it is reported for inclusion in income), and how Section 409A may accelerate taxation.

## Section 11.1 Income Tax Reporting and Withholding

### A. Form W-2 and Form 1099 Reporting

When deferred compensation is includible in an employee's income, the employer should report the taxable amount to the employee using IRS Form W-2. The employer is required to identify the compensation using either Code Y or Code Z on an employee's W-2.[1] Code Y reporting is for any deferred compensation subject to Section 409A during the fiscal year. Code Z reporting is when the employer must report any taxable deferred compensation because of a 409A violation. Under Code Z (violation of Section 409A), an employer must treat the deferred compensation that violates Section 409A as "supplemental wages" and withhold federal taxes. There is no requirement for the employer to withhold the 20 percent penalty tax under Section 409A. Currently, the IRS has suspended Code Y reporting (deferred compensation compliant with 409A) pending the issuance of more regulations, but Code Z is in effect (deferred compensation violating 409A).[2]

---

1. I.R.S., Cat. No. 25979S, General Instructions for Forms W-2 and W-3 (2021), https://www.irs.gov/pub/irs-pdf/iw2w3.pdf. *See also* I.R.S. Notice 2008-115, 2008-52 I.R.B. 1367.

2. I.R.S. Notice 2008-115, 2008-52 I.R.B. 1367; I.R.S., General Instructions for Forms W-2 and W-3 (2021), https://www.irs.gov/pub/irs-pdf/iw2w3.pdf.

If the deferred compensation is payable to someone other than a current or former employee, then the employer will use Form 1099 to report the income to such individual and should report the income as subject to IRC Section 409A in box 15b of Form 1099.[3]

## B. Withholding

Income tax withholding should occur when the deferred compensation is distributed to the individual, which is not necessarily when it is earned or includible in income. In situations where the income is included in a year prior to the distribution, this can create practical issues for the company and executive to manage. This is particularly likely to occur in 457(f) plans for tax-exempt employers or other circumstances where taxation is accelerated.[4] (Section 457(f) is discussed in chapter 13).

As an example, assume an ineligible 457(f) plan of a tax-exempt employer provides that payment will occur no later than two-and-a-half months after the end of the year in which the substantial risk of forfeiture lapses. The employee has a $50,000 benefit under the plan. The substantial risk of forfeiture lapses June 30, 2021. The company can pay the benefit any time between June 30, 2021 and March 15, 2022. However, regardless of when the amount is paid, the executive will have to take the $50,000 into income in 2021 and the company will report the benefit on the executive's 2021 Form W-2. If the company pays the amount to the employee in 2021, then the tax withholding will occur in 2021 and be reported on the executive's 2021 Form W-2. If, however, the company pays the amount in 2022, the withholding will occur in 2022 and the taxes paid will show in the executive's 2022 Form W-2. The executive's 2021 Form W-2 will show $50,000 of income with $0 tax withholding, which means the executive will need to pay the tax out of pocket when he or she files her 2021 income tax return, and then will presumably get a refund of the unnecessary tax withholding that is made in 2022.

The timing difference in the above example could create an unintended hardship (and certainly an unintended surprise) for the executive who receives a payment less tax withholdings but still must pay out of pocket to cover the taxes because they were withheld in the wrong year. Note that this would not have been a problem for a for-profit entity because the executive would have been taxed in 2022 when the payment was made, and therefore, the income inclusion and tax withholding would occur in the same year. It is the accelerated taxation of Section 457(f) that creates the mismatch in timing. When possible, it is usually best for the parties to design the plan so distributions occur in the same calendar year as the employee includes the amount in income.

3. I.R.S. Notice 2008-115, 2008-52 I.R.B. 1367.
4. I.R.C. § 457(f) (2018).

# Section 11.2 Payroll Tax Reporting and Withholding

FICA is the Federal Insurance Contributions Act, which requires that the company and the executive both pay a share of Social Security and Medicare taxes applicable to wages.[5] FUTA is the Federal Unemployment Tax Act, which is an employer-paid tax on the first $7,000 of wages each year.[6] The timing for FUTA and FICA withholdings and payment is generally the same.

Generally, wages are taken into account for FICA purposes at the same time as they are included in income—when they are actually or constructively paid.[7] However, amounts deferred under a NQDCP are subject to a special timing rule that may accelerate when these wages are included for FICA purposes.[8] Under the special timing rule, amounts deferred are taken into account as FICA wages as of the later of (1) the date the services giving rise to the compensation are performed or (2) the date on which the right to receive the amounts deferred is no longer subject to a substantial risk of forfeiture.[9] Thus, deferred compensation plan benefits generally are included in FICA wages when the executive vests in the benefit.

There is another special rule for non-account balance plans (such as a defined benefit SERP). A benefit is not required to be included as FICA wages until it is reasonably ascertainable. A benefit is reasonably ascertainable when the amount, form, and commencement date of the benefit are known, and the only actuarial or other assumptions regarding future events or circumstances needed to determine the benefit are interest and mortality.[10] In the case of a non-account balance plan (such as a SERP-type benefit), the amount deferred for a period is the present value of the additional future payment or payments to which the individual has obtained a legally binding right during the period.[11]

If the deferred compensation is not taken into FICA wages under the special timing rule (i.e., when it vested), then the deferred compensation is included as FICA wages in accordance with the general timing rule (i.e., when the deferred compensation is actually or constructively paid).[12] This often would result in additional taxation to the executive because executives are often over the Social Security wage limit when the amounts vest and/or the general timing rule would result in payments over multiple years and, therefore, would apply multiple Social Security wage limits. For example, assume an executive who makes more

5. I.R.C. §§ 3101-3128 (2018).

6. I.R.C. §§ 3301-3311 (2018); *Topic No. 759 Form 940—Employer's Annual Federal Unemployment (FUTA) Tax Return —Filing and Depositing Requirements*, I.R.S. (Mar. 8, 2021), https://www.irs.gov/taxtopics/tc759.

7. Treas. Reg. § 31.3121(v)(2)-1(a)(1) (2020).

8. Treas. Reg. § 31.3121(v)(2)-1(a)(2) (2020).

9. Treas. Reg. §§ 31.3121(v)(2)-1(a)(2)(ii)(A), (B) (2020).

10. Treas. Reg. § 31.3121(v)(2)-1(e)(4)(i)(B) (2020).

11. Treas. Reg. § 31.3121(v)(2)-1(c)(2)(i) (2020).

12. Treas. Reg. § 31.3121(v)(2)-1(d)(1)(ii)(A) (2020).

than $200,000 has a $500,000 deferred compensation benefit that will pay in five annual installments of $100,000 beginning in the calendar year after he or she has a separation from service with the company. The executive vests in that amount in 2021, separates from service in 2024, and receives payments in the years 2025 through 2029. Under the special timing rule, the $500,000 should be included in FICA wages in 2021 (when it vests). In 2021, the executive already has wages over the Social Security wage limit, so he or she will owe only the Medicare tax on the $500,000. If, however, the amount is not treated as FICA wages in that year, he or she will have to treat the five $100,000 payments as FICA wages in the years 2025 through 2029. Assuming he or she doesn't have other income, the entire amount will be below the Social Security wage limit and he or she will owe 7.65 percent FICA tax (using current rates) on the entire $500,000—an additional $26,500 in taxes.[13]

The FUTA taxation provisions applicable with respect to nonqualified deferred compensation are similar to the FICA provisions, except that only the employer pays the tax imposed under FUTA.[14] Therefore, if amounts deferred were taken into account previously as FUTA wages and FUTA taxes paid by the company, then payment to the former employee of benefits attributable to the deferred compensation, including income on amounts deferred, will be exempt from FUTA taxation at the time of payment. Otherwise, benefits attributable to the deferred compensation, including income, are considered wages subject to FUTA taxation at the time of payment.

## Section 11.3 Section 409A Failure Reporting

If a company determines that an arrangement violates Section 409A during a tax year and is, therefore, includible in income, then the amounts not subject to a substantial risk of forfeiture as of the last day of the taxable year[15] should be reported to the executive on Form W-2 using Code Z in box 12.[16] However, amounts that were already included in income are not required to be reported again as taxable income. The 409A violation does not change the timing of inclusion for FICA and FUTA wages. Although the 409A violation will result in an additional 20 percent penalty tax, the amount the employer is required to withhold will not change. However, the executive will be required to pay the amount of any underpayment upon filing of his or her Form 1040 for that year.

Often, 409A errors are discovered after the executive has already received his or her W-2 for the year(s) in question. Often, companies are naturally reluctant

13. *Topic No. 751 Social Security and Medicare Withholding Rates*, I.R.S. (Mar. 10, 2021), https://www.irs.gov/taxtopics/tc751.

14. *See* I.R.C. §§ 3301, 3306(b), 3306(r)(2) (2018); Treas. Reg. §§ 31.3301-1, 31.3301-2, 31,3301-3, 31.3301-4, 31.3302(d)-1, 31.3306(b), 31.3306(c)(6)-1, 31.3306(p)-1, 31.3306(r)(2)-1, 31.3308-1, 31.6302(c)-3 (2020).

15. I.R.C. § 409A(a)(1) (2018).

16. I.R.S. Notice 2005-1, 2005-2 I.R.B. 274. If the payee is not an employee, the amount is reported on Form 1099-MISC. I.R.S. Notice 2005-1, 2005-2 I.R.B. 274, Q&A 30.

to go back and amend prior Form W-2s. However, the company and the practitioner should keep in mind that failure to properly report income, including income due to Section 409A violations could subject the company to interest and penalty assessments, such as the following:

- *Interest on Underpaid Withholdings.* Interest (which varies quarterly) is generally imposed on the underpayment of income tax withholding.[17]
- *Failure to File a Correct W-2.* A penalty of $100 per return is imposed, subject to a reasonable cause exception; however, this penalty is replaced with a penalty of 10 percent of the aggregate amount of the items required to be reported correctly if there is an intentional disregard of the filing requirements, with no maximum on the amount of the penalty.[18]
- *Failure to Furnish a Correct W-2.* A penalty of $100 per return is imposed, subject to a reasonable cause exception; however, this penalty is replaced with a penalty of 10 percent of the aggregate amount of the items required to be reported correctly if there is an intentional disregard of the filing requirements, with no maximum on the amount of the penalty.[19]
- *Failure to Withhold.* If the employer willfully (i.e., voluntary, consciously, and intentionally) fails to collect and pay the tax, the employer is liable for 100 percent of the underpayment of the income tax withholding under IRC 6672.
- *Failure to Pay Tax Form 941.* A penalty of 0.5 percent of the tax due per month (to a maximum of 25 percent) is imposed for failure to pay tax.[20]
- *Accuracy-Related Penalty.* Failure to properly report on Form W-2 and the underpayment of tax on Form 941 due to negligence or disregard of rules or regulations results in a penalty of 20 percent of the tax underpaid under Sections 6662(a) and 6662(b)(1). Under IRC 6662, this penalty is not combined with the penalty for failure to file. Alternatively, if the underpayment is substantial the 20 percent penalty will apply (but not both the negligence penalty and this penalty) An underpayment may be substantial if it exceeds the lesser of (1) 10 percent of correct tax (or, if greater, $10,000) or (2) $10 million.[21]
- *Civil and Criminal Fraud Penalties.* The IRS may also impose civil or criminal fraud penalties or both under IRC Sections 6663, 6674, 7201, 7202, 7203, 7204, and 7207. For example, willful failure to collect any tax is a felony, and, upon conviction, the guilty party will be fined not more than $10,000, or imprisoned not more than five years, or both, and will be liable for the costs for prosecution under IRC 7202.

The executive may similarly be penalized for failing to timely report income arising from a Section 409A violation, including the following:

17. I.R.C. §§ 6601(a), 6205(b); Treas. Reg. § 31.6205-1 (2021).
18. I.R.C. § 6721 (2018).
19. I.R.C. § 6722 (2018).
20. I.R.C. § 6722 (2018).
21. I.R.C. § 6662(d) (2018).

- *Failure to Pay Tax on Form 1040.* A penalty of 0.5 percent of the tax due per month is imposed with a maximum penalty equal to 25 percent of the tax due; a reasonable cause exception to the penalty is available.[22]
- *Failure to Pay Estimated Income Tax.* The penalty for underpayment of estimated tax is calculated over quarterly periods, beginning on the installment due date, and is based on the underpayment rate under IRC Section 6621.[23]
- *Accuracy-Related Penalty.* Failure to properly report on Form 1040 the underpayment of tax that results in a substantial understatement of tax or is due to negligence or disregard of rules or regulations may result in a penalty of 20 percent of the tax underpaid.[24]
- *Interest on Underpayment.* Interest is imposed on the underpayment of federal income taxes; the rate varies quarterly under IRC Sections 6601(a) and 6621.

The rules surrounding taxation and withholding on deferred compensation are at the best of times, confusing, and at the worst of times, costly, to either the employer, the employee, or both.

---

22. I.R.C. § 6651(a)(2) (2018).
23. I.R.C. § 6654 (2018).
24. I.R.C. § 6662(b)(1) (2018).

CHAPTER **12**

# Nonqualified Deferred Compensation Plans in Mergers/Acquisitions

## Section 12.1 Why Deferred Compensation Plans Matter in Mergers and Acquisitions

When companies engage in mergers, acquisitions, or similar transactions (collectively, corporate transactions), nonqualified deferred compensation plans (NQDCPs) become a significant consideration for at least three reasons: (1) they often represent material unfunded liabilities that need to be accounted for in the transaction; (2) they often cover key employees and therefore treatment of such plans (and any compliance failures uncovered during a buyer's due diligence) may cause important employee relations concerns; and (3) they can raise concerns about key employee retention if the corporate transaction will result in accelerated vesting or payment of substantial amounts. This chapter provides an overview of some of the most common considerations that arise with NQDCPs in corporate transactions.

## Section 12.2 The Due Diligence Process

Before entering into a corporate transaction, a prospective buyer should obtain disclosure about any NQDCPs maintained by the target company. Such disclosure should include at least: (1) the name of each benefit and compensation plan (2) a copy of each plan's formal plan document, (3) a schedule of the amount of liability under each plan that is believed to be a NQDCP, and (4) information about any funding arrangements (e.g., a rabbi trust) related to NQDCPs.

## A. Understanding Plan-Related Liabilities

Material unfunded liability is often associated with NQDCPs. Accordingly, information about the liabilities under a target company's NQDCPs and any related funding arrangements should be reviewed and analyzed as part of a buyer's financial due diligence.

## B. Reviewing Plan Documents

The plan document for each benefit and compensation arrangement maintained by a target company (including employment agreements) should be reviewed to identify: (1) any arrangements that are NQDCPs, but that were not understood as such by the target company, (2) any arrangements that raise concerns about undisclosed material liability, and (3) any legal compliance concerns.

*Accidental deferred compensation.* Section 409A of the Internal Revenue Code (IRC), which sets out detailed rules for deferred compensation plans, is broad enough in scope to cover compensation arrangements that are not commonly thought of as deferred compensation. For example, many employment agreements include promises to pay compensation in future years that qualify as deferred compensation. Similarly, restricted stock units under stock incentive plans may have vesting features that cause them to be nonqualified deferred compensation. If the target company did not know an arrangement was a NQDCP, it is unlikely to have administered it in compliance with Section 409A.

*Undisclosed material liability.* At their simplest, undisclosed material liabilities are deferred compensation benefits not reflected in a seller's financial disclosures. However, there are at least two other common forms of potential undisclosed liability a buyer will want to be aware of when reviewing the target company's plans. First, companies sometimes promise to indemnify or gross-up employees (particularly key executives) for taxes owed on deferred compensation. Such promises can vary in scope, but they are important to be aware of because of their ability to increase materially the cost of paying deferred compensation. For example, if the company must gross-up a payment of $1,000,000 to an executive with a combined federal and state tax rate of 40 percent, the payment would become $1,000,000 / (1 – 0.40) = $1,666,666.67.

In the right circumstances, a corporate transaction can also cause payments under deferred compensation plans to be nondeductible to the company under IRC Section 280G. This occurs whenever payments to disqualified individuals (generally, certain highly compensated individuals, officers, and shareholders) that are contingent on a change in control of the company exceed two times the disqualified individual's prior five-year average W-2 compensation.[1] The rules of Section 280G are complex and beyond the scope of this chapter, but it is important to bear Section 280G in mind when evaluating a target's deferred compensation arrangements.

1. I.R.C. § 280G(c) (2018).

*Legal compliance.* Section 409A requires that a plan be both properly documented *and* properly operated. While it can be difficult to determine operational compliance during a typical due diligence process, reasonable assurance about documentary compliance can be gained by reading the plan document. For example, plan provisions specifying payment timing that do not comply with Section 409A are fairly common and can be identified by simply reading the plan.

While the penalties for violating Section 409A fall primarily on the employee or other service provider, rather than the company, legal compliance failures are relevant to a prospective buyer because (1) adverse tax consequences for plan participants might raise employee relations concerns, and even litigation concerns, that might affect the post-closing business, and (2) there could be some direct liability to the company to the extent its tax reporting of plan participants' compensation was incorrect.

*Employee retention.* Section 409A allows benefits under a NQDCP to be paid only at a specified time or upon the occurrence of certain specified events. Of relevance in a corporate transaction, deferred compensation may be paid upon the occurrence of a separation from service or upon a change in the ownership or effective control of a corporation, or in the ownership of a substantial portion of a corporation's assets.[2] Accordingly, a corporate transaction may result in the payment of deferred compensation to employees the buyer might want to retain to run the business. If these payments are large enough, they might cause concerns about employee retention.

## C. Deciding What Matters

While it is a good idea for every party to a corporate transaction to have a good understanding of the other party's deferred compensation liabilities, the type of corporate transaction and other considerations unique to the parties and the transaction will often determine which issues matter to a prospective buyer and how much they matter.

*Mergers and stock purchases.* In a merger or stock purchase, a prospective buyer or merger party will want to be keenly aware of any liabilities and compliance failures related to the target entity's deferred compensation plans because the plans (and their liabilities and failures) will generally belong to the buyer once the transaction closes.

*Asset purchases.* In an asset purchase, deferred compensation plans and their associated liabilities and failures do not automatically transfer to the buyer. Accordingly, a prospective asset buyer's concerns might be limited to any employee relations or retention problems related to transferring employees' participation in the target's deferred compensation plans.

2. I.R.C. § 409A(a)(2)(A) (2018).

# Section 12.3 The Transaction Agreement

The stock purchase, asset purchase, merger, or other definitive agreement in a corporate transaction (the transaction agreement) sets forth the understanding of the parties about the terms of the corporation transaction. It typically includes representations and warranties of each party asserting certain information about the businesses (including the nature and legal compliance of compensation arrangements, and the impact of the transaction on those arrangements); covenants promising that the parties will take, or refrain from taking, various actions; and indemnity provisions governing the parties' liability for breaches of the representations, warranties, and covenants, and sometimes for specific known liabilities. The transaction agreement provides a buyer the ability to affect the treatment of deferred compensation plans in the transaction and take steps to protect itself from liability.

## A. Treatment of Equity-Based Compensation

Typically, most equity-based compensation (e.g., stock options, stock appreciation rights, restricted stock, and restricted stock units) is not deferred compensation subject to Section 409A. Restricted stock is taxed under IRC Section 83 and is exempt from Section 409A.[3] Most stock options and stock appreciation rights are structured to satisfy a specific exemption from Section 409A, and many restricted stock units are structured to be exempt from Section 409A as short-term deferrals. However, even if all the equity-based compensation in a corporate transaction is exempt from Section 409A, the parties to a transaction often wish to specify in the transaction agreement that payments related to equity-based compensation will be delayed in ways that implicate Section 409A (e.g., partial payment at closing with the remainder paid when deferred transaction consideration or earn-outs are received).

*Transaction-based compensation.* Fortunately, Section 409A allows equity-based compensation to be paid on the same schedule and according to the same conditions applicable to shareholders generally if certain conditions are met.[4] Specifically, payments must be related to a Section 409A change in the ownership of a company or change in the ownership of a substantial portion of the company's assets, and payment must occur because the company purchases its stock held by the employee or because the employer or a third party purchases a stock right held by a service provider, or be calculated by reference to the value of stock of the company. Such payments may be treated as paid at a designated date or pursuant to a payment schedule that complies with the requirements of Section 409A if it is paid on the same schedule and under the same terms and conditions that apply to payments to shareholders generally with respect to stock of the company pursuant to a change in the ownership of the company or as apply to payments to the company pursuant to a change in the ownership of a

3. I.R.C. § 83(i)(2)(A) (2018).

4. Treas. Reg. § 1.409A-3(i)(5)(iv)(A) (2020).

substantial portion of the company's assets, and must be paid not later than five years after the change in control event.[5] If the parties to a corporate transaction wish to use this payment timing rule, it is typically reflected in the transaction agreement.

*Substitutions and assumptions by reason of a corporate transaction.* The Section 409A regulations provide specific guidance on how parties to a corporate transaction can preserve the 409A-exempt status of stock options and stock appreciation rights when substituting a new stock option or stock appreciation right for an existing one in connection with the transaction.[6] The 409A regulations generally follow similar guidance for incentive stock options under the IRC Section 424 regulations, but allow somewhat more flexibility.[7]

## B. Representations and Warranties

Typically, a buyer will want to include representations and warranties in the transaction agreement that require the seller to do at least the following:

- Provide a list of, and complete documentation related to, each of its compensation and benefit plans.

  Example 1: "Section X.XX of the disclosure schedules contains a true and complete list of each . . . deferred compensation . . . and other similar agreement, plan, contract, policy, program, practice, or arrangement."

  Example 2: "With respect to each Benefit Plan, the Companies have delivered or made available to the Buyer a complete copy of the plan document and all amendments thereto (or, to the extent no such plan document exists, an accurate written description of the Benefit Plan)."

- Represent that all arrangements have been maintained in compliance with applicable law, including Section 409A, and that the target company has not taken upon itself any obligation to indemnify participants for taxes related to Section 409A.

  Example 1: "Each Benefit Plan has been established, maintained, operated, and administered in material compliance with its terms and all applicable laws."

  Example 2: "Each Benefit Plan that is a 'nonqualified deferred compensation plan' (as defined in Section 409A(d)(1) of the code) has been maintained and operated, in all material respects, in compliance with Section 409A of the code and applicable guidance thereunder. The Company does not have any obligation to indemnify, hold harmless, or provide any tax gross-up payment to any individual

5. Treas. Reg. § 1.409A-3(i)(5)(v) (2020).
6. Treas. Reg. § 1.409A-1(b)(5)(iii)(E)(4) (2020).
7. Treas. Reg. § 1.409A-1(b)(5)(v)(D) (2020).

with respect to any penalty tax, interest payments or other liability such individual may incur under Section 409A of the code."

- Represent that the company has no undisclosed liabilities.

  Example: "Except as reflected or reserved against in the Balance Sheet or the notes thereto and liabilities incurred in the ordinary course of business consistent with past practice since the date of the Balance Sheet, the Company has no liabilities."

- Represent that the transaction will not cause any acceleration of vesting or payment, or increase the amount of a participant's benefits under any of the target company's compensation plans, and that it will not result in excess parachute payments under IRC Section 280G.

  Example: "Neither the execution of this Agreement nor the consummation of the transactions contemplated by this Agreement will (either alone or upon the occurrence of any additional or subsequent events): (i) entitle any individual to any payment; (ii) accelerate the time of payment, funding, or vesting, or increase the amount of compensation due to any such individual; or (iii) result in excess parachute payments within the meaning of Section 280G of the code."

## C. Covenants

Covenants allow a party to a corporate transaction to obtain commitments that the other parties will act or refrain from acting in a particular manner. While covenants can cover a variety of issues related to deferred compensation, below are three special situations of which to be aware.

*Termination of deferred compensation plans in connection with a transaction.* Although Section 409A generally restricts changes to the time and form of payment of deferred compensation, it includes a rule allowing deferred compensation plans to be terminated and liquidated in connection with a change of control transaction.[8] This termination rule requires that the company take irrevocable action within thirty days before or twelve months following a change in control event to terminate and liquidate all deferred compensation plans of the same type with respect to each participant that experienced the change in control event, so that under the terms of the termination and liquidation, all such participants are required to receive all amounts of compensation deferred under the terminated plans within twelve months of the date the company irrevocably takes all action necessary to terminate and liquidate the plans.[9] Whether to use this rule is sometimes the subject of purchase agreement covenants. For example, if a seller intended to retain its deferred compensation arrangements, but a buyer wanted to ensure transferring employees would be paid (and not subject to the seller's creditor risk), it might seek to require that the seller use this

8. Treas. Reg. § 1.409A-3(j)(4)(ix)(B) (2020).
9. Treas. Reg. § 1.409A-3(j)(4)(ix)(B) (2020).

rule to terminate and liquidate its deferred compensation plans with respect to employees affected by the corporate transaction.

> Example: "On or before the Closing Date, the Company shall have terminated and liquidated the XYZ Corporation Deferred Compensation Plan in accordance with Treas. Reg. § 1.409A-3(j)(4)(ix)(B) and to Buyer's reasonable satisfaction."

*Transfer or spinoff of deferred compensation plans in connection with a transaction.* Rather than seeking termination of a target company's deferred compensation plans, a buyer might wish for such plans to transfer with the business and its employees as part of the corporate transaction, or it might wish to transfer the liabilities (and any related assets) to one of its deferred compensation plans. If so, the terms of the transfer would generally be included as a covenant in the transaction agreement.

> Example: "Effective at Closing, Buyer shall establish or designate a nonqualified deferred compensation plan (the Buyer Deferred Compensation Plans) for the benefit of the Transferred Employees who participated in the XYZ Deferred Compensation Plan immediately prior to Closing. From and after Closing, Buyer and the Buyer Deferred Compensation Plans shall assume all liabilities with respect to such Transferred Employees under the XYZ Deferred Compensation Plan, and the grantor trust related to the XYZ Deferred Compensation Plan shall be transferred to Buyer at Closing."

*Agreement not to treat an asset sale as a separation from service.* Section 409A provides a special rule for the treatment of deferred compensation in an asset sale when the deferred compensation is payable on a separation from service.[10] Because an asset sale will result in a separation from service for any transferring employees, the sale would generally cause payment to be made. Under the special rule, unrelated parties in a bona fide, arm's length asset sale may agree in advance not to treat the sale as a separation from service triggering payment. To use this rule, all employees providing services to the seller immediately before the asset sale and providing services to the buyer after and in connection with the asset sale must be treated consistently in applying the provisions of any NQDCP, and the treatment must be specified in writing no later than the closing date of the asset sale.[11] This treatment might be preferable to an asset buyer and its transferred employees because it potentially avoids large payments to transferring employees that might cause the buyer concerns about employee retention, and it preserves the intended deferral of taxation for the transferring employees.

> Example: "The Transferred Employees shall not be considered to have a 'separation from service' for purposes of Section 409A of the Code as a result of their transfer of employment from Seller to Buyer."

---

10. Treas. Reg. § 1.409A-1(h)(4) (2020).
11. Treas. Reg. § 1.409A-1(h)(4) (2020).

*Private company shareholder vote for Section 280G.* If a buyer is concerned that compensation might be nondeductible under Section 280G (and that the excise tax under Section 4999 of the code might apply to transferring employees), it might seek to address this in the purchase agreement. If the target company is not publicly traded, it has the option of conducting a shareholder vote to approve the compensation in question and avoid the consequences of Section 280G and 4999.[12] To be effective, the shareholder vote requires that the payments be approved by more than 75 percent of the voting power of all outstanding stock of the company entitled to vote immediately before the change in control, and that adequate disclosure of all material facts concerning the payments be provided in advance to all persons entitled to vote.[13] When this option is available, it is common for a buyer to include a covenant in the purchase agreement requiring the seller to conduct such a shareholder vote.

> Example: "Prior to Closing, the Company shall submit to a shareholder vote in a manner satisfying Treas. Reg. § 1.280G Q/A-6(a)(2) the right of any 'disqualified individual' to receive any payment that would constitute a 'parachute payment' to the extent necessary to cause such payment not to constitute an 'excess parachute payment' within the meaning of Section 280G of the Code. To the extent any 'disqualified individual' has the right to receive payments that could constitute 'parachute payments,' the Company shall obtain waivers of such rights prior to soliciting the shareholder vote such that the vote shall establish each 'disqualified individual's' right to the payment."

## D. Indemnities

Indemnities can provide a prospective buyer some assurance that it will not be liable for deferred compensation liabilities or compliance failures caused by the seller prior to closing. If the parties are aware of specific liabilities that are not intended to be the buyer's responsibility, they should consider expressly listing them as seller liabilities. This could include specific items about which there is some particular concern (e.g., liability related to John Doe's benefit under the XYZ Corporation Deferred Compensation Plan) or general categories (e.g., all excluded liabilities in an asset sale, which are defined to cover all of the sellers benefit plans).

It is important to bear in mind, indemnities are only as useful to a buyer as its ability to be paid under them. Accordingly, a buyer should consider whether it will have effective and practical recourse against the seller post-closing. If the seller is a large, solvent corporation, a simple contractual promise to pay might provide sufficient protection. If the seller is an individual or a group of

12. Treas. Reg. § 1.280G Q/A-6(a)(2) (2020).
13. Treas. Reg. § 1.280G Q/A-6(a)(2) (2020).

shareholders, a buyer might want to consider negotiating for some of the purchase price to be held in escrow for a period of time post-closing to provide a source of funds to cover the seller's indemnity obligations.

# Section 12.4 Six-Month Delay for Specified Employees

## A. Specified Employees under Section 409A

Section 409A requires that payments made to certain specified employees of publicly traded companies due to a separation from service be delayed by six months.[14] A company must identify its specified employees each year, generally as of December 31 (the specified employee identification date) based on status during the prior calendar year. This list of specified employees then typically becomes effective the following April 1 (the specified employee effective date).

## B. Determining Specified Employees Post-Closing

When a public company is involved in a corporate transaction, its workforce typically changes. How, if at all, should such a change affect its list of specified employees subject to the six-month delay? Under the Section 409A regulations, the treatment depends on the type of transaction.[15] The following rules are of particular relevance:

*Mergers and acquisitions of public companies.* If a corporate transaction causes two or more publicly traded companies to become a single publicly traded company, the resulting public company's next specified employee identification date and specified employee effective date after the corporate transaction are the specified employee identification date and specified employee effective date that the acquiring company would have been required to use in the absence of the transaction (e.g., the surviving company in a merger). For the period between the transaction and the next specified employee effective date, the list of specified employees of the resulting public company is generally determined by combining the lists of specified employees of the companies participating in the transaction that were in effect on the date of the transaction, ranking the specified employees in order of the amount of compensation used to determine their status as specified employees, and treating the top fifty, plus any 1 percent and 5 percent owners, as specified employees.[16]

*Mergers and acquisitions of non-public companies.* If a corporate transaction causes a private company and a publicly traded company to become a single, publicly traded company, the resulting public company's next specified

14. Treas. Reg. § 1.409A-1(i) (2020).
15. Treas. Reg. § 1.409A-1(i)(6) (2020).
16. Treas. Reg. § 1.409A-1(i)(6) (2020).

employee identification date and specified employee effective date following the transaction are the specified employee identification date and specified employee effective date that the initial publicly traded company would have been required to use in the absence of the transaction.[17] For the period after the date of the transaction and before the next specified employee effective date, the specified employees of the initial publicly traded company before the transaction continue to be the specified employees of the resulting publicly traded company, and no service providers of the private company are required to be treated as specified employees.

17. Treas. Reg. § 1.409A-1(i)(6) (2020).

*CHAPTER* **13**

# Executive Compensation for Tax-Exempt and Government Entities[1]

## Section 13.1 Introduction: Leaving the For-Profit Sphere

Tax-exempt employers must compete for talent just as for-profit employers do, and similarly, they turn to deferred compensation plans as vehicles for providing executive compensation. However, as discussed in chapter 3, the tax status of the entity employing the executive has important consequences on the deferred compensation options available to the entity and that executive. The tax code includes a special provision limiting the tax deferral for employees of these tax-exempt entities. The executive of a for-profit company may vest in a deferred compensation amount today, receive payment three years from now, and take the amount into income in that later year of payment. Meanwhile, an executive of a tax-exempt organization generally would be taxed on that amount in the year the amount vests (or, technically speaking, is no longer subject to a substantial risk of forfeiture) rather than the year in which the amount is received by the executive.[2] Thus, in addition to taking into account the ERISA considerations and general tax principles, such as constructive receipt, discussed in earlier chapters, tax exempt entities must design plans around the requirements of Internal Revenue Code (IRC) Section 457.

This dramatically changes the design of executive compensation for many tax-exempt entities as the tax deferral in a nonqualified plan often is limited to the amount of time which the executive is willing to remain subject to a substantial risk of forfeiture. This chapter will explore the deferred compensation arrangements of these tax-exempt entities.

1. Special thanks to Hannah Munn, Esq. for her contribution to this chapter
2. I.R.C. § 457(f) (2018).

# Section 13.2 Section 457 Plans

Nonqualified deferred compensation plans (NQDCPs) sponsored by a tax-exempt organization, including a governmental employer, generally are subject to the rules set forth in IRC Section 457.[3] Broadly, there are two types of NQDCPs under Section 457: (1) eligible deferred compensation plans or Section 457(b) plans (plans meeting the requirements of Section 457(b)) and (2) ineligible deferred compensation plans or Section 457(f) plans (plans subject to Section 457(f)). Although these plans share a number of characteristics, they each carry their own unique requirements and may be used to serve different business purposes. These similarities and differences are explored below.

## A. Section 457(b) Plans

Section 457(b) plans, otherwise known as eligible deferred compensation plans, may be thought of as something akin to defined contribution plans in the qualified plan sphere. These plans provide an important exception to the general rule under Section 457 that an executive of a tax-exempt organization will be taxed on deferred compensation in the year the amount vests. Instead, amounts deferred under a Section 457(b) plan will be taxed when they are made available[4]—providing much more favorable tax-deferral treatment to the executive.[5] In exchange for such tax-favored treatment, however, these arrangements must comply with the strict requirements of Section 457(b), discussed below.

*Participation.* Section 457(b) plans may offer eligibility to both employees and independent contractors who perform services for the tax-exempt plan sponsor. Because the ERISA-considerations discussed in chapter 5 still apply, plans sponsored by ERISA-covered tax-exempt entities must limit participation to a select group of management or highly compensated individuals. Plans sponsored by other tax-exempt entities, such as governmental employers, are not so restricted and can permit participation by any class of individuals.

*Contributions.* Section 457(b) plans may permit employer and/or employee contributions. However, the annual contributions and other additions to a Section 457(b) plan may not exceed the lesser of: (1) 100 percent of a participant's compensation (as defined in IRC Section 415(c)(3)) or (2) the contribution limit set forth in Section 457(e)(15) ($19,500 for 2021 and indexed annually).[6]

There are also two types of catch-up contributions that may be permitted above the normal contribution limit. All Section 457(b) plans may permit special catch-up contributions for participants in the three years prior to the

3. Note, though, plans sponsored by churches or certain church-controlled organizations are not subject to Section 457, as discussed briefly in Section 13.5 of this chapter. IRC 457(e)(13)

4. IRC 457(a)

5 5 Robert L. Abramowitz & Mark J. Simons, *Plans for Tax-Exempt Entities*, *in* Section 409A Handbook § 20.II (BNA) (Regina Olshan & Erica F. Schohn eds., 2016).

6. I.R.C. §§ 457(b)(2), (e)(15) (2018); Treas. Reg. § 1.457-4(c)(1) (2020); *Retirement Topics—457(b) Contribution Limits*, I.R.S. (Nov. 10, 2020), https://www.irs.gov/retirement-plans/plan-participant-employee/retirement-topics-457b-contribution-limits.

plan's normal retirement age.[7] These special catch-up contributions are limited to the lesser of: (1) the annual contribution limit described above, and (2) the basic annual contribution limit not used in prior years.[8] The plan will define the term "normal retirement age," which generally must be between age 65 and age 70.5 (although it may be earlier if the entity sponsors a defined benefit plan under which the participant can retire and receive immediate benefits without an actuarial reduction).[9] Only Section 457(b) plans sponsored by governmental entities may also permit catch-up contributions for participants who are age 50 or older—equal to the catch-up contribution permitted for elective deferrals ($6,500 for 2021 and indexed annually).[10]

Importantly, these contribution limits are *not* coordinated with the limits for 401(k) and 403(b) plans. The limits for Section 457(b) plans are coordinated only with other Section 457(b) plans.[11] A participant who, for example, participates in both a 401(k) plan and a Section 457(b) plan of his or her tax-exempt employer may contribute to or receive the maximum allowable amount under both plans.[12] Thus, tax-exempt employers who sponsor both a 401(k)/403(b) plan and a Section 457(b) plan present employees with significant opportunities for retirement savings.

Importantly however, if an amount deferred to the plan is subject to a substantial risk of forfeiture, then such amount is not treated as contributed to the plan (and therefore is not counted toward the annual deferral limit) until it is no longer subject to a substantial risk of forfeiture.[13] This is unlike a 401(k) or 403(b) plan, where a contribution is counted in the year it is made even if the participant is not vested in such amount. If a 457(b) contribution is subject to a vesting schedule, that amount (and any earnings) will be treated as a contribution subject to the annual limits when it vests, and, therefore, care must be taken to ensure the contribution limits are not exceeded in that year (which can be extremely difficult if the amount is credited with variable earnings). Due to this complication, most 457(b) plans do not subject contributions to a vesting schedule.

Section 457(b) plans sponsored by a government entity may permit rollovers both to and from the plan. These must be eligible rollover distributions under Section 457(e)(16), meaning they may be rolled over to or from a qualified plan, a Section 403(b) plan, an IRA, or another governmental Section 457(b) plans.[14]

---

7. I.R.C. § 457(b)(3) (2018); Treas. Reg. § 1.457-4(c)(2) (2020).

8. I.R.C. § 457(b)(2) (2018); *Retirement Topics—457(b) Contribution Limits*, I.R.S. (Nov. 10, 2020), https://www.irs.gov/retirement-plans/plan-participant-employee/retirement-topics-457b-contribution-limits.

9. Treas. Reg. § 1.457-4(c)(3)(v) (2020).

10. I.R.C. § 457(e)(18) (2018); *Retirement Topics—Catch-Up Contributions*, I.R.S. (Nov. 10, 2020), https://www.irs.gov/retirement-plans/plan-participant-employee/retirement-topics-catch-up-contributions.

11. Treas. Reg. § 1.457-4(c)(2)(ii) (2020).

12. *See How Much Salary Can You Defer if You're Eligible for More Than One Retirement Plan?*, I.R.S. (Nov. 12, 2020), https://www.irs.gov/retirement-plans/how-much-salary-can-you-defer-if-youre-eligible-for-more-than-one-retirement-plan.

13. A substantial risk forfeiture is defined for these purposes in Treas. Reg. § 1.457-2(b)(2) (2020).

14. I.R.C. § 457(e)(15) (2018).

In contrast, Section 457(b) plans that are sponsored by a tax-exempt entity generally may *not* permit rollovers to or from the plan.[15] Note, however, both governmental and nongovernmental Section 457(b) plans may generally permit direct plan-to-plan transfers.

*Taxation.* Benefits under a Section 457(b) plan sponsored by a government entity are taxed upon distribution (subject to deferred taxation due to a rollover).[16] Benefits under a Section 457(b) plan sponsored by a tax-exempt entity, however, generally are taxed when they are first made available to the plan participant or beneficiary (i.e., when a plan permits distributions), even if they are not actually distributed.[17] However, as discussed below, the availability of certain in-service distributions and post-employment deferral elections will not cause the account to have been made available and have, therefore, become taxable. In these instances, the benefit is only taxable when actually paid (or later made available).[18]

*Vesting.* Section 457(b) plans may permit employee deferrals and/or employer contributions. As with other retirement plans, employee deferrals are always fully vested. Plan sponsors have the option to impose a vesting schedule for employer contributions. For the reasons discussed above, however, contributions are generally vested when made.

*Distributions.* Generally, Section 457(b) plans may permit distribution: (1) upon severance from employment, (2) upon attainment of age 70.5, (3) in the event of an unforeseeable emergency, and (4) under certain circumstances, from small balance accounts.[19]

- A participant has a severance from employment when she dies, retires, or otherwise has a severance from employment.[20]
- A participant has an unforeseeable emergency when she suffers severe financial hardship resulting from: (1) an illness or accident of herself or her beneficiary, of her spouse or dependent, or of her beneficiary's spouse or dependent; (2) the loss of her or her beneficiary's property due to casualty (including the need to rebuild a home following damage not otherwise covered by homeowner's insurance); and/or (3) "other similar or extraordinary and unforeseeable circumstances arising as a result of events beyond the control of the participant or beneficiary."[21]

---

15. I.R.C. § 457(e)(16) (2018).
16. Treas. Reg. § 1.457-7(a) (2020).
17. Treas. Reg. § 1.457-7(c) (2020).
18. Treas. Reg. § 1.457-7(c) (2020).
19. Treas. Reg. § 1.457-6(a) (2020).
20. Treas. Reg. §§ 1.457-6(b)(1) (2020).
21. Treas. Reg. § 1.457-6(c)(2)(i) (2020). Events that might be covered in this third category include the imminent foreclosure of or eviction from the participant's or beneficiary's primary residence, the need to pay for medical expenses, and the need to pay for funeral expenses of a spouse or dependent. The regulations here provide specifically unforeseeable emergencies do not include the purchase of a home and the payment of college tuition. Note that the standard for unforeseeable emergency is generally thought of as much higher and more difficult to meet than the standard for hardship withdrawals in 401(k) plans. *Id.*

- A participant may take an in-service distribution of small accounts (generally under $5,000) only if: (1) no amount has been deferred by or on behalf of the participant during the two years preceding the distribution, and (2) she has not received a prior distribution of a small account.[22]

Unlike with the 457(f) plans, 457(b) plans are permitted to give executives some ability to control the timing of payment. For governmental plans, the plan may permit unlimited deferrals and flexibility so long as the plan requires distribution in accordance with the Section 401(a)(9) required minimum distribution rules.[23] Section 457(b) plans of other tax-exempt entities may permit the executive to select a certain fixed or determinable future time to begin distributions as long as the election is made before any such amounts could be considered to have been made available to the individual. This is the initial deferral election. If a participant or beneficiary makes an initial deferral election, the plan may permit him or her to make one additional election to delay when the distributions will begin. This election, in turn, generally must be made before distributions have begun under the terms of the first election.[24] Though this flexibility is certainly attractive to participants and beneficiaries, the interaction of these deferral election periods can be complex and often requires careful planning as a participant cannot elect to accelerate distributions—only delay them.

Distributions from a governmental 457(b) plan are treated as eligible rollover distributions—meaning the recipient may further delay taxation by rolling them over into another eligible retirement plan.[25] While most distributions from a 457(b) plan are not subject to the early distribution penalties in IRC Section 72(t) (generally applicable if received before age 59.5), distributions of rollovers from a Section 401(a) plan, a Section 403(b) plan, or an IRA, *are* subject to the early distribution penalties.

*Funding.* Like many other requirements of Section 457(b) plans, the rules regarding how these arrangements are funded differ depending on whether the plan is sponsored by a governmental or other tax-exempt employer. A governmental 457(b) plan must hold the plan assets in a trust that is maintained for the exclusive benefit of plan participants and beneficiaries.[26] By contrast, Section 457(b) plans sponsored by a tax-exempt employer must remain unfunded (although they may employ certain funding mechanisms, like rabbi trusts, discussed in chapter 6).[27]

22. Treas. Reg. § 1.457-6(e) (2020).
23. Treas. Reg. § 1.457-6(d) (2020).
24. Treas. Reg. § 1.457-7(c)(2)(iii) (2020).
25. Treas. Reg. § 1.457-10(b)(1), (e) (2020).
26. I.R.C. § 457(g) (2018).
27. I.R.C. § 457(b) (2018).

**457(b) Quick Reference Chart: What a Difference the Plan Sponsor Makes**

| | Sponsored by Government Entity | Sponsored by Tax-Exempt Entity |
|---|---|---|
| ***Participation*** | Employee or independent contractor; not limited to select group | Employee or independent contractor; must limit to select top hat group |
| ***Contributions*** | Both age 50 catch-up contributions and special catch-up contributions permitted | Only special catch-up contributions permitted |
| ***Taxation*** | Benefits are taxable when actually paid (subject to rollover) | Benefits are taxable when made available (for distribution), subject to certain exceptions |
| ***Vesting*** | Generally the same | Generally the same |
| ***Distributions*** | • May permit participant unlimited ability to select when to receive payment following distributable event, subject to required minimum distribution rules<br>• Eligible for rollover to another plan or IRA | • Plan will specify distribution date and may allow participant up to two opportunities to delay the date of the distribution<br>• Not eligible for rollover to another plan or IRA |
| ***Funding*** | Funds must be held in qualified trust | Plan must be unfunded |

## B. Section 457(f) Plans

Deferred compensation plans sponsored by a tax-exempt entity that do not satisfy the IRC Section 457(b) requirements are known as ineligible deferred compensation plans and are subject to taxation under Section 457(f) and are also subject to Section 409A. Importantly, plans that are intended to be Section 457(b) plans, but fail to fully meet the Section 457(b) requirements generally become subject to Section 457(f).

Unlike the strict limits on 457(b) plans, 457(f) plans have broad flexibility on amount, design, vesting, and other features. Section 457(f) plans (1) have no limits on benefits, (2) provide more flexibility to apply a vesting schedule and place more money at risk (i.e., subject to a substantial risk of forfeiture), and (3) more broadly permit payment of benefits during employment.[28] Practically, the only limitations are understanding and planning for the taxation upon vesting (or, more technically, upon the lapse of a substantial risk of forfeiture). The guidance on those points is somewhat limited, however. The IRS has proposed

28. *See, e.g.*, *Non-Governmental 457(b) Deferred Compensation Plans*, I.R.S. (Sept. 8, 2021), https://www.irs.gov/retirement-plans/non-governmental-457b-deferred-compensation-plans.

additional regulations interpreting Section 457(f) plans, which, while not finalized, do provide a window into how the IRS likely views 457(f) arrangements.[29]

*Participation.* As with Section 457(b) plans, the ERISA-considerations discussed in Chapter 5 also apply to Section 457(f) arrangements. Thus, plans sponsored by ERISA-covered tax-exempt entities must limit participation to a select group of management or highly compensated employees. Plans sponsored by other tax-exempt entities, such as governmental employers, are not so restricted and can permit participation by any class of individuals.

*Contributions.* Contributions to Section 457(f) plans may consist of employee contributions and/or employer contributions.[30] However, because taxation to the executive is deferred only if amounts are subject to a risk of forfeiture, it is uncommon for these plans to include employee contributions. Contributions to Section 457(f) plans also are unlimited, making them an attractive vehicle for employers hoping to provide substantial additional benefits to executives.

*Taxation.* Amounts deferred under a Section 457(f) plan are taxable to the executive when they vest, even if they are unpaid and unavailable for distribution. More technically, the general rule is that deferred compensation is included in the executive's gross income upon the *later* of: (1) the date an employee obtains a legally binding right to compensation, or (2) the first taxable year in which there is no longer a substantial risk of forfeiture of the rights to the compensation (regardless of whether the benefit is paid or otherwise made available).[31] While relatively simple to state, the rule can become extremely intricate in practice.

*When is compensation deferred and when is there a legally binding right to compensation?* Generally, there is a deferral of compensation if an arrangement provides for payment of compensation in a tax year after the year in which the executive obtains a legally binding right to receive the compensation. For instance, I sign a contract today that says I will be paid $1,000 on December 1 of next year. I have a legally binding right to $1,000 today that will be paid in a later year. That $1,000 is deferred compensation.

In addition, a participant generally does not have a legally binding right to compensation if that right may be unilaterally reduced or eliminated by the employer after the employee-participant has performed the services creating that right. In determining whether the employer has the unilateral ability to reduce or eliminate compensation, the IRS will perform a facts-and-circumstance analysis.

Importantly, Section 457(f) plans also are subject to Section 409A. This means that a deferral of compensation may be subject to both the rules under Section 457(f) and Section 409A. Though the two sections use similar vocabulary, they often do not have the same meaning and practitioners are encouraged to carefully consider the implications of both. As an example, the term "substantial risk of forfeiture" is used in both statutes, but defined differently in

29. Prop. Treas. Reg. § 1.457-13, 81 Fed. Reg. 40,548 (June 22, 2016).

30. I.R.C. § 457(f) (2018).

31. Prop. Treas. Reg. § 1.457-13, 81 Fed. Reg. 40,548, 40,568 (June 22, 2016).

each.[32] This chapter limits discussion generally to the definitions and guidance connected with Section 457(f).

*What is a substantial risk of forfeiture?* The definition of "substantial risk of forfeiture" under Section 457(f) is similar, but not identical, to the term's definition under Section 409A. Benefits are subject to a substantial risk of forfeiture for Section 457 purposes when a participant's right to the benefit is conditioned upon the participant's future performance of substantial services.[33] Because the definition in 457(f) adopts the same general rule as that under Section 83, the IRS has often looked to Section 83 in evaluating issues related to a substantial risk of forfeiture under Section 457(f).[34]

First, the risk of forfeiture must itself be substantial. This is a facts-and-circumstances analysis.[35] Informal IRS guidance provides that "[a] substantial risk of forfeiture exists where rights in property that are transferred are conditioned, directly, or indirectly, upon the future performance (or refraining from performance) of substantial services by any person, or the occurrence of a condition related to a purpose of the transfer, and the possibility of forfeiture is substantial if such condition is not satisfied."[36] The risk of forfeiture is *not* substantial if forfeiture is imposed only upon the employee's death, age, or insolvency. A noncompete agreement may constitute a substantial risk in certain circumstances.[37]

Second, the services upon which the benefit is conditioned must also be substantial. Here, the IRS also generally looks to Section 83. To determine whether service is substantial, practitioners should look at both the regularity of the performance of services and the time spent in performing such services. Performance or nonperformance over a period of less than twenty-four months may indicate that the services required are not substantial.[38] Similarly, a person's ability to decline to perform services without forfeiture may also indicate that the services are not substantial.

Certain circumstances, such as an initial election to defer, a second or subsequent deferral, or an acceleration upon termination of employment (unless limited to death, disability, or involuntary termination without cause), may negate the existence of a substantial risk of forfeiture.[39]

---

32. I.R.C. § 457(f)(3)(B) (2018); I.R.C. § 409A(d)(4) (2018).

33. 457(f)(3), 81 Fed. Reg. 40,548, 40,568 (June 22, 2016); Robert L. Abramowitz & Mark J. Simons, *Plans for Tax-Exempt Entities*, *in* Section 409A Handbook § 20.VIII (BNA) (Regina Olshan & Erica F. Schohn eds., 2016).

34. *See, e.g.*, I.R.S. Tech. Adv. Mem. 1999-03-032 (Oct. 2, 1998). Robert L. Abramowitz & Mark J. Simons, *Plans for Tax-Exempt Entities*, *in* Section 409A Handbook § 20.III (BNA) (Regina Olshan & Erica F. Schohn eds., 2016).

35. Treas. Reg. § 1.83-3(c)(1) (2020).

36. Cheryl Press & Robert Patchell, *Section 457 Deferred Compensation Plans of State and Local Government and Tax-Exempt Employers*, *in* Exempt Organizations Continuing Professional Education Technical Instruction Program (I.R.S., 1997), https://www.irs.gov/pub/irs-tege/eotopicm97.pdf.

37. *See* Treas. Reg. § 1.83-3(c)(2) (2020); Prop. Treas. Reg. § 1.457-12(e)(iv), 81 Fed. Reg. 40,548, 40,567 (June 22, 2016).

38. Treas. Reg. § 1.83-3(c)(2) (2020).

39. Carol V. Calhoun, *Substantial Risk of Forfeiture Comparison Chart*, Emp. Benefits Legal Res. Site (May 29, 2018), https://benefitsattorney.com/charts/substantial-risk-of-forfeiture-definition-comparison-chart/.

*How is value determined for taxation?* Broadly, the value generally is equal to the present value of the future payments to which the participant has a legally binding right, as of the date the benefit is includible in a participant's gross income. However, the proposed Section 457 regulations provide rather detailed instructions for calculating the value of a benefit at taxation that practitioners may find helpful.[40] After this initial inclusion in income, the tax-exempt entity will have to pay close attention to taxation at the actual payment event as well. Payments of the principal amount (already included in income) will not be taxable to the executive when paid, but any earnings accrued after the initial inclusion in income will be taxable when paid.

*Vesting.* Other than the timing of taxation, few restrictions are tied to vesting. Therefore, tax-exempt employers can get creative in designing vesting schedules. The schedule may be tied to nearly anything from the passage of time to the attainment of corporate goals, with no limit on how long the schedule can run. The primary consideration when creating a vesting structure in Section 457(f) plans is its inextricable tie to taxation, as discussed above.

*Distributions.* Distributions from Section 457(f) plans are most often made close in time to when the substantial risk of forfeiture lapses. This is because the entire amount deferred is taxed at that time and, thus, the executive often wants the benefit at that time as well. However, payment is not required to be made based on that date. It may also be based on any of the permissible 409A payment events, including (1) separation from employment, (2) death, (3) disability, (4) corporate change of control, or (5) a particular date.[41] Plan sponsors have only a limited ability to change distribution timing once a deferral has been made, so the plan should be carefully designed to meet the organization's and executive's objectives up front.

*Funding.* Section 457(f) plans generally must remain unfunded. As with Section 457(b) plans sponsored by a tax-exempt entity and deferred compensation plans sponsored by for-profit entities, sponsoring employers may choose to use a rabbi trust or other mechanism discussed in chapter 6.[42]

*Section 457(b) Plans May Become Section 457(f) Plans.* Many sponsors intentionally choose Section 457(f) plans as a vehicle for providing executive compensation. However, plans may also become Section 457(f) plans unintentionally. As a general rule—and subject to certain exceptions—deferred compensation plans that fail to comply with Section 457(b) automatically become subject to Section 457(f).[43] There are, however, certain types of plans, such as

---

40. Prop. Treas. Reg. § 1.457-12(e)(iv), 81 Fed. Reg. 40,548, 40,553, 40,563 (June 22, 2016); Robert L. Abramowitz & Mark J. Simons, *Plans for Tax-Exempt Entities*, *in* SECTION 409A HANDBOOK § 20.VIII (BNA) (Regina Olshan & Erica F. Schohn eds., 2016).

41. *See, e.g.*, I.R.S. Priv. Ltr. Rul. 2003-21-002 (May 23, 2003); I.R.S. Priv. Ltr. Rul. 99-16-037 (Apr. 22, 1999); I.R.S. Priv. Ltr. Rul. 94-29-007 (July 22, 1994); I.R.S. Priv. Ltr. Rul. 98-22-030 (May 29, 1998).

42. I.R.C. § 457(f)(2) (2018).

43. Section 457(b) plans sponsored by government entities that fail to meet the attendant requirements are converted to Section 457(f) plans on the first day of the plan year beginning more than 180 days after the IRS provides written notice to the government entity of its compliance failure(s). Section 457(b) plans sponsored by tax-exempt entities, in sharp contrast, become Section 457(f) plans on the first day of a compliance failure. I.R.C. § 457(b) (2018).

bona fide severance pay plans, vacation pay plans, retention plans, and other arrangements governed by different sections of the tax code that are not subject to 457(f) even though they might be seen as deferring compensation under the general rule.[44]

## C. Summary Chart

| | Section 457(b) Plan | Section 457(f) Plan |
|---|---|---|
| **Contributions** | • Annual benefit accruals are subject to statutory limits that are indexed each year<br>• May permit employee deferrals and/or employer contributions<br>• Generally, may allow participants to make catch-up contributions (Government sponsors can permit age 50 and special catch—ups; tax-exempt can permit only special catch-ups) | • No limit on annual benefit accrual<br>• Generally only permit employer contributions |
| **Taxation** | Amounts deferred are taxable when actually paid (governmental) or when made available (tax-exempt) | Amounts deferred are taxable when they vest, even if not yet paid or made available |
| **Vesting** | Practically, contributions must be vested when made | Vesting of contributions may be tied to a number of events, length of time, accomplishment of metrics, etc. |
| **Distributions** | Generally, only after severance of employment | Generally, at any time established at the time of deferral (with some limits) |
| **Funding** | • Governmental plans must hold benefits in a qualified trust<br>• Tax-exempt plans must remain unfunded | Plans must remain unfunded |

44. I.R.C. § 457(e)(11) (2018).

## Section 13.3 Additional Option for Governmental Employers: 415(m) Plans

Section 415(m) plans—also known as qualified excess benefit arrangements or QEBAs—are plans unique to public employers and other governmental entities. Section 415(m) plans may be used as an additional vehicle for providing deferred executive compensation. Described broadly, the 415(m) plan "sits on top" of a qualified plan and provides benefits that would have been provided in an employer's qualified plan but for the limits on benefits imposed in Section 415.[45] Accruals to 415(m) plans are unlimited, and benefits are taxed in the same way that deferred compensation programs for for-profit entities would be taxed (meaning, that subject to Section 409A, they are not taxed until they are paid, even if already vested). Benefits under a 415(m) plan cannot be paid at the participant's election. Private letter rulings issued on these plans suggest that tying the payment to the participant's elections in the employer's qualified plan—meaning that the participant would receive the benefit at the same time and in the same form as she elects to receive her qualified plan benefit—is not an impermissible election.[46] Because private letter rulings cannot be relied upon, however, practitioners should carefully evaluate any payment timing that might be seen as giving the participant a direct or indirect election as to payment timing.

## Section 13.4 What About Churches?

The rules under Section 457 do not apply to churches and certain church organizations. Specifically, churches and qualified church controlled organizations (QCCO) are not subject to the special taxation under Section 457 and, therefore, are treated the same as for-profit employers and would not establish a Section 457(b) or a Section 457(f) plan.[47] Tax-exempt nonqualified church controlled organizations (non-QCCO), on the other hand, are treated the same as other tax-exempt entities and *may* establish plans under Section 457. These terms have specific meanings that practitioners should evaluate carefully when working with any organization affiliated with a church.

- Broadly, the term "church" is understood to mean an entity operated for religious purposes, including both religious orders and religious organizations. Religious organizations are treated as churches depending on a number of factors, including whether the organization has a recognized creed and form of worship, a definite and distinct ecclesiastical

45. I.R.C. § 415(m)(3) (2018).

46. *See, e.g.*, I.R.S. Priv. Ltr. Rul. 2016-43-014 (Oct. 21, 2016).

47. Churches and qualified church-controlled organizations are not eligible employers under Section 457. I.R.C. § 457(e)(1) (2018)

leadership, a distinct religious history, an organization of ordained ministers, and literature of its own.[48] Churches cannot sponsor Code Section 457 plans.

- A QCCO is defined in IRC Section 3121(w)(3)(B) as a church-controlled tax-exempt organization described in IRC Section 501(c)(3), other than an organization which: (1) offers goods, services, or facilities for sale, other than on an incidental basis and (2) normally receives more than 25 percent of its support from either these sales, governmental sources, or both.[49] QCCOs cannot sponsor Section 457 plans.
- A non-QCCO is a church-controlled tax-exempt organization that does not meet the definition of a QCCO. These commonly include organizations such as hospitals and universities or colleges that are controlled by a church. Non-QCCOs can sponsor Section 457 plans.[50]

# Section 13.5 Special Considerations for Tax-Exempt Entities

## A. Compensation Must be Reasonable

Certain tax-exempt entities are prohibited from using their income or assets to benefit persons with a significant relationship to the organization for a private, non-exempt purpose.[51] This is known as private inurement and, the IRS views this as any circumstance "where the financial benefit represents a transfer of the organization's financial resources to an individual solely by virtue of the individual's relationship with the organization, and without regard to accomplishing exempt purposes."[52]

For many years, the only penalty the IRS could impose on an exempt organization engaging in a private inurement transaction was the revocation of the organization's tax-exempt status. Since 1996, however, the IRS has had another enforcement option—civil penalties under IRC Section 4958. These penalties are commonly known as intermediate sanctions, and they are imposed not on the exempt organization, but instead on the person or persons responsible for managing the organization and the individual or individuals benefited by the private inurement transaction.[53]

---

48. Tax Guide for Churches & Religious Organizations, Pub. 1828, I.R.S. 33 (2015), https://www.irs.gov/pub/irs-pdf/p1828.pdf. *See also* Tara Schulstad, *Church Retirement Plans*, w-002-8456, PRAC. L. (2017).

49. I.R.C. § 3121(w)(3)(B) (2018).

50. I.R.C. § 3121(w) (2018).

51. Tax-exempt organizations described in IRC Section 501(c)(3), (4), or (29) are subject to these rules. I.R.C. § 4958(e) (2018).

52. *See* I.R.S. Gen. Couns. Mem. 38,459 (June 24, 2016).

53. I.R.C. § 4958 (2018); *Intermediate Sanctions*, I.R.S. (Aug. 18, 2021), https://www.irs.gov/charities-non-profits/charitable-organizations/intermediate-sanctions.

Intermediate sanctions generally apply to transactions where a person with substantial influence over a covered tax-exempt organization (referred to as a disqualified person) engages in a transaction with the organization that is not at fair market value. Such a transaction is called an excess benefit transaction.[54] The payment of unreasonable compensation to a disqualified person is one example of an excess benefit transaction. For example, certain compensation arrangements designed to be proportionate to the organization's revenues or income may be challenged on private inurement grounds.[55] Intermediate sanctions can be imposed by the IRS on the individuals who benefit from an excess benefit transaction and on the persons who authorize the transaction. They are intermediate in the sense that they do not affect the tax-exempt status of the organization itself.[56]

Certain executive officers (including CEOs, CFOs, presidents, and board members) are automatically classified as disqualified persons for purposes of Section 4958.[57] Accordingly, if an organization pays unreasonable compensation to its CEO or president, then that transaction would be an excess benefit transaction and penalties could be imposed under the intermediate sanctions provision. Compensation is reasonable if a like amount would ordinarily be paid for like services by a like enterprise, under like circumstances. In determining reasonableness, the law generally takes into account (with certain limited exceptions) the dollar value of all economic benefits the individual receives from the organization, including both taxable and non-taxable benefits and any deferred compensation.[58] The reasonableness of a contract with a fixed payment generally is determined as of the date the contract is entered into; while the reasonableness of a non-fixed payment considers all facts up to and including the actual date of payment.

---

54 *Intermediate Sanctions*, I.R.S. (Aug. 18, 2021), https://www.irs.gov/charities-non-profits/charitable-organizations/intermediate-sanctions.

55. *See* Church of Scientology v. Comm'r, 823 F.2d 1310 (9th Cir. 1987), *cert. denied*, 486 US 1015 (1988) (payments to founder of percentage of church's receipts); Birmingham Bus. Coll., Inc. v. Comm'r, 276 F.2d 476 (5th Cir. 1960) (compensation proportionate to stock ownership); Gemological Inst. of Am. v. Comm'r, 17 T.C. 1604 (1952), *aff'd per curiam*, 212 F.2d 205 (9th Cir. 1954) (founder paid salary plus 50 percent of net earnings); Kemper Military Sch. v. Crutchley, 274 F. 125 (W.D. Mo. 1921) (6 percent dividend to principal and teachers of school, who were shareholders of corporation); Sonora Cmty. Hosp. v. Comm'r, 46 T.C. 519 (1966), *aff'd per curiam*, 397 F.2d 814 (9th Cir. 1968) (inurement to founding doctors through arrangement for sharing in fees of hospital's laboratory and x-ray operations); Maynard Hosp., Inc. v. Comm'r, 52 T.C. 1006 (1969), *supp. opinion*, 54 T.C. 1675 (1970) (pharmacy's income paid to stockholders of hospital).

56. The IRS still can revoke an organization's tax-exempt status for engaging in one or more transactions causing private inurement if the IRS determines that: (1) in the aggregate, the private inurement transactions are significant; (2) the organization did not implement reasonable procedures to prevent the private inurement; and (3) the organization does not correct the transactions. I.R.C. §4958(c)(4) (2018).

57. I.R.C. § 4958(f)(1) (2018).

58. *See* Larence M. Brauer, Toussaint T. Tyson, Leonard J. Henzke & Debra J. Kawecki, *An Introduction to I.R.C 458 (Intermediate Sanctions), in* Exempt Organizations Continuing Professional Education Technical Instruction Program (2002), https://www.irs.gov/pub/irs-tege/eotopich02.pdf.

The amount of compensation in excess of the reasonable amount would be considered an excess benefit.[59] The recipient of compensation that is determined to be an excess benefit must (1) pay the IRS the excise tax of 25 percent of the excess benefit; and (2) return the entire amount of the excess benefit to the organization.[60] If the excess benefit is not returned to the organization, the recipient could be liable for an additional tax equal to 200 percent of the amount of the excess benefit.[61]

In addition, any officer or director of the exempt organization who knowingly and willfully participated in the transaction approving the compensation could be liable for payment of an excise tax equal to 10 percent of the excess benefit; provided that the total amount collected from all such individuals could not exceed $20,000.[62] If this penalty were assessed against more than one officer or director, then each would be jointly and severally liable for payment of the excise tax, which means that one individual could be liable to pay the full 10 percent even though other officers or directors were involved in approving the compensation.[63]

Further, the penalty ordinarily is not imposed if the officer or director disclosed the factual situation to an appropriate professional and, in making his or her decision, relied upon a well-reasoned, written opinion of that professional that the compensation is reasonable.[64] An appropriate professional includes only: (1) legal counsel, (2) CPAs with expertise regarding the relevant tax law matters, and (3) independent valuation experts who hold themselves out to the public as appraisers or compensation consultants, perform the relevant valuations on a regular basis, are qualified to make valuations of the type of property or services involved, and certify in the written opinion that they meet these three criteria.[65]

---

59. I.R.C. § 4958(c)(1) (2018).
60. I.R.C. § 4958(a)(1) (2018).
61. I.R.C. § 4958(b) (2018).
62. I.R.C. § 4958(a)(2) (2018). An officer or director's participation is knowing only if the officer or director: (1) has actual knowledge of sufficient facts that would show that the transaction is an excess benefit transaction; (2) is aware that such an act under these circumstances may violate federal tax law; and (3) knows, or negligently fails to make reasonable attempts to ascertain whether, the transaction is an excess benefit transaction. Willful participation is also required to assess a penalty against an officer or director. An officer or director's participation is willful only if he or she knows the transaction is an excess benefit transaction and his or her participation is voluntary, conscious, and intentional. No motive to avoid the law or the incidence of any tax is necessary to make the participation willful. Finally, if an officer or director participated knowingly and willfully, but acted with reasonable cause, meaning with ordinary business care and prudence, then a penalty would not be imposed. *Intermediate Sanctions—Excise Taxes*, I.R.S. (Sept. 7, 2021), https://www.irs.gov/charities-non-profits/charitable-organizations/intermediate-sanctions-excise-taxes.
63. I.R.C. § 4958(d)(1) (2018); Treas. Reg. § 53.4958-1(d) (2020); *Intermediate Sanctions—Excise Taxes*, I.R.S. (Sept. 7, 2021), https://www.irs.gov/charities-non-profits/charitable-organizations/intermediate-sanctions-excise-taxes.
64. *Intermediate Sanctions—Excise Taxes*, I.R.S. (Sept. 7, 2021), https://www.irs.gov/charities-non-profits/charitable-organizations/intermediate-sanctions-excise-taxes.
65. Treas. Reg. § 53.4958-1(d)(4)(iii) (2020).

As such, it is common for practitioners advising tax-exempt organizations subject to these rules to provide advice regarding reasonableness of any deferred compensation arrangement under consideration and/or assist them in securing outside professional advice. Further, if the organization follows certain procedures, the organization can create a rebuttable presumption that the deferred compensation plan (together with other compensation) complies with the private inurement restrictions. Practitioners working with tax-exempt entities subject to these rules should ensure familiarity with these regulations when any executive compensation program is being considered.

## B. Compensation Over $1 Million May be Subject to an Excise Tax

Pursuant to the 2017 Tax Cuts and Jobs Act, both tax-exempt and government organizations must now pay a 21 percent excise tax on any compensation paid to covered employees that is in excess of $1 million in a taxable year.[66] This rule operates separately from the private inurement rules applicable to a tax-exempt organization's executive compensation structure.

- An employee is a covered employee if he or she is one of the organization's five highest-paid employee for any tax year after 2016.[67] Importantly, this list is cumulative—once an employee joins the list, he or she will remain a covered employee for all subsequent years (*even if* he or she is no longer one of the five highest-paid employees and *even if* he or she no longer works with the organization).[68]
- In considering whether compensation exceeds $1 million, generally all taxable wages, other than designated Roth contributions to an employer-sponsored plan, are taken into account.[69] This would include deferred compensation amounts, such as amounts deferred under Section 457(b) and Section 457(f) plans, in the year in which it is included in taxable income.

Because amounts are included when vested under IRC Section 457(f), those plans result in periodic inclusion of significant amounts in income. For example, an executive making $300,000 per year could easily exceed the $1 million limit in the year or years in which his or her deferred compensation vests. If not considered at the outset, this may result in the organization inadvertently triggering the excise tax, which may cause surprising, additional tax liability.

66. I.R.C. § 4960(a) (2018).
67. I.R.C. § 4960(c)(2) (2018).
68. I.R.C. § 4960(c)(2) (2018).
69. I.R.C. § 4960(c)(3) (2018).

# Section 13.6 Summary

Employers in the nonprofit space often choose IRC Section 457 plans as a means of providing additional compensation to top executives. Though Section 457(b) plans and Section 457(f) plans have much in common, they also have many unique characteristics that require attentive advance planning. In assisting clients who are considering establishing a Section 457 plan, practitioners should carefully consider both the employer's motivation in establishing the plan and the design and taxation implications of each.

*CHAPTER* **14**

# Applicability of Federal Securities Law to Nonqualified Deferred Compensation Plans

## Section 14.1 Relevance of Securities Laws

Most nonqualified deferred compensation plans (NQDCPs) do not involve securities of the sponsoring company. Accordingly, federal securities laws generally will not directly impact such plans in the way that they often do a company's equity compensation plan. However, some securities-related compensation arrangements are structured in a way that technically are NQDCPs (although the sponsoring company might not think of them as such). For example, unless they are structured as short-term deferrals, restricted stock units generally are NQDCPs and are often settled by issuing shares of the sponsoring company's stock. Similarly, although stock options are usually structured to be exempt from Section 409A, they can instead be structured to be Section 409A compliant. For these plans, the federal securities laws are highly relevant.

For companies subject to the reporting rules of the federal securities laws, a number of disclosure provisions require information even about traditional NQDCPs. In addition, Section 409A, itself, includes a special payment timing rule related to a company's compliance with federal securities laws.

## Section 14.2 Section 409A Securities Law Payment Timing Rule

Although Section 409A generally restricts acceleration and delay of payment timing, it includes a rule allowing payments to be delayed where the company reasonably anticipates making the payment will violate federal securities laws or other applicable law.[1] If this rule is used, payment must be made at the earliest

1. Treas. Reg. § 1.409A-1(b)(4)(ii) (2020).

date the company reasonably anticipates that the making of the payment will not cause such a violation.[2]

Proposed regulations under Section 409A issued in June 2016 extended this rule to short-term deferrals.[3] Under the proposed rule, payment may be made after the short-term deferral period under an arrangement that otherwise qualifies as a short-term deferral if the company reasonably anticipates making the payment within the short-term deferral period would violate federal securities laws or other applicable law, and the delayed payment is made as soon as reasonably practicable after the first date on which the company anticipates or reasonably should anticipate that making the payment will not cause a violation.[4]

# Section 14.3 Nonqualified Plans and the Issuance of Securities

Federal securities laws generally require that any offer or sale of securities be registered with the Securities and Exchange Commission (SEC) unless an exemption applies.[5] Granting equity compensation to employees and directors is considered an offer or sale of securities for this purpose. Accordingly, unless an exemption applies, any shares used for equity compensation would need to be federally registered.

## A. Rule 701

While several exemptions are available to the federal securities law registration requirements, Rule 701 is the exemption most commonly used for equity-based compensation plans. This rule allows a company to issue securities to its service providers without registering if its requirements are met, including that:

- The securities must be issued under a written compensatory benefit plan (or contract) established by the issuer of the securities, its parents, its majority-owned subsidiaries or majority-owned subsidiaries of the issuer's parent. (And the company must provide a copy of the plan or contract to each person receiving such compensation.)[6]
- Participation generally must be limited to employees, directors, general partners, trustees, consultants, and advisors who are natural persons providing bona fide services to the company and which services are

2. Treas. Reg. § 1.409A-2(b)(7)(ii) (2020).
3. Application of Section 409A to Nonqualified Deferred Compensation Plans, 81 Fed. Reg. 40,569 (June 22, 2016).
4. Application of Section 409A to Nonqualified Deferred Compensation Plans, 81 Fed. Reg. 40,569, 40,578-79 (June 22, 2016).
5. 15 U.S.C. § 77e (2018).
6. 17 C.F.R. § 230.701(c) (2020).

not in connection with the offer or sale of securities in a capital-raising transaction.[7]

- The amount of securities the company issues under Rule 701 in any twelve-month period may not exceed: (1) $1 million, (2) 15 percent of the company's total assets as of its most recent balance sheet date (but no older than its last fiscal year end), and (3) 15 percent of the outstanding amount of the class of securities being offered and sold, measured at the most recent balance sheet date (but no older than its last fiscal year end).[8]
- If the aggregate sale price of the securities issued in a twelve-month period under Rule 701 exceeds $10 million, the company must provide additional disclosure.[9]

### B. Form S-8

When a company has registered securities, any securities related to its equity compensation plans must be registered. Fortunately, federal law provides a short-form registration statement (Form S-8) that such companies may use in place of the lengthy and burdensome full registration statement (Form S-1). To be eligible to use Form S-8, a company must have filed all of its Exchange Act reports during the prior twelve-month period.[10]

### C. State Securities Laws

Although beyond the focus of this chapter, it is important to bear in mind that state securities laws might impose requirements on a company wishing to issue securities as compensation to its service providers. These requirements vary by state.

## Section 14.4 Nonqualified Plans and Section 16

As discussed previously, most NQDCPs will not directly involve securities of the sponsoring company and, therefore, will not raise issues under Section 16 of the Securities Exchange Act of 1934 (Exchange Act).[11] However, equity compensation plans often will, and equity compensation plans can be NQDCPs (sometimes unintentionally).

7. 17 C.F.R. § 230.701(c) (2020).
8. 17 C.F.R. § 230.701(d) (2020).
9. 17 C.F.R. § 230.701(e) (2020).
10. Form S-8: Registration Statement Under the Securities Act of 1933, SEC, https://www.sec.gov/files/forms-8.pdf (last accessed Sept. 15, 2021).
11. 17 C.F.R. § 240.16a-2 (2020).

## A. Reporting Requirements

Directors, officers, and more-than-10-percent shareholders of publicly traded companies are required to file certain information statements with the SEC. These include:

*Form 3.* This report must be filed when a person becomes a Section 16 insider. On Form 3, the new insider will disclose his or her ownership of the company's equity securities (or that he or she does not own any of the company's equity securities). Form 3 must be filed within ten days of becoming an insider or the day the company's registration statement is effective if filed in connection with an initial public offering.[12]

*Form 4.* The most common of the Section 16 reports, Form 4 is intended to make the public aware of transactions by Section 16 insiders involving the company's equity securities, and generally, it must be filed whenever a Section 16 insider executes such a transaction.[13] Form 4 must be filed within two business days following the date of the transaction. Because its purpose is to inform the public about insiders' transactions, Form 4 includes a number of codes used to describe the nature of the transaction being reported. Of particular relevance to nonqualified deferred compensation plans involving securities of the company are:

- A – Grant, award, or other acquisition of securities from the company (e.g., an option);
- D – Sale or transfer of securities back to the company;
- F – Payment of the exercise price or tax liability using a portion of the securities received from the company;
- M – Exercise or conversion of derivative security received from the company (such as an option).[14]

*Form 5.* This report must be filed by an insider when a transaction, because of an exemption or failure to report earlier, was not reported on Form 4 during the year. Form 5 generally must be filed within forty-five days after the end of the company's fiscal year.[15]

## B. Short-Swing Profit Rule

Section 16 generally provides that profits realized by directors, officers, and more-than-10-percent shareholders of a company with equity securities registered under Section 12 of the Exchange Act from the purchase and sale (or sale and purchase) of the company's equity securities within a period of less than

12. Form 3: Initial Statement of Beneficial Ownership in Securities, SEC, https://www.sec.gov/files/form3data.pdf (last accessed Sept. 15, 2021).

13. Form 4: Statement of Changes of Beneficial Ownership of Securities, SEC, https://www.sec.gov/files/form4data%2C0.pdf (last accessed Sept. 15, 2021).

14. Form 4: Statement of Changes of Beneficial Ownership of Securities, SEC, https://www.sec.gov/files/form4data%2C0.pdf (last accessed Sept. 15, 2021).

15. Form 5: Annual Statement of Beneficial Ownership of Securities, SEC, https://www.sec.gov/files/form5data%2C0.pdf (last accessed Sept. 15, 2021).

six months is recoverable by the company.[16] The company may bring suit, or if it fails to do so, the owner of any security of the company may bring suit to recover the profit. This rule is intended to prevent insiders from unfairly profiting from their access to information about the company. Important exceptions to the general rule are provided in Rule 16(b)-3. Of particular importance to deferred compensation plans involving employer securities, Rule 16(b)-3(d)-(e) exempts certain acquisitions from and dispositions to the company that issued the securities.[17]

*Exception for acquisition from the issuer.* Under Rule 16(b)-3(d), a transaction (other than a discretionary transaction) involving the acquisition of securities from the issuer (including a grant or award) is exempt if:

- the transaction is approved by the board of directors, or a committee of the board composed solely of two or more non-employee directors; or
- the transaction is approved or ratified by the affirmative votes of the holders of a majority of the issuer's securities at a meeting or the written consent of the holders of a majority of the securities of the issuer entitled to vote, as long as ratification occurs no later than the date of the next annual meeting of shareholders.[18]

*Exception for dispositions to the issuer.* Under Rule 16(b)-3(e), a transaction (other than a discretionary transaction) involving disposition of securities to the issuer is exempt if the terms of the disposition are approved in advance in the manner described above for acquisitions.[19]

In some instances, shareholders have alleged that withholding shares from an executive's equity compensation award to pay taxes violated the short-swing profit rule. To date, such lawsuits have not succeeded because courts found the equity compensation plans in question to satisfy the requirements of Rule 16(b)-3 described above.

# Section 14.5 Securities Disclosure Requirements Related to Nonqualified Plans

## A. Proxy Disclosure

Companies that have a class of securities registered under Section 12 of the Exchange Act are subject to federal securities rules regarding the disclosures they provide each year in connection with soliciting proxies for their shareholder meetings. Of particular relevance to NQDCPs, Schedule 14A sets out various

---

16. 17 C.F.R. §§ 240.16b-1 – 240.16b-8 (2020).
17. 17 C.F.R. § 240.16b-3 (2020).
18. 17 C.F.R. § 240.16b-3 (2020).
19. 17 C.F.R. § 240.16b-3(e) (2020).

content requirements for companies' proxy statements, including a requirement to provide compensation-related information under Item 402 of Regulations S-K.[20] While compensation-related proxy disclosure requirements are subject to full treatises of their own, below is a high-level summary of the requirements applicable to NQDCPs. Bear in mind that the disclosure requirements vary for certain companies (e.g., smaller reporting companies and emerging growth companies).

*Compensation discussion and analysis.* The company must provide a narrative discussion of all material elements of the compensation of its chief executive officer, chief financial officer and its next three most highly compensated officers (collectively, the named executive officers or NEOs). This discussion should include, at a minimum, (1) the objectives of the company's compensation programs; (2) what the compensation program is designed to reward; (3) each element of compensation; (4) why the company chooses to pay each element; (5) how the company determines the amount (and, where applicable, the formula) for each element to pay; (6) how each compensation element and the company's decisions regarding that element fit into its overall compensation objectives and affect decisions regarding other elements; and (7) whether and, if so, how the company considered the results of the most recent shareholder advisory vote on executive compensation required by Section 14A of the Exchange Act (15 U.S.C. 78n–1) or 17 C.F.R. §240.14a–20 in determining compensation policies and decisions and, if so how that consideration has affected the company's executive compensation decisions and policies.[21]

*Summary compensation table.* The company must provide information in tabular format regarding specific elements of each NEO's compensation for the last three completed fiscal years. These include (1) the name and principal position of each NEO; (2) the fiscal years covered in the table; (3) the dollar value of base salary (cash and non-cash) earned by each NEO during the fiscal year; (4) the dollar value of bonus (cash and non-cash) earned by each NEO during the fiscal year; (5) for awards of stock, the aggregate grant date fair value computed in accordance with FASB ASC Topic 718; (6) for awards of options, the aggregate grant date fair value computed in accordance with FASB ASC Topic 718; (7) the dollar value of all earnings for services performed during the fiscal year pursuant to awards under non-equity incentive plans and all earnings on any outstanding awards; (8) the sum of (a) the aggregate change in the actuarial present value of each NEO's accumulated benefit under all defined benefit and actuarial pension plans (including supplemental plans) from the pension plan measurement date used for financial statement reporting purposes with respect to the company's audited financial statements for the prior completed fiscal year to the pension plan measurement date used for financial statement reporting purposes with respect to the company's audited financial statements for the covered fiscal year; and (b) above-market or preferential earnings on compensation that is deferred on a basis that is not tax-qualified, including such earnings on nonqualified

---

20. 17 CFR § 240.14a-101 (2020); 17 C.F.R. § 229.402 (2020).
21. 17 C.F.R. § 229.402(b)(1)(i)-(vii) (2020).

defined contribution plans; (9) all other compensation for the covered fiscal year that the company could not properly report in any other column of the table; and (10) the dollar value of total compensation for the covered fiscal year.[22]

*Nonqualified deferred compensation table.* The company must provide information in tabular format regarding each defined contribution or other plan that provides for nonqualified deferred compensation, including (1) the name of each NEO; (2) the dollar amount of aggregate executive contributions during the company's last fiscal year; (3) the dollar amount of aggregate company contributions during the company's last fiscal year; (4) the dollar amount of aggregate interest or other earnings accrued during the company's last fiscal year; (5) the aggregate dollar amount of all withdrawals by, and distributions to, the executive during the company's last fiscal year; and (6) the total balance of the NEO's account as of the end of the company's last fiscal year.[23] The company must also provide a narrative description of any material factors necessary to an understanding of the plans covered by the disclosures in the table, such as the types of compensation that can be deferred and any limitations on the extent to which deferral is permitted; "the measures for calculating interest or other plan earnings (including whether such measure(s) are selected by the [NEO or the company] and the frequency and manner in which selections may be changed), quantifying interest rates and other earnings measures applicable during the [company's] last fiscal year; and material terms with respect to payouts, withdrawals and other distributions."[24]

*Other tables.* Companies must also include tables covering (1) the grant of plan-based awards (e.g., stock options), (2) outstanding equity awards at fiscal year-end, (3) option exercises and stock vested, (4) pension benefits, and (5) certain additional narrative disclosures.[25]

*Description of any termination, severance provisions, or agreements applicable to the NEOs.* For each contract, agreement, plan, or arrangement that provides for payment to an NEO at, following, or in connection with any termination, a change in control of the company, or a change in the NEO's responsibilities, the company must: (1) describe and explain the specific circumstances that would trigger payment or the provision of other benefits, including perquisites and health care benefits; (2) describe and quantify the estimated payments and benefits that would be provided in each covered circumstance, whether they would or could be lump sum, or annual, disclosing the duration, and by whom they would be provided; (3) describe and explain how the appropriate payment and benefit levels are determined under the various circumstances that trigger payments or provision of benefits; (4) describe and explain any material conditions or obligations applicable to the receipt of payments or benefits, including but not limited to non-compete, non-solicitation, non-disparagement or confidentiality agreements, including the duration of such agreements and provisions regarding

22. 17 C.F.R. § 229.402(c) (2020).
23. 17 C.F.R. § 229.402(i) (2020).
24. 17 C.F.R. § 229.402(i)(2) (2020).
25. 17 C.F.R. §§ 229.402(f), (g), (h), (o), (q), (s) (2020);

waiver of breach of such agreements; and (4) describe any other material factors regarding each such contract, agreement, plan or arrangement.[26]

*Disclosure of director compensation.* The company must provide information in tabular format regarding the compensation of its directors for the last fiscal year. This includes: (1) the name of each director unless the director is also an NEO and his or her compensation for service as a director is fully reflected in the summary compensation table and other NEO disclosures; (2) the aggregate dollar amount of all fees earned or paid in cash for services as a director, including annual retainer fees, committee and/or chairmanship fees, and meeting fees; (3) the aggregate grant date fair value computed in accordance with FASB ASC Topic 718 for awards of stock; (4) the aggregate grant date fair value computed in accordance with FASB ASC Topic 718 for awards of options; (5) the dollar value of all earnings for services performed during the fiscal year pursuant to non-equity incentive plans and all earnings on any outstanding awards; (6) the sum of (a) the aggregate change in the actuarial present value of the director's accumulated benefit under all defined benefit and actuarial pension plans (including supplemental plans) from the pension plan measurement date used for financial statement reporting purposes with respect to the company's audited financial statements for the prior completed fiscal year to the pension plan measurement date used for financial statement reporting purposes with respect to the company's audited financial statements for the covered fiscal year; and (b) above-market or preferential earnings on compensation that is deferred on a basis that is not tax-qualified, including such earnings on nonqualified defined contribution plans; (7) all other compensation for the covered fiscal year that the company could not properly report in any other column of the director compensation table; and (8) the dollar value of total compensation for the covered fiscal year for each director.[27]

The company must also provide a narrative description of any material factors necessary to understand the director compensation disclosed in the table. This might include a description of standard compensation arrangements. Standard compensation arrangements might include fees for retainer, committee service, service as chairman of the board or a committee, and meeting attendance.[28] The narrative may also include whether any director has a different compensation arrangement and identifying that director and describing the terms of the director's compensation arrangement.[29]

*Pay ratio.* The company must disclose: (1) the median of the annual total compensation of all its employees, except the CEO; (2) the annual total compensation of the CEO; and (3) the ratio of the median amount, from number 1, to the annual total compensation of the CEO, in number 2.[30]

---

26. 17 C.F.R. § 229.402(j) (2020).
27. 17 C.F.R. § 229.402(k) (2020).
28. 17 C.F.R. § 229.402(k)(3) (2020).
29. 17 C.F.R. § 229.402(k)(3) (2020).
30. 17 C.F.R. § 229.402(u) (2020).

## B. Form 10-K

While executive compensation information is required to be included in annual reports on Form 10-K, typically companies provide this information by referencing their annual proxy statements.[31]

## C. Form 8-K

Some executive compensation-related events must be "currently" reported (i.e., within four business days) on Form 8-K under Item 5.02. Of particular relevance to NQDCPs, current disclosure is required if a company "enters into, adopts, or otherwise commences a material compensatory plan, contract or arrangement . . . as to which a [NEO] participates or is a party, or such [an arrangement] is materially amended or modified, or a material grant or award under any such [arrangement to a NEO] is made or materially modified."[32] In such situations, the company must provide a brief description of the terms and conditions of the arrangement and the amounts payable to the NEO under the arrangement.

# Section 14.6 Say-on-pay Votes

At least once every three years, companies subject to the proxy disclosure rules, discussed above, generally must include in their proxy or consent or authorization for an annual or other meeting of shareholders a separate resolution subject to shareholder vote to approve the compensation of executives as disclosed under the proxy disclosure rules (say-on-pay votes).[33] In addition, at least once every six years, the company must include a separate resolution subject to shareholder vote to determine whether the say-on-pay vote will occur every one, two, or three years (say-on-frequency votes).[34]

---

31. Form 10-K: Annual Report Pursuant to Section 13 or 15(d) of the Securities and Exchange Act of 1934, SEC https://www.sec.gov/files/form10-k.pdf (last visited Sept. 16, 2021).

32. Form 8-K: Current Report, SEC 16, https://www.sec.gov/files/form8-k.pdf (last accessed Sept. 16, 2021).

33. 17 C.F.R. § 240.14a-21 (2020).

34. 17 C.F.R. § 240.14a-21 (2020).

CHAPTER **15**

# Partnerships and LLCs Taxed as Partnerships

Partnerships have unique considerations when it comes to designing executive compensation due to their treatment under the Internal Revenue Code (IRC). In addition, limited liability companies (LLCs) may be treated as partnerships for tax purposes and the same considerations may apply. For simplicity, these entities will be referred to collectively as partnerships throughout this section.

## Section 15.1 Types of Partnership Interests (Profits, Capital)

Interests in a partnership take on two main forms: capital interests and profits interests. A capital interest is most equivalent to a share of stock in a corporation. It grants the holder a right to a share of the total value of the company on liquidation, including the existing capital value of the company.[1] A profits interest, on the other hand, entitles the holder to a share of the income of a partnership, but not the existing capital value of the company (meaning that if the company were liquidated on the grant date, the holder of the profits interest would receive $0).[2] There also are blends of the two interests.

## Section 15.2 Consequences of Granting Partnership Interest

The grant of a partnership interest is a transfer of property under IRC Section 83.[3] Thus, the rules discussed in chapter 3 will apply to the transfer. However, the type of interest granted will make a difference in the taxation at the time of grant. In

1. Rev. Proc. 93-27, 1993-24 I.R.B. 63.
2. Rev. Proc. 93-27, 1993-24 I.R.B. 63.
3. Notice 2005-1, 2005-2 I.R.B. 274.

either case, when an executive is compensated with a partnership interest, the fair market value (FMV) of the interest received as compensation is generally included in the executive's income in the year the executive can transfer the interest or the interest is not subject to a substantial risk of forfeiture.[4] Generally, a capital interest may have a FMV because the company itself has a liquidation value, whereas, a strict profits interest is treated as not having a present value. As such, the grant of a capital interest may result in a taxable event to the executive, whereas, the grant of a profits interest generally does not create a tax liability. However, if a profits interest relates to a substantially certain and predictable stream of income from partnership assets, such as income from high-quality debt securities or a high-quality net lease, the partner disposes of the profits interest within two years, or the interest is in a publicly traded partnership, the interest may be scrutinized under general principles to determine whether the grant results in a taxable event.[5]

Grants of partnership interests, both capital and profits, may be subjected to a vesting schedule or other risk of forfeiture. As explained in chapter 3, this risk of forfeiture may delay taxation unless the executive makes an election under Section 83(b). However, there is a special rule for profits interests. A strict profits interest will not be treated as a taxable event at the time of grant or the time the interest becomes substantially vested—and an 83(b) election is unnecessary.[6] However, this special rule applies only to strict profits interests that comply with the rules of Revenue Procedure 93-27. If a profits interest does not fall neatly in that construction, an 83(b) election may be necessary to ensure the grant date (when the FMV is lowest and likely $0) is treated as the taxable event. As such, it is common for all grants of a profits interest or a capital interest to be conditioned on the executive filing an 83(b) election.

For executives considering taking a capital or profits interest, it is important to consider the impact of such an interest on their treatment as employees. In a corporation, receipt of an equity interest does not change the individual's status as an employee—in other words, one can hold an equity interest and be treated the same as any other employee (receiving a W-2, participating in pre-tax benefits, etc.). In a partnership, on the other hand, the holder of a capital interest or a profits interest is treated as a partner, not an employee.[7] This means the individual will receive a Schedule K-1 statement reflecting their share of ownership, must pay estimated income taxes (on their share of income from the partnership and self-employment taxes on their salary), and will not be permitted to participate in certain pre-tax benefits (such as pre-tax payment of health premiums and flexible spending accounts).[8]

---

4. Alessandra K. Murata, Partnerships, *in* Section 409A Handbook § 19.III (BNA) (Regina Olshan & Erica F. Schohn eds., 2016).

5. Rev. Proc. 93-27, 1993-24 I.R.B. 63 (Section 4).

6. Rev. Proc. 2001-43, 2001-34 I.R.B. 191.

7. If the interest is not vested when granted, the executive will not be treated as a partner until the interest is vested, unless a Section 83(b) election is made or it is a profits interest falling under Revenue Procedure 2001-43. This additional uncertainty makes the filing of an 83(b) election in all instances where an interest is granted a common practice.

8. *About Schedule K-1 (Form 1065), Partner's Share of Income, Deductions, Credits, Etc.*, I.R.S. (July 12, 2021), https://www.irs.gov/forms-pubs/about-schedule-k-1-form-1065.

## Section 15.3 Alternatives to Granting Partnership Interests

Partnerships may wish to avoid the consequences described above by using options or phantom interest plans instead of an outright grant of equity. Phantom plans are discussed in chapter 5 and could, generally, mimic the income of a capital interest without actually granting the interest.

Options are somewhat uncommon in the partnership context because a profits interest is very similar in economic effect and, generally, considered to be more favorable. For instance, generally, a profits interest is issued for no cost, while an option requires payment of an exercise price. The taxable event for an option occurs when it is exercised. Therefore, if there is current value when the option is exercised, then the executive will have a tax consequence on the date of exercise, where there would have been no taxable event when a profits interest was granted.

However, the option does come with some meaningful benefits over issuance of a profits interest. For instance, if an option is granted, then the partnership will be allowed a deduction when the option is exercised. That deduction, would result in a direct benefit to other partners and may be more valuable than if a profits interest had been granted. Further, the executive would remain an employee, enjoying the benefits of that status, unless and until the option is exercised.

## Section 15.3 Section 409A

Currently, the grant of capital or profits interests in a partnership are not treated as a deferred compensation subject to Section 409A. However, the Treasury Department and the IRS did create a placeholder in the regulations, so this may change in the future—particularly for equity grants that are somehow designed to defer compensation.

*CHAPTER* **16**

# Terminating a Nonqualified Deferred Compensation Plan

## Section 16.1 General Information

The right to establish, amend, or terminate a plan reflects the discretionary aspect and flexibility employers rely on when they voluntarily establish a plan.[1]

The termination of a nonqualified deferred compensation plan (NQDCP) disrupts certain rules and policies under Section 409A. Therefore, certain guardrails are established for termination to minimize any disruption to the purposes of section 409A.

Since payments under a NQDCP represent an unfunded promise to pay the deferred amounts in the future, if the employer terminates the plan during a period of financial uncertainty, the executive may lose the entire deferred amounts. The employer could also terminate a plan to accelerate payments, and then, turn around and reestablish a new plan. Termination can benefit the company since acceleration of a taxable event for the executive, opens the opportunity for a deduction for the company. In addition, the unilateral decision to terminate a NQDCP can create a conflict of interest between the company and the executive, who benefits from continued deferral.

Since termination of a NQDCP accelerates payments of the deferred compensation it violates the prohibition on acceleration of payments. As discussed in chapter 9, Section 409A specifically prohibits the acceleration of deferred compensation payments from NQDCPs.[2] However, the regulations provide an exception to the anti-acceleration of payments rules to allow plan terminations.[3] This relief from the anti-acceleration rules for plan terminations is accompanied by many conditions and restrictions.

A NQDCP can be terminated for: (1) no articulable reason, this is sometimes referred to as a discretionary termination, (2) due to a change in control

---

1. *See, e.g.*, Curtiss-Wright Corp. v. Schoonejongen, 514 U. S. 73 (1995); McGann v H. & H. Music Co., 946 F.2d 401 (5th Cir.1991).
2. Treas. Reg. § 1.409A-3(j) (2007).
3. Treas. Reg. § 1.409A-3(j)(4)(ix) (2007).

of the company, or (3) due to liquidation or reorganization of the company pursuant to the bankruptcy laws.[4] A plan document may also provide or restrict the conditions under which termination can occur.[5] Generally, approval by action of the governing board of the employer is necessary in order for the employer to terminate a plan, cease deferrals, and provide for acceleration of payments of the deferred amounts under the plan.[6]

If an arrangement is exempt from Section 409A, then only rules on termination specifically applicable to that arrangement, (such as requirements to terminate defined benefit plans using PBGC procedures), will apply. For arrangements subject to Section 409A, an employer can exercise its discretion to terminate a plan provided that all the following conditions are satisfied:

1. The termination and distribution of deferrals does not occur proximate to a downturn in the employer's financial condition.[7] Some posit that the downturn must be sufficient to threaten the payment of the deferred compensation for this restriction to prevent plan termination.[8]
2. Termination cannot be selective, in that the company must terminate and liquidate all agreements, methods, programs and arrangements that would be aggregated with the terminated plan.[9] In addition, certain similar arrangements must be terminated; this includes individual accounts maintained for all employees and all other arrangements that would be classified as a single plan if the same executive participated in the plan. Plans of subsidiaries of the company must also be terminated since an employer and a wholly owned subsidiary are considered a single employer.[10] It is irrelevant that the plans have different terms and conditions.
3. Payments after termination cannot be immediate. No payments from the NQDCP may occur within twelve months of board action to irrevocably terminate the NQDCP.[11] This means that within the twelve months after the resolution to terminate, the plan should continue to operate under its terms. The plan may be able to be frozen during this

---

4. Treas. Reg. § 1.409A-3(j)(4)(ix) (2007).

5. Taylor v. NCR Corp., 61 Employee Benefits Cas. (BL) 2434 (N.D. Ga. Sept. 23, 2015).

6. Barry K. Downey, Henry A. Smith III & Michael P. Connors, Nonqualified Deferred Compensation Answer Book Q 12:18 (8th ed. 2017).

7. Treas. Reg. § 1.409A-3(j)(4)(ix)(C)(1) (2007); Regina Olshan, *Acceleration of Payments, in* Section 409A Handbook (BNA) 11-23 to -24 (Regina Olshan & Erica F. Schohn eds., 2016).

8. Regina Olshan, *Acceleration of Payments, in* Section 409A Handbook (BNA) 11-24 to -26 (Regina Olshan & Erica F. Schohn eds., 2016).

9. Treas. Reg. § 1.409A-3(j)(4)(ix)(C)(2) (2007); Regina Olshan, *Acceleration of Payments, in* Section 409A Handbook (BNA) 11-23 to -24 (Regina Olshan & Erica F. Schohn eds., 2016). *See also* Prop. Treas. Reg. § 1.409A-3(j)(4)(ix)(C)(2), 81 Fed. Reg. 40,569, 40,575, 40,583 (June 22, 2016) (clarifying rules).

10. Regina Olshan, *Acceleration of Payments, in* Section 409A Handbook (BNA) 11-23 to -24 (Regina Olshan & Erica F. Schohn eds., 2016).

11. Treas. Reg. § 1.409A-3(j)(4)(ix)(C)(3) (2007); Mark P. Altieri, *Modifying or Terminating Nonqualified Deferred Compensation Plans*, Tax Advisor 5 (May 1, 2013), https://www.thetaxadviser.com/issues/2013/may/altieri-may2013.html.

period, but deferred amounts cannot be paid out (unless done under the pre-termination payment timing).

4. After the twelve-month period, all payments due to the termination must be made no later than twenty-four months after the termination resolution by the board.[12]
5. The employer cannot adopt a new similar-type of NQDCP for three years after the date of the board action to irrevocably terminate the plan.[13]

As an example, if on July 1, 2020, the company's board of directors authorizes termination of its NQDCP and the termination is not "proximate to a downturn in the financial health of the [employer],"[14] the distribution of the deferred compensation will not be deemed an impermissible acceleration of payment, provided the distributions do not begin earlier than July 1, 2021, (twelve months after all action to make the termination effective has been completed). Further, the distributions must be completed by July 1, 2022, (twenty-four months after all action necessary to make the termination effective has been completed). In addition, the employer cannot establish a new plan even with different terms for the existing executive or for any newly hired executives until July 1, 2023. If a plan were to be established earlier than the three years post termination, the previously terminated plan distributions would be deemed impermissible accelerations of payments in violation of 409A and the deferred payments would be subject to the triple tax effects of income taxation, a 20 percent penalty, and interest.[15]

An employer may seek to terminate the plan and accelerate payment within twelve months of a corporate dissolution or by filing for bankruptcy. The amounts deferred must be distributed by the later of the calendar year of the plan termination, or the first calendar year in which the right to the deferred amounts vests, or the first calendar year that payments are administratively feasible.[16]

An example of this type of termination exists where there is a significant downturn in the financial condition of the employer such that the discretionary termination is not an option. In such a case, the employer may decide to file for reorganization under chapter 11 of the bankruptcy code and seek the approval

---

12. Treas. Reg. § 1.409A-3(j)(4)(ix)(C)(4) (2007); Mark P. Altieri, *Modifying or Terminating Nonqualified Deferred Compensation Plans*, TAX ADVISOR 5 (May 1, 2013), https://www.thetaxadviser.com/issues/2013/may/altieri-may2013.html.

13. Treas. Reg. § 1.409A-3(j)(4)(ix)(C)(5) (2007); Mark P. Altieri, *Modifying or Terminating Nonqualified Deferred Compensation Plans*, TAX ADVISOR 5 (May 1, 2013), https://www.thetaxadviser.com/issues/2013/may/altieri-may2013.html. ). *See also* Prop. Treas. Reg. § 1.409A-3(j)(4)(ix)(C)(5), 81 Fed. Reg. 40,569, 40,575, 40,583 (June 22, 2016) (clarifying rules).

14. Regina Olshan, *Acceleration of Payments, in* SECTION 409A HANDBOOK (BNA) 11-20 (Regina Olshan & Erica F. Schohn eds., 2016).

15. Regina Olshan, *Acceleration of Payments, in* SECTION 409A HANDBOOK (BNA) 11-25 (Regina Olshan & Erica F. Schohn eds., 2016); I.R.C. § 409A(a)(1)(A), (B) (2018); Daniel Hogans, *Deferral Election Deadlines Under Section 409A Chart*, WESTLAW PRACTICAL LAW PRACTICE NOTE (2018).

16. Treas. Reg. § 1.409A-3(j)(4)(ix)(A) (2007).

of the bankruptcy court for the termination of the NQDCP. If approved, distributions must be made and the deferred compensation must be included in the gross income of the executive in the latest of: (1) the calendar year in which the plan termination and liquidation occurs; or (2) if later, the first calendar year in which the amount of the compensation vests; or (3) the first calendar year in which the payment is administratively practicable.[17]

A company can also terminate a plan after a change-in-control event as described in the Section 409A.[18] An irrevocable board action to terminate the plan due to a change-in-control event must occur within thirty days preceding or twelve months after the change-in-control event. The plan must complete distributing deferred compensation within twelve months after the resolution to terminate is adopted, and the termination does not apply to employees of the acquiring corporation. In addition, all plans of the same type maintained by the company *after* the transaction must be terminated. Thus, if the acquiring company assumes a NQDCP and also maintains its own NQDCPs, the company may have to terminate one or more of its own plans in order to terminate the acquired plan.

If the company terminates a plan in accordance with the requirements in the regulations the rules governing irrevocability of initial deferral elections and the prohibition of accelerated payment of all benefits accrued under the plan will not apply.[19]

If the plan is informally funded utilizing a rabbi trust, the trustee must make distributions and terminate the trust after all benefits under the plan are distributed.[20]

---

17. Regina Olshan, *Acceleration of Payments, in* SECTION 409A HANDBOOK (BNA) 11-25 (Regina Olshan & Erica F. Schohn eds., 2016); Treas. Reg. §§ 1.409A-3(j)(4)(ix)(A)(1) - (3) (2007).

18. Treas. Reg. § 1.409A-3(i)(5) (2007).

19. Regina Olshan, *Acceleration of Payments, in* SECTION 409A HANDBOOK (BNA) 11-21 (Regina Olshan & Erica F. Schohn eds., 2016).

20. *Terminating and Liquidating a Non-Qualified Deferred Compensation Plan* (Newport Group White Paper, 2018), https://www.newportgroup.com/knowledge-center/august-2018-(1)/terminating-and liquidating-a-non-qualified defer/.

*CHAPTER* **17**

# Enforcement of Executive Agreements

## Section 17.1 Introduction

The enforcement issues surrounding executive compensation are potentially as complex as the rules themselves. Disputes and settlements involving executive compensation can potentially result in Section 409A violations and attendant penalties. This chapter discusses the implications of disputes and settlements involving executive compensation arrangements.

## Section 17.2 Timing of Disputed Payments under Section 409A

As discussed previously, Section 409A of the Internal Revenue Code (IRC) prohibits a change in the time and form of payment after deferral, and a substitution of one payment for another may be treated as the same deferred compensation. Thus, an employer's failure to pay deferred compensation when due or the settlement of a dispute could theoretically cause problems under Section 409A. Thus, where a claim or dispute is being settled, counsel should take care to ensure the timing rules are not violated. Thankfully, Section 409A does include some relief to permit the settlement of disputes involving deferred compensation.

First, Section 409A provides that a payment of deferred compensation will be treated as having been made timely if:

- the company fails to make all or a portion of the payment (rather than the executive requesting that payment not be made);[1]

1. The executive, not the company, is deemed to have requested that a payment not be made, rather than the company having failed to make such payment, if the decision to not make the payment is made by the executive, a member of the executive's family (including the spouse of any member of the family), anyone over whom the executive (or a family member) has effective control, or anyone whose compensation is controlled by the executive (or a family member). Treas. Reg. § 1.409A-3(g).

- the executive accepts the portion (if any) of the payment that the company is willing to make (unless such acceptance will result in a relinquishment of the claim to all or part of the remaining amount);
- the executive makes prompt and reasonable, good faith efforts to collect the remaining portion of the payment; and
- any further payment (including payment of a lesser amount that satisfies the obligation) is made by the end of the executive's first taxable year in which the executive and company resolve the dispute (such as entering into a legally binding settlement of such dispute, the company conceding that the amount is payable, or a final and non-appealable judgment or other binding decision is entered).[2]

For purposes of the second bullet, the executive must notify the company within ninety days of the latest date on which the payment could have been timely and, if not paid, must take further enforcement measures within 180 days after that latest date.[3]

However, the above merely treats the payment as having been made timely even though the payment was delayed by the company. It does not provide relief from the rules that would treat settlements as substitutions or provide relief from the rules preventing a change in the time and form of payment. A separate provision of Section 409A does provide some limited relief in that regard, however. A payment subject to Section 409A may be accelerated as part of a settlement between the company and the executive only if there has been "an arm's length, bona fide dispute as to the [executive's] right to the deferred amount."[4] The regulations provide that whether a payment qualifies for the exception is based on all relevant facts and circumstances. However, a payment will be presumed *not* to meet this exception if the payment is:

- not subject to substantial reduction in value, compared to the amount that would have been payable had there been no dispute, and/or
- made proximate to a downturn in the financial health of the company.[5]

For purposes of the first bullet, generally the reduction must be at least 25 percent of the present value of the deferred amount in dispute to be considered a substantial reduction.[6] Thus, to avoid Section 409A violations, the settlement of a disputed claim may need to be paid under the terms of the arrangement (rather than in the common lump sum settlement) if the parties agree on a settlement that is close to present value of the deferred compensation.

---

2. Treas. Reg. § 1.409A-3(g) (2020).
3. Treas. Reg. § 1.409A-3(g) (2020).
4. Treas. Reg. § 1.409A-3(j)(4)(xiv) (2020).
5. Treas. Reg. § 1.409A-3(j)(4)(xiv) (2020).
6. Treas. Reg. § 1.409A-3(j)(4)(xiv) (2020).

## Section 17.3 Settlement of Claims

As noted above, the settlement of claims involving deferred compensation may need to be structured in a specific manner to comply with Section 409A. Not infrequently, however, an executive's claims to deferred compensation are mixed with other claims. For instance, the executive might claim discrimination and constructive termination that should result in vesting under a deferred compensation plan. The settlement of these mixed claims warrants close attention.

Settlement agreements, like any other agreement between a company and executive, could result in deferred compensation. However, an agreement will not be treated as deferred compensation if it resolves bona fide legal claims based on the following:

- wrongful termination,
- employment discrimination,
- Fair Labor Standards Act, or
- worker's compensation statutes.[7]

The above claims would include claims for reasonable attorneys' fees or other reasonable expenses related to such bona fide legal claims, regardless of whether such settlements are treated as compensation or wages for federal tax purposes. Thus, settlement of these claims is not subject to Section 409A and the attendant rules on time and form of payment. This exception from application of Section 409A does not apply to amounts that would have been deferred or paid regardless of the existence of a claim (or other amounts not arising from the claim), even if such amounts are paid or modified as part of a settlement or award resolving an actual bona fide claim.[8]

Thus, when settling an executive's claims, certain portions of a settlement may need to be paid at different times and/or in different forms than other portions. Commonly, employment and compensation claims are settled in a lump sum without clear itemization of what amount of the settlement is for particular portions of the claim. When settling claims for deferred compensation, this may be problematic if the parties cannot support that the Section 409A bona fide dispute exceptions are satisfied. Itemizing the settlement, at least with respect to the settlement of deferred compensation claims, may assist the parties in memorializing how the settlement satisfies Section 409A (and may ensure the parties properly consider the issue in the first place).

## Section 17.4 Enforcement Schemes

As noted in chapter 5, certain deferred compensation arrangements will be subject to ERISA either as pension plans covering a select group of management or highly compensated employees (top hat plans) or as welfare plans (such as

7. Treas. Reg. § 1.409A-1(b)(11) (2020).
8. Treas. Reg. § 1.409A-1(b)(11) (2020).

severance arrangements). Other plans will be merely non-ERISA contractual promises to pay. The difference can be very important.

## A. ERISA Plans

If the deferred compensation arrangement is subject to ERISA, then ERISA will provide the enforcement scheme.[9] Notably, the arrangement is required to provide for an administrative claims procedure and the remedies will be limited to those provided in ERISA.[10]

With regard to the claims procedure, many arrangements provide that the executive is required to exhaust internal administrative remedies before filing suit regarding any dispute. The plan may also provide certain timeframes and procedures that must be followed to correctly complete the internal claim and appeals process. Further, the plan may also provide a deadline for filing suit and the venue in which any such suit must be filed. This means it is critical for an executive to review the arrangement's claims procedure as soon as any dispute arises. Failing to follow the timeline or procedures outlined in the claim's procedure could effectively foreclose the executive's ability to pursue the claim in court.

In addition, even once the administrative procedures are satisfied, the executive's claims may be limited by ERISA. In general, if the company followed its claims procedures, it may be entitled to a favorable standard of review by the court, and the company's decision may be subject to reversal only if the executive can show the decision was an abuse of discretion. Discovery is generally limited to the administrative record that was developed during the claim and appeals process—making the internal claims process even more critical.

Finally, the remedies under ERISA will generally be limited to the disputed benefits and any harm arising from a breach of fiduciary duty.[11] Attorneys' fees can also be awarded.[12] However, punitive damages, the doubling or trebling of damages, and right to a jury trial often seen under state law are not available.

## B. State Law Enforcement

Arrangements not subject to ERISA generally are enforceable under state laws—both contract laws and wage and hour laws may apply. These laws vary significantly from state to state. However, it is not uncommon for a state to provide an enforcement mechanism that could result in double or even treble damages. The arrangement may provide for choice of law and the venue in which any litigation must be brought and also may attempt to establish a deadline for filing suit. Thus, counsel should carefully review the arrangement in assessing an executive's claims.

---

9. Employee Retirement Income Security Act of 1974 (ERISA), Pub. L. No. 93-406, 88 Stat. 829 (codified as amended at 29 U.S.C. §§ 1001-1461 and scattered sections of 5, 18, and 26 U.S.C.).

10. 29 C.F.R. § 2560.503-1 (2020).

11. 29 U.S.C. § 1132 (2018). The fiduciary rules of ERISA do not apply to top hat plans.

12. 29 U.S.C. § 1132(g) (2018).

# Section 17.5 Non-Compete/Non-Solicitation/ Non-Disclosure/Non-Disparagement Covenants

Like state contract laws, statutes regarding the enforcement of restrictive covenants vary significantly from state to state. A non-compete provision may be enforceable in state A and completely impermissible in state B and, further, even within the same state may be enforceable as a forfeiture condition on deferred compensation but not enforceable as an actual restriction on the executive's ability to compete. Restrictive covenants may or may not be enforceable by injunctive relief, depending on the state. A fifty-state survey of this area of law is outside the scope of this publication. However, counsel should review the applicable law in assessing the enforceability of any restrictive covenant.

# About the Authors

**Kelsey Mayo** is an employee benefits and executive compensation partner with the law firm Poyner Spruill LLP. She works with executives, vendors, business owners, and HR teams to understand and manage all types of employee benefits and executive compensation arrangements. Kelsey enjoys helping professionals decipher the most complex areas of this field and speaks regularly with industry organizations. She also serves the American Retirement Association's Government Affairs Team, which works with government agencies and Congress to develop workable regulations and legislation for the retirement industry. She earned her B.S. degree in Accounting from North Carolina State University and her J.D. degree from Wake Forest University School of Law.

**Sharon Reece** has taught in the area of taxation and employee benefits for several years. Currently she is a Visiting Associate Law Professor at the University of Maryland Francis King Carey School of Law. She earned a J.D. from Hofstra University School of Law and an LL.M in Taxation from New York University School of Law. Professor Reece has published in the areas of Taxation and Employee Benefits Law, and has coauthored two books on the Employee Retirement Income Security Act of 1974 (ERISA).

**Jesse St. Cyr** practices employee benefits and executive compensation as a partner with the law firm Poyner Spruill LLP. He has extensive experience working on executive compensation matters with a variety of employers, including public and private companies, governmental employers, and churches. Jesse received his B.A. degree from George Mason University and his J.D. degree from William & Mary School of Law.

# Table of Cases

# Index